Gay on God's Campus

Gay on God's Campus

Mobilizing for LGBT Equality at Christian Colleges and Universities

Jonathan S. Coley

The University of North Carolina Press CHAPEL HILL

This book was published with the assistance of the Authors Fund of the University of North Carolina Press.

The University of North Carolina Press has been a member of the Green Press Initiative since 2003.

Library of Congress Cataloging-in-Publication Data
Names: Coley, Jonathan S., author.
Title: Gay on God's campus : mobilizing for LGBT equality at Christian colleges and universities / Jonathan S. Coley.
Description: Chapel Hill : University of North Carolina Press, [2018] | Includes bibliographical references and index.
Identifiers: LCCN 2017020716 | ISBN 9781469636214 (cloth : alk. paper) | ISBN 9781469636221 (pbk : alk. paper) | ISBN 9781469636238 (ebook)
Subjects: LCSH: Gay college students—Political activity—United States. | Christian college students—Political activity—United States. | Student movements—United States. | Sexual minorities—Political activity—United States.
Classification: LCC LC2575 .C65 2018 | DDC 378.0086/64—dc23
LC record available at https://lccn.loc.gov/2017020716

Cover illustration: © iStock.com/neyro2008

Portions of chapter one were previously published as "Reconciling Religion and LGBT Rights: Christian Universities, Theological Orientations, and LGBT Inclusion," *Social Currents* 4, no.1 (2017): 87–106. Portions of chapter four were previously published as "Social Movements and Bridge Building: Religious and Sexual Identity Conflicts," *Research in Social Movements, Conflicts, and Change* 37 (2014): 125–51.

To Hugh Floyd and Theresa Davidson—
for inspiring my sociological journey

Contents

For more information about this project's research methodology and theoretical grounding, please visit http://jonathancoley.com/book.

Figure and Tables

Acknowledgments

I have many people to thank for their support as I wrote this book. In many ways, this book is a biographical consequence of my time as an undergraduate student at Samford University, a Baptist university in Birmingham, Alabama. Beginning in 2009, other students, faculty members, and I worked together to form an unofficial support group for LGBT students and promote LGBT inclusion in a conservative religious environment. I would not be where I am today if it were not for Hugh Floyd and Theresa Davidson, two faculty members in Samford's Department of Sociology, who showed enormous courage in supporting this fledgling LGBT group and who ultimately inspired my career in sociology. Similarly, I am forever grateful to Fred Shepherd, chair of Samford's Department of Political Science, who did more than any other person to support me and broaden my worldview throughout my time at Samford.

I began the research for this book at Vanderbilt University. I had the pleasure of working under Larry Isaac and Dan Cornfield, who enthusiastically supported this research beginning at its earliest stages while also granting me the space to forge my own scholarly path. They are two of the most generous people I have ever met. I am also grateful for the support of other members of Vanderbilt's faculty, such as David Hess and Melissa Snarr, who provided extensive feedback on this project, and George Becker, Karen Campbell, Laura Carpenter, Shaul Kelner, Richard Lloyd, Holly McCammon, Mariano Sana, and Steven Tepper, who encouraged me to engage with a variety of subfields and methodological approaches that inform this book. Finally, Vanderbilt's Robert Penn Warren Center provided crucial financial support as I undertook this project. I thank executive director Mona Frederick and my "fellow Fellows" of the Warren Center for their encouragement and feedback on the book.

At Monmouth College, my colleagues in the Department of Sociology and Anthropology, Petra Kuppinger, Judi Kessler, Megan Hinrichsen, and Wendel Hunigan, have been highly supportive of my research and have been a pleasure to work alongside. Similarly, my colleagues in Religious Studies, Hannah Schell and Dan Ott, have been eager to engage in conversations about the intersections of religion and social change. I am grateful for all of my colleagues and for the friends I have made here, and for the amazing students in the Spring 2017 Methods of Social Research class at Monmouth, who read over a draft of this book.

A number of sociologists outside of my own institutions have provided professional support over the years, including Bernadette Barton, Jason Crockett, David Cunningham, Terrence Hill, Lauren Joseph, Melinda Kane, Tom Ratliff, and Yvonne Zylan. Other sociologists, including James Cavendish, Adam Mayer, Doug McAdam, Andrew Whitehead, and Stacy Williams, provided helpful comments on previous versions of the chapters. I am thankful not only for these sociologists but also for other sociological co-travelers who have provided both their professional expertise and their friendship over the years; Pallavi Banerjee, Anna Jacobs, Heather Kettrey, Dan Morrison, Peter Viehlehr, and especially Becky Conway and Quan Mai have been ongoing sources of encouragement.

The expert editorial team at the University of North Carolina Press deserves special praise. Joseph Parsons reached out to me before I had put a pen to paper to encourage me to write this book, and Lucas Church ensured this book made it across the finish line. Becki Reibman, Alison Shay, Stephanie Wenzel, and others provided helpful editorial support.

My sincere gratitude also goes to the editors of *Social Currents*, Toni Calisanti and Vincent Roscigno, who published an earlier version of chapter one, and to the guest editor of *Research in Social Movements, Conflicts, and Change*, Lynne Woehrle, who published an earlier version of chapter four. The anonymous reviewers of those journals and this book helped shaped the book in its current form, so I thank them for their close readings of my work.

Finally, I cannot forget to thank my respondents, who are perhaps my biggest source of inspiration. Many of them came of age at a political moment where the surest way to get elected was to denigrate people who identified as lesbian, gay, bisexual, or transgender. Even as the political climate grows more accepting of LGBT rights, many of my respondents continue to face rejection from their closest family members, faith communities, and schools. Others come from more accepting backgrounds, but they still assume considerable risk by speaking up for others in their community. I am so glad they let me in on their journeys, and I hope I have done their stories justice.

Gay on God's Campus

Introduction

What do an anarchist, a former fundamentalist Christian, and a relatively apolitical and nonreligious student have in common? Conventional explanations of activist group participation, and perhaps human sociality more generally, would suggest very little. Common sense might suggest that these three people would occupy different social spheres and advocate for different causes—if they advocated for certain causes at all. But in a fledgling lesbian, gay, bisexual, and transgender (LGBT) organization at the Catholic University of America, a conservative religious university in Washington, D.C., these students represented three of the most passionate people banding together to promote LGBT equality at their school.

Neil, the anarchist in this account, was one of the most politicized students at his university. An atheist, Neil came to Catholic University not because of the school's religious identity but because of his desire to be at the center of political action in the nation's capital. For most of his college career, he spent very little time at the university itself, instead involving himself in an antiwar organization off campus.

Yet a startling incident on campus made Neil realize that some of the change he needed to work for was on Catholic University's campus itself. Walking through the parking lot at his school one night, Neil encountered several people slashing the tires of his car and spray-painting the word "faggot" on it. Although he approached school administrators about the incident, he alleges that the leaders were more interested in brushing the hate crime under the rug than in broaching difficult conversations about sexual identity on campus. Thus, his initial desire to become involved in LGBT activism at his school was sparked.

Ashley, a graduate student studying religion, had a very different background than Neil, having enrolled at Catholic University because of its religious identity and her desire to study at one of the most high-profile Catholic theology programs in the United States. Indeed, Ashley had a conservative Catholic upbringing, telling me that she had come to identify as a "fundamentalist Christian" when she was nineteen and that she remained in that mind-set for the next eight years. "I think if I had been anything" during those years, she says, "I would have been someone who . . . would have been writing letters opposing [LGBT] groups at Christian universities."

Despite her conservative convictions, Ashley slowly became aware of her attraction to other women. Believing that she could not be a gay Christian, and fearing that she would be sent to hell if she entered into a relationship with another woman, she took a number of steps to resist her same-sex attractions, including by enrolling in reorientation therapy and praying to God to change her. She also had passive suicidal thoughts.

By her mid-twenties, Ashley knew something had to change. She began reviewing church teachings and scriptures so she could confirm for herself that same-sex relationships were wrong. But this led her to commentaries of biblical texts and books on church history that convinced her that so many arguments against same-sex relationships were inconsistent—"it was just one argument after another argument that slowly began to fade away and lose its support." After two or three years of extensive reinvestigation, she finally decided for herself that homosexuality was okay, and another year later, she came out as a lesbian.

When she finally came to Catholic University, Ashley decided that she did not want the undergraduates on campus to undergo their own struggles with self-doubt and internal torment—rather, she wanted to affirm the message that one could be gay and Christian. After reading op-eds in the campus newspaper condemning homosexuality, she decided to enter into the campus debate and—despite some reservations as one who had never been involved in an activist group before—decided to seek out a new outlet to promote LGBT equality on campus.

The final student in this account, Julie, was neither a committed activist nor a regular churchgoer at the time she joined the LGBT group at Catholic University. Rather, for most of her college career, she kept her head down and applied herself to her studies. Although she would speak out in class if she disagreed with something or otherwise "felt something was off," she was never heavily involved in social justice groups on campus or LGBT advocacy off campus.

Even so, as a lesbian at a conservative university, she routinely encountered discrimination and microaggressions ("brief, everyday exchanges that send denigrating messages to certain individuals because of their group membership"; Sue 2010, xvi). For example, she described an interaction with a professor, who was also a priest, who told her that she was "going to hell and that [she] should just date and marry a man and that [she] would learn to love him." Thus, she became aware of the need for a safe space for LGBT students on campus, and when other students told her about a new LGBT group they were hoping to start, she happily joined.

Although these three students hailed from different backgrounds and maintained very different political and religious perspectives—if they held strong political and religious views at all—they nonetheless all joined the unofficial LGBT group on their campus and dedicated themselves to that cause until graduation. They are also broadly representative of their peers involved in LGBT activism at other Christian universities in the United States. Like Neil, many participants maintain well-cultivated activist identities and dedicate themselves to direct action groups throughout much of their lives. But like Ashley and Julie, other participants are relative strangers to activist groups; many join activist causes only after undergoing resocialization, and they bring about social change by educating their wider communities on LGBT issues or otherwise influencing their families and friends.

These students may not all readily resemble the people usually portrayed in scholarship on activist organizations. Yet, as I will argue in the pages that follow, each of these types of students is actively pursuing social change. Although their motivations for joining LGBT groups may differ—with some seeking policy changes, others hoping for campus-wide dialogue, and still others hoping to create a safe space for people like themselves—these students are taking on risk (McAdam 1986; Taylor and Raeburn 1995; Wiltfang and McAdam 1991), engaging in collective action in pursuit of their goals, and in many cases succeeding in transforming the policies and cultures of their institutions. In short, these students are all in some sense activists.

Understanding Activist Group Participation

This book is premised on the idea that something important can be learned from the stories of seemingly disparate people, connected only by their common pursuit of LGBT equality on their campuses. Sociologist C. Wright Mills ([1959] 2000, 6) famously argued that "no social study that does not come back to the problems of biography, of history, and of their intersections within a society has completed its intellectual journey." The sociology he championed took seriously the role of social structures in shaping everyday life—structures that have long been perceived as the "stuff" of sociology. Nevertheless, he also advocated linking visible public issues to seemingly personal troubles, illuminating how changes in society over time intersect with and help us make sense of changes in people's personal lives.

The many movements for minority-group inclusion over the past few decades—and the unusually rapid evolution in attitudes and rights for sexual and gender minorities over the past few years—have certainly reverberated through the biographies of LGBT youths and young adults, many of whom would not have been able to envision a place for themselves on their college and university campuses even a few years ago. In this book, I draw on historical evidence about the growing success of LGBT movements, quantitative data on the spread of LGBT groups and inclusive nondiscrimination policies across Christian colleges and universities, and in-depth interviews with sixty-five student activists at four Christian colleges and universities (Belmont University, the Catholic University of America, Goshen College, and Loyola University Chicago) to illuminate how and why LGBT and allied students, at this historical juncture, have come to embrace their role as change agents on college campuses and beyond. Specifically, I address the following research questions:

(1) Why do students participate in LGBT activism at Christian colleges and universities?
(2) Why do students commit to LGBT activism at Christian colleges and universities?
(3) How do LGBT activist groups at Christian colleges and universities impact their participants?

The book's central insights are that there is more than one way to be an activist, and thus there are multiple pathways to activism, patterns of commitment to activist groups, and biographical consequences of activism. Specifically, I identify three groups of participants in LGBT groups—politicized participants, religious participants, and LGBT participants; pinpoint differences in the LGBT groups to which they commit—direct action groups, educational groups, and solidarity groups; and demonstrate the various ways they embody activism in their lives—through continued social movement participation, humanistic careers, and intentional relationships.

These insights have significant implications for the body of literature on activist group participation, which has focused almost entirely on a group of activists whom I call *politicized participants*, including Neil, rather than students who are motivated by a specific set of religious values (*religious participants*) or by their sexual or gender identity (*LGBT participants*), such as Ashley and Julie. In historical-biographical terms, history has flowed most naturally through the biographies of participants like Neil—politicized participants foresaw where society was heading in terms of LGBT inclusion, and history was seemingly catching up with them. Much like the people portrayed in the literature on activist group participation, prior to coming to his university, Neil had undergone an extensive process of *socialization* into left-wing political ideologies that embraced the inclusion of minority groups.[1] Neil also reported *prior activist group participation* (such as in an antiwar organization) that had solidified his own identity as an organizer and ensured that his transition to LGBT activism was relatively smooth.[2]

Neil, as with most politicized participants, thus possessed a number of personal characteristics that made him a prime target for *micromobilization*—that is, recruitment into activist groups. First, given his socialization into left-wing political ideologies, Neil exhibited *attitudinal affinity* with LGBT movements, or agreement with the values, tactics, and goals of LGBT movements.[3] Next, especially because of his prior movement participation, Neil exhibited *microstructural availability*, or embeddedness in personal (friendship) networks that reaffirmed his attitudes and organizational networks that linked him with other activist groups.[4] Finally, because he was still quite young and lacked major personal and professional responsibilities outside of school, Neil happened to exhibit *biographical availability*, or a lack of personal constraints (such as a full-time job, a marital partner, or children) that might have detracted from participation.[5]

Once politicized participants are recruited into an activist group, scholars of activist group commitment presume that people like Neil will commit to their group, and thus take on increased responsibilities and devote increased amounts of time, on two conditions. First, they must continue to exhibit characteristics such as attitudinal affinity, microstructural availability, and biographical availability.[6] Second, they must not face certain *meso-level* (organizational) *constraints*, such as overly hierarchical and bureaucratic organizational structures that might inhibit their ability to devote large amounts of time and energy to an activist group.[7] In this case, Neil indeed continued to exhibit characteristics such as attitudinal affinity, microstructural availability, and biographical availability, and the LGBT group he joined at Catholic was indeed nonhierarchical and nonbureaucratic.

In university-based groups like the LGBT groups examined here, graduation presents a natural end point for participation in an activist organization. Nevertheless, literature on biographical consequences of activist groups shows that these groups have enduring consequences on the lives of politicized participants. For example, following graduation, Neil participated in subsequent activist groups, in a local organization that coordinates direct action campaigns in Washington, D.C. Naturally, Neil also became further and further entrenched in his left-wing political views.[8] Finally, Neil's involvement in LGBT activism impacted his personal life—given both his engagement with queer theory and his continued dedication to direct action groups, Neil refuses to enter into marriage (which he views as an assimilationist institution) and reports no plans to raise children.[9]

Neil is perhaps the prototypical activist, at least according to past literature on activist group participation. Nevertheless, a quick consideration of the biographies of Ashley and Julie—students who were also deeply involved in LGBT activism—quickly adds doubt to the assumptions in this literature. Religious participants like Ashley, at least during earlier parts of their lives, were more likely to "stand athwart history, yelling stop!" (Buckley 1955, 1). Prior to becoming involved in an LGBT group, religious participants such as Ashley were not socialized into values conducive to LGBT activism but were instead socialized into more conservative, religious worldviews that viewed non-heterosexual and non-cisgender (i.e., non-normative gender) identities as worthy of condemnation. Indeed, Ashley says she sided with anti-LGBT campaigns growing up. After her lengthy period of self-reflection, Ashley eventually exhibited attitudinal affinity with the LGBT group she joined, but she had few friends and few organizational connections (i.e., microstructural availability) that would affirm or facilitate her involvement in the LGBT group. She also lacked biographical availability, given that she worked and had a dedicated partner outside of school, and she had never been involved in other activist groups. Because she lacked characteristics such as microstructural availability and biographical availability, existing explanations for commitment to activist groups similarly do not apply to participants like Ashley. Finally, although Ashley engaged in a political campaign promoting marriage equality after graduation, she was most interested in promoting social change outside the confines of formal activist organizations—in her case, by transforming students' views through her job in higher education—so literature on biographical consequences of activist groups sometimes fails to fully capture stories like hers.

Scholarship on activist group participation also misses the many nuances in Julie's story, who participated in an LGBT group mainly because of her own sexual identity. Participants with salient LGBT identities have often been socialized into accepting values (if not overarching political ideologies), and they do all report attitudinal affinity. Furthermore, many participants with salient LGBT identities exhibit microstructural availability (they have accepting friends) and biographical availability. However, they are distinct from politicized participants in that few had been involved in previous activist groups. Although, on paper, Julie shares many of the characteristics of committed activist group participants, characteristics like attitudinal affinity, microstructural availability, and biographical availability fail to truly capture the essence of why she was so drawn to an LGBT group—to connect with other LGBT students on campus in a safe space. Finally, following graduation, rather than continue to participate in a formal LGBT activist group, Julie mostly sought to bring about social change through conversations on LGBT issues with family, friends, and neighbors.

In the following chapters, I make the argument that scholars should take into account the multiple ways one can be an activist and thus come to join, commit, and emerge out of an activist group. I argue that Neil, Ashley, and Julie represent three types of activists whose biographies cohere around three basic types of identities—a so-called *activist identity* (held by politicized participants), a *value-based identity* (held by religious participants), and a *solidary identity* (held by LGBT participants) (Corrigall-Brown 2012; Gamson 1991; Gecas 2000; Simon and Klandermans 2001; Valocchi 2013). Addressing the first research question about why people join activist groups, and contributing to the literature on micromobilization, I show that scholars have identified most of the components crucial to explaining activist group participation—concepts like socialization, prior activist group participation, attitudinal affinity, microstructural availability, and biographical availability. Nevertheless, studies wrongly assume that activists possess each of these characteristics; instead, different configurations of these characteristics matter for each type of activist.

Addressing the second research question, and contributing to the literature on activist group commitment, I next show that scholars have failed to account for why some participants take on increasing responsibilities and devote an increasing amount of time to activist organizations while others do not. Rational choice calculations based on factors like attitudinal affinity, microstructural availability, and biographical availability may matter in some cases, and meso-level constraints (e.g., bureaucratic complexity and hierarchical organizational structures) may detract from participation in others. However, I suggest that activist group commitment is best explained by the correspondence ("fit") between one's most salient identity and the group ethos of the LGBT organization one joins. Politicized participants will feel most at home in what I call *direct action groups*—groups engaged in extra-institutional collective action, often through some form of civil disobedience. Religious participants will be most dedicated to *educational groups*—organizations dedicated to hammering out their collective values and sharing those values with their wider communities. Finally, those with salient LGBT identities will devote the most time and energy to *solidarity groups*—groups that offer a safe space for, and a chance to connect with, those who identify as LGBT and that facilitate their members' personal development.

Addressing the third research question, and contributing to the literature on biographical consequences of activist groups, I finally argue that not all participants in LGBT groups go on to pursue, or express plans to pursue, involvement in formal activist groups following graduation. Although most politicized participants do tend to become involved in other direct action groups, religious participants usually enter into humanistic careers (e.g., as teachers or social workers) through which they seek to make existing institutions more inclusive of LGBT people. Furthermore, LGBT participants are most interested in pursuing more intentional personal lives—starting conversations on LGBT issues with friends and families, entering into equal marital partnerships, and raising children with values of tolerance and acceptance. In other words, these varieties of activists will pursue varieties of activism.

Moving toward an Inclusive Understanding of Activism

This book's goal of offering explanations for students' pathways to activism, decisions to commit to activism, and biographical consequences of activism is motivated by questions that occur for many people when they first hear that students are mobilizing around LGBT issues at such seemingly unlikely places, Christian colleges and universities. Why do LGBT students attend Christian schools in the first place, and how do students find themselves in such groups? The book's engagement with theories of activist group participation also stems from broader questions we hear about modern-day, campus-based identity politics. Who comprises this new generation of student activists—are they similar to "red-diaper babies" of previous generations (see Kaplan and Shapiro 1998)? Are students who join LGBT (and other identity-based) groups merely involved in "slacktivism"—are students really that committed to their cause? And is students' involvement in campus activism—their work to create safe spaces, to combat microaggressions—merely a naive, fleeting "phase" that students will drop when they enter the "real world," rather than something that will significantly change their biographical trajectories?

This book addresses these questions through its exploration of the biographical trajectories of LGBT student activists, but beyond that, the book speaks to our understanding of activism itself. As I initially researched past insights on activist group participation, I found that scholars were contributing almost exclusively to a subfield of sociology known as *social movement studies*. Thus, as I entered into the field, I initially expected that the students whom I would talk to would be *social movement participants* who were members of *social movement organizations*. In their well-regarded work, sociologists David Snow, Sarah Soule, and Hanspeter Kriesi (2004, 11) define social movements as "collectivities acting with some degree of organization and continuity outside of institutional or organizational channels for the purpose of challenging or defending extant authority, whether it is institutionally or culturally based, in the group, organization, society, or world order of which they are a part." In the strictest formulations, these social movements are further said to be challenging political authorities and thus seeking changes in policies or overthrows of governments (see critiques by Armstrong and Bernstein 2008; Van Dyke, Soule, and Taylor 2004; Yukich 2013). The students I interviewed met many of the qualifications of social movement participants—they are members of groups that act collectively, with some degree of organization and planning, in an attempt to challenge (if seldom defend) the status quo. Yet the tactics that they were deploying were not always outside of institutional or organizational channels—that is, the tactics were not always part of the traditional social movement repertoire of rallies, marches, pickets, sit-ins, or occupations—and the status quo they were challenging was not always embodied in a tangible authority, certainly not one that was always part of the political sphere.

What kind of collective action, then, does this book focus on? Although some students were certainly part of LGBT groups that could be classified as social movement organizations, I argue that the substantial attention these kinds of groups receive from scholars may be due to the disproportionate amount of disruption they cause and the enormous media attention they receive, because in my sample of respondents, a minority of students participated in such groups. For example, some activist groups that I encountered were composed of groups of people who, although still acting with "some degree of organization and continuity," worked mostly within existing institutions and deployed more conciliatory consciousness-raising tactics throughout their communities to achieve goals that were more cultural in nature, such as changes in intergroup attitudes.[10] Other activist groups seemed to take most seriously the feminist notion that the personal is political, working to create safe spaces that were often closed off from their wider communities and that intentionally sought to facilitate personal change, including changes in members' identities.[11] Thus, I found that the social change activist groups sought to promote came about through multiple means and in multiple forms.

Although I have found that scholars of women's and LGBT movements in particular are increasingly sensitive to the multiple types of goals (e.g., political, cultural, and occasionally intentionally personal goals) that activist groups pursue and the multiple kinds of tactics (e.g., extra-institutional and institutional tactics) that activists deploy to promote social change,[12] I argue that scholars still exhibit an overwhelming tendency to squeeze all groups promoting social change into the category of social movements. Sociologist Doug McAdam and his colleagues (McAdam and Boudet 2012; McAdam, Sampson, Weffer, and MacIndoe 2005) have recently called on scholars of social change to "put social movements in their place" (McAdam and Boudet 2012), to examine social movements in conjunction with the wider range of organizations involved in promoting social change. Yet, I find few recent systematic efforts to map out the varieties of organizations and activists involved in social change processes. Armstrong's (2002, 1) book on lesbian and gay activism in San Francisco contributes a typology of traditional social movement organizations (focused on societal transformation through direct action), interest group organizations (which hoped to "improve life for homosexuals by educating the mainstream public"), and identity organizations (which sought to help LGBT people to live more authentic lives). Armstrong's typology of organizations is similar to mine, but her book is primarily focused on mapping out the range of activist organizations focused on lesbian and gay issues rather than identifying the types of activists involved in these organizations. A more recent exception is Cornfield's (2015) book on artist activists in Nashville, which develops a helpful typology of trade union reformers, social entrepreneurs, and enterprising artists who facilitate broader-scale collective changes, interpersonal changes, and personal changes, respectively. But although Cornfield's conceptualization of the methods and scale on which actors seek social change is similar to mine, the book does not contribute distinct insights on the ways these actors may come to join, commit to, and emerge out of activist groups.

This book thus seeks to move beyond the confines of social movement studies and build a more holistic, inclusive understanding of the ways that people engage in activism, which I define simply as the pursuit of social change. As noted above, in investigating paths to joining LGBT groups at Christian colleges and universities, I profile not only those politicized participants who are committed to direct action—those who most resemble the prototypical social movement participants—but also those who hold salient religious and LGBT identities and who may ultimately be drawn to other ways of promoting social change. In analyzing commitment to LGBT groups at Christian colleges and universities, I map out a range of activist groups, or organizations that promote social change, to which these participants are drawn—not only direct action groups, the organizations that resemble traditional social movement organizations by deploying extra-institutional tactics in pursuit of policy changes, but also educational groups and solidarity groups, which are more focused on meaning making or "everyday activism" (Mansbridge 2013) and that maintain goals that are cultural or personal in nature. Finally, in investigating the biographical consequences of LGBT activist group participation, I identify several ways in which students engage in activism postgraduation—not necessarily through continued social movement activity but also through humanistic careers and more intentional family lives.

Although the book engages with theories on activist group participation, it is about more than that. While privileging the personal, individual-level narratives of students who progress through LGBT groups at Christian colleges and universities, the book contributes to a more inclusive understanding of activism itself. The book is about the many ways that people work to promote more welcoming, inclusive campuses in places where they are often scorned. It is about the multiple ways that people are working to help conservative college campuses and (after graduation) governments, workplaces, and families adapt to our increasingly diverse, multicultural society. The book is about activists, activist groups, and activisms—in the distinct forms they come in—in places where we might not even think to expect them.

Background on LGBT Issues at Christian Colleges and Universities

This book not only contributes to our understanding of activist group participation and the nature of activism itself but also draws attention to our substantive and practical understanding of discrimination against LGBT students, staff, and faculty across often ignored sites (Guhin 2014), Christian colleges and universities in the United States.

Issues facing LGBT people in the United States have, by now, reached the level of widespread public awareness. Although same-sex couples have now gained formal marital rights, youths who identify as lesbian, gay, bisexual, or transgender continue to face much higher rates of bullying and harassment than their straight peers, which in turn contribute to higher rates of suicide among LGBT youths.[13] Despite Americans' increasing willingness to offer formal legal benefits to LGBT people, same-sex couples continue to lack many informal privileges that straight couples enjoy, such as the basic ability to hold a partner's hand without fear of violence or disapproval (Doan, Loehr, and Miller 2014).

In many ways, the problems facing LGBT people at Christian colleges and universities are quite similar to problems facing LGBT people in the United States at large—LGBT students on Christian campuses are more vulnerable to discrimination, bullying, and harassment than their straight or cisgender counterparts.[14] Indeed, their struggles are perhaps more severe given continued links between conservative religiosity and homophobia.[15] Nevertheless, issues facing LGBT students on Christian campuses have historically been hidden from public awareness, in part because of a basic objection—are Christian colleges and universities not well within their First Amendment rights to discriminate against LGBT students (see discussion by Hotchkiss 2013)? And could LGBT students not simply attend public colleges and universities that are more accepting of LGBT students? Currently, it is indeed true that Christian universities are within their rights to discriminate against LGBT people. Although the federal government bars Christian schools receiving federal grants from discriminating on the basis of factors such as race and sex, the Obama administration began the practice of granting individual waivers to religious employers who discriminated on the basis of sexual orientation (Zoll 2014), and in one of its earliest actions, the Trump administration completely withdrew Title IX protections for transgender students (Fain 2017). Furthermore, it is certainly true that LGBT people are not compelled (by law, at least) to attend these schools. Given such skepticism, then, it is worth considering a basic question about these cases: why care? Why be concerned about any issues facing LGBT students on Christian campuses when Christian schools are breaking no laws and LGBT students could avert discrimination by attending other schools?

A first potential response to this question (and often missed in conversations about LGBT issues on Christian campuses) is that some Christian colleges and universities actively recruit LGBT students, promising them a hospitable environment. Consider, for example, one of the four schools I spotlight in this book—Goshen College in Goshen, Indiana. Goshen College belongs to the Mennonite Church USA, one of the historic peace churches of Protestantism, often known for its involvement in traditionally left-wing causes such as peace and antiwar movements. Currently, the school is home to two officially approved LGBT student groups—Advocates, a group dedicated to raising awareness about LGBT issues, and PRISM, a confidential social support group for students who identify as LGBT. In these ways, as I discuss in chapter one, Goshen is like the hundreds of other (45 percent of all) Christian colleges and universities in the United States that officially recognize LGBT student groups. At Goshen and similar colleges, prospective LGBT students are informed about these official forms of support and told they will feel supported and accepted.

Despite such official forms of support, LGBT students who decide to attend Goshen quickly discover that the campus has issues. For example, the Mennonite Church USA continues to resist full equality for LGBT members and, at the time of my fieldwork, was actively discouraging the adoption of inclusive policies at Mennonite schools. Indeed, as late as 2014, faculty and staff who came out as LGBT were fired or pressured to resign from the school (Pfund 2014). Although the Goshen board voted to add sexual orientation and gender identity to the school's nondiscrimination statement in July 2015, at the time of my fieldwork Goshen was like the 45 percent of Christian colleges and universities that lack nondiscrimination statements inclusive of sexual orientation and the 90 percent of Christian campuses that lack nondiscrimination statements inclusive of gender identity. This fact had given rise to a student-based Open Letter movement, which petitioned the school to add nondiscrimination protections for LGBT people and which was very active during the time I interviewed students at Goshen.

LGBT students also reported that, despite being recruited to the school, they sometimes found a chilly reception from other students in practice. Indeed, the groups Advocates and PRISM originally formed following acts of hate on campus. In one episode, as relayed to me by nearly every student I interviewed at Goshen, some members of the Goshen community reportedly spray-painted the outline of a human body across train tracks that ran through the campus, along with the words "Another Dead Fag." In another case, after some pro-LGBT messages were posted on a campus bulletin board, a student reportedly set the bulletin board on fire.

A second school in this study, Loyola University Chicago, is quite similar to Goshen College in that it actively recruits LGBT students and supports multiple LGBT student groups. In fact, for the past few years, Loyola Chicago has maintained a nondiscrimination statement inclusive of both sexual orientation and gender identity. Nevertheless, Loyola students have also encountered problems at the school. For example, for years, the university simply denied the campus LGBT group's request to hold a drag ball (an event that had its root in 1920s and 1930s queer underground Chicago). Beginning a few years ago, the university began allowing students to hold a more traditional drag show on campus, but this event was immediately met with resistance from one student and two Jesuit priests who believed the event "promotes a lifestyle that is not aligned with the teachings of Saint Ignatius and the Catholic Church" (Advocate 2010). Eventually, the university ordered the group to hold the drag show in a closed-off room on campus that students could only see if they were intentionally going to the event (and not simply walking by). The event remains in that space as of this writing.

More recently, after Illinois legalized same-sex marriage in 2013, a lesbian couple expressed interested in holding their wedding at the school. However, the university denied the couple the opportunity to host their wedding ceremony at the school and quickly announced a new rule stating that only "Catholic weddings" (between Catholic opposite-sex couples) would be allowed on campus, alienating many LGBT students (Kubicki 2014).

For these reasons, it is perhaps unfair to blame LGBT students for attending many Christian colleges and universities in the United States; they have been recruited to a campus only to discover it is less than welcoming in some respects. Still, it remains true that other Christian campuses show no official signs of support for LGBT students—indeed, the majority (55 percent) of Christian colleges and universities continue to lack officially approved LGBT student groups, and many even include so-called homosexual acts on their list of banned behaviors. Why would LGBT students choose to attend those schools?

Another potential response to this question is to offer another question: why would any student (straight or gay) attend a Christian college or university? To this question, the potential responses are numerous. For example, like their straight peers, many LGBT students do identify as religious, and often deeply so; they may seek an environment where they can grow in their faith at the same time that they work toward a college degree. There is also the issue of academics: many religious universities are highly regarded academically, and these schools may have been the best to which students were admitted. Some students seek a college close to home or in a large, LGBT-friendly city (e.g., Catholic University is in Washington, D.C., and Loyola University Chicago is in Chicago, IL). Still other students, eyeing mounting tuition costs, choose to attend the school their parents will agree to pay for or that has given them the best scholarship, which is often a Christian school. Finally, we live in a time of rapid social change, and many students attend their colleges or universities believing that it is only a matter of time before their schools adopt LGBT-inclusive policies.

Another of the four schools I spotlight in this book—Belmont University, which was affiliated with the conservative Tennessee Baptist Convention until 2006 and still identifies as a conservative Christian institution—is instructive for many of the reasons offered above. The school was very attractive to the majority of the students I interviewed because of its highly regarded school of music business. Still, at the time I began my study, Belmont University was a less-than-hospitable environment for LGBT students. For example, until 2009, Belmont not only lacked nondiscrimination protections but also formally prohibited any forms of "homosexual behavior" on campus. Some students on Belmont's campus also reported that they not only heard their peers casually use words like "fag" or phrases such as "that's so gay" in everyday conversation but that they were also the targets of bullying.

The final straw for many students came in 2010, when a lesbian soccer coach suddenly left the school after announcing to her team that she and her same-sex partner would soon have a baby. Although the exact circumstances of her departure have been shrouded by a nondisclosure agreement, most students whom I talked to believe she was forced to leave by the school.

Although, given such details, one might be tempted to "blame the victim" for choosing to attend this school, the case of Belmont is instructive because it demonstrates the real possibility for LGBT students to bring about change even on conservative campuses. Specifically, following the departure of the aforementioned soccer coach, students across the campus, many associated with a newly formed, unofficial LGBT student group called Bridge Builders, coordinated rallies, letter-writing drives, sit-ins, and media appearances at the school to call for new nondiscrimination protections inclusive of sexual orientation. Only days after these protests began, the school not only announced that it would adopt such nondiscrimination protections but also stated that it was initiating the process to formally approve Bridge Builders as an official student organization. Although LGBT students at the school still face many issues—and although the school has not yet adopted nondiscrimination policies protective of gender identity—the case of Belmont challenges those who might write off the possibility for LGBT inclusion on conservative Christian campuses.

Catholic University, referenced at the beginning of the chapter, is likely the most conservative of the four universities studied here. The beginning of the study referenced many of the personal troubles of Catholic University students, but as at Belmont, the university has also adopted official discriminatory policies toward LGBT students. Over the past several years, the university has continually denied recognition to an unofficial LGBT student organization known as CUAllies and indeed has gone so far as to cancel pro-LGBT events scheduled by other student organizations (such as the College Democrats). The university also continually schedules events promoting traditional views of marriage and sexuality—including by a cardinal who compared the LGBT movement to the Ku Klux Klan (DeBernardo 2012).

Still, Catholic University continues to attract many LGBT students who hold strong Catholic identities and seek a distinctly Catholic education, as well as LGBT students who are attracted by the politically active and LGBT-friendly city of Washington, D.C. Furthermore, as at Belmont, many LGBT students enroll at Catholic believing change might be just around the corner. This is not a crazy thought—in fact, for a period in the 1980s and 1990s, the university officially recognized an LGBT student group and included sexual orientation in its nondiscrimination statement. Finally, LGBT students have succeeded in bringing about some change on campus—for example, all students are now required to sign a personal code of honor saying they will not bully or disparage other students on the basis of characteristics that include sexual orientation.

Whether students come to a religious university that openly recruits LGBT students or whether students arrive at their religious university because of other characteristics that appeal to them (such as the school's religious identity, location, or academic programs), most LGBT students attend religious schools because they want to be there, and they seek to cultivate a more inclusive campus community in good faith. LGBT students face many problems at these colleges—from official policies banning same-sex behaviors to chilly campus climates that seem to foster discrimination and harassment—but they come to their colleges at a historical juncture in which it is quite plausible that even conservative Christian schools could come to embrace their LGBT student populations. A study of LGBT activism at Christian colleges and universities, then, has the potential to shed light on an often hidden group of students who are continually fighting institutional heterosexism, homophobia, and transphobia in their day-to-day lives. Because studies have shown that LGBT groups have a positive impact on students' health, academic achievement, and safety,[16] a study of participation in LGBT groups promises to show how and why students come to join and commit to organizations that may improve their lives, and thus how and why students come to pursue empowerment and resiliency even in these conservative environments.

Data and Methods

In selecting the four Christian colleges and universities that I feature in this book—Belmont University in Nashville, Tennessee; the Catholic University of America in Washington, D.C.; Goshen College in Goshen, Indiana; and Loyola University Chicago in Chicago, Illinois—I sought to achieve variation in levels of LGBT inclusion or repression at Christian colleges and universities. Specifically, as Table I.1 shows, I selected the four schools because they varied along the dimensions of (a) denominational affiliation, either with a communalist religious tradition that values social justice or with an individualist religious tradition that emphasizes personal piety;[17] and (b) location, either in a Democratic-leaning state or a Republican-leaning state, characteristics consistently associated with the presence of LGBT groups and inclusive nondiscrimination statements at Christian colleges and universities (see chapter one). Although my interviews showed me that different campus environments seemed to make certain types of participants or activist groups more likely, I also found that the politicized, religious, and LGBT participants and direct action, educational, and solidarity groups were present on each campus at different points in time, lending credence to the idea that the book's core theoretical framework is generalizable to a broad cross-section of Christian colleges and universities (and helping me to eliminate the possibility that a particular kind of campus environment is driving my findings).

I interviewed sixty-five students who had been actively involved in LGBT student groups across these four Christian colleges and universities.[18] (Occasionally, I also draw on twelve additional interviews with faculty, staff members, and community members who provided insights into the history of LGBT activism at their schools.) I conducted most of these interviews during the 2013–14 school year by traveling to each of the four schools and interviewing twelve to fifteen participants at each school. However, I also draw on an earlier wave of interviews that I conducted during the 2010–11 school year at Belmont University, during which time I interviewed eighteen students protesting that school's discriminatory policy on sexual orientation.[19] I identified potential respondents first by contacting group

TABLE I.1 Case selection

Variables	Communalist theological tradition	Individualist theological tradition
Blue state/district	Loyola University Chicago (Catholic–Jesuit; Illinois)	Catholic University of America (Catholic; Washington, D.C.)
Red state/district	Goshen College (Mennonite; Indiana)	Belmont University (historically Southern Baptist; Tennessee)

leaders listed on organizational websites or Facebook groups. I not only asked for their participation in interviews but also requested personal recommendations of current students or alumni who had participated in the group. Furthermore, I asked group leaders to issue a call for interview participants either to a Listserv or a physical meeting of their group. This call for participants included a special request for students who had participated only for a short length of time, given that these students might otherwise shy away from interviews. I stopped interviewing students at each school after I noticed continued repetition in students' perspectives and experiences. The interviews ranged from forty-five minutes to three hours, with an average length of ninety minutes, contingent on the extent of participants' involvement.

I found that my final sample of student participants contained a healthy mix of the progressive politicized participants, the more conservative religious participants, and those who joined an LGBT group simply because they themselves identified as LGBT. This variation was valuable for understanding the multiple pathways to participation that I identify in chapter two. Furthermore, my final sample includes not only students who had served as leaders of each group but also students who had served as active group members, students who had participated in the group for a short period of time, and students who had once participated in the group but later dropped out; this kind of variation was particularly important for my investigation of activist commitment in chapter three. Finally, around half of the respondents at each college or university were current students, while the other half of the respondents at each college or university were alumni. These alumni include some of the founders or earliest participants of the groups at Goshen College, Catholic University, and Belmont University.[20] The interviews with alumni were particularly helpful in my

TABLE 1.2 Sample characteristics

Characteristic	Overall	Loyola	Goshen	Catholic	Belmont
Age (mean)	21	21	20	23	21
Race (proportion non-white)	0.15	0.20	0.17	0.15	0.12
Sex (proportion female)	0.46	0.27	0.58	0.46	0.52
Sexual orientation (proportion LGB)	0.77	1.00	0.42	0.84	0.76
Gender identity and expression (proportion transgender or gender fluid)	0.08	0.27	0.08	0	0
n	65	15	12	13	25*

*The Belmont data collection occurred during two waves.

analysis of biographical consequences of activist group participation in chapter five.

The final sample of student participants is also fairly diverse demographically, as Table 1.2 shows.[21] A few respondents at each site identified as people of color, but most respondents were white. These numbers are reflective of the campuses under study; according to the National Center for Educational Statistics, as of 2012, just 26 percent of Loyola students, 17 percent of Catholic students, 14 percent of Goshen students, and 9 percent of Belmont students identify as nonwhite. The respondents are roughly evenly divided in terms of sex, although women made up only a quarter of the respondents at Loyola.[22] Unsurprisingly, the majority of respondents are lesbian, gay, or bisexual, although straight students comprise the majority of respondents at the Goshen site.[23] Finally, although the Loyola and Goshen sites contained some students who self-identified as transgender or gender fluid, none of the Catholic or Belmont respondents identified as transgender or gender fluid, reflecting the more conservative nature of those campuses, at least at the time I visited. Overall, of the people I personally contacted, the response rate was very high (over 80 percent), with the groups at Catholic and Goshen achieving response rates of over 90 percent.

The interviews themselves covered a wide range of topics (see the online supplement for the full interview schedule). A first section of questions examined circumstances surrounding respondents' initial participation, including how and when they found out about the groups; why they participated in the groups; what they initially expected from the groups; whether they personally identified as activists, people of faith, sexual minorities, or transgender; whether they had any work or family responsibilities at the time they joined the organizations; whether they told friends or family members they were joining the organizations; and whether they feared backlash in response to their joining the organizations. A second set of questions examined their lives before they joined the groups, including whether their family, church, or school was accepting of sexual minorities and transgender people, as well as whether they had previously been involved in LGBT groups or other activist groups. A third set of questions then surveyed students on their leadership responsibilities and levels of activity in the group, while the final set of questions attempted to understand students' postgraduation work, family, political, and religious trajectories (or at least their postgraduation plans). In general, the interviews yielded strong support to the basic insight that grounded this study—varieties of activism exist, and consequently multiple paths to joining activist groups, committing to activist groups, and emerging out of activist groups exist.

Outline

This introduction has provided a broad framework for the book that follows, including its theoretical claims and empirical basis. The remaining chapters flesh out the arguments presented above. Chapter one provides context for the present study through an original argument about the historical developments that have created opportunities for LGBT activism at Christian colleges and universities. I not only discuss the LGBT movement's increasing victories in public policy and influences on public opinion, but I also highlight LGBT activists' organizing efforts within religious denominations; as former religious foes have become receptive to LGBT rights, students have found cover in pushing for LGBT rights even at conservative Christian campuses. I also present data on the presence of LGBT groups and inclusive nondiscrimination policies across all Christian colleges and universities, again showing that it is the recent embrace of LGBT rights by many U.S. religious denominations that has facilitated the emergence of LGBT groups and inclusive nondiscrimination policies on Christian campuses.

Chapters two through five comprise the core of the book and draw from my interview data with participants in LGBT groups at four Christian colleges and universities. Why do students join LGBT activist groups? Chapter two analyzes the multiple pathways that students follow into LGBT groups. As I show, participants with salient political identities were generally raised in like-minded families and had participated in prior activist groups. In comparison, participants with salient religious identities were socialized into values quite hostile to LGBT activism and had never previously participated in activist groups, while participants with sexual identities are best characterized by their attitudinal affinity with the group they join.

Why do students commit to LGBT activist groups? Chapter three focuses on this question. I do not assume that any of the three types of activists discussed above are better suited or more predisposed to LGBT activism than others. Rather, I show that whether students commit to LGBT activist groups depends on whether each of their most salient social identities corresponds with what I call the group ethos or nature of the group in which they are joining, with politicized participants being most drawn to direct action groups, religious participants being most drawn to educational groups, and LGBT participants being most drawn to solidarity groups.

What type of impact do these LGBT activist groups have? Chapter four briefly departs from the focus on student participants to examine how the various LGBT activist groups examined above have succeeded (or failed) to change campus policies regarding LGBT issues and campus climates toward LGBT people. Generally, direct action groups are best suited for achieving policy change, and educational groups are most adept at facilitating changes in campus climate, but at Christian colleges and universities in particular, it is these groups' ability to challenge conventional understandings of religion and LGBT rights that determines their success. Chapter five then focuses on the impacts of LGBT groups on their participants, exploring divergences in the postgraduation political, work, family, and personal lives of these activists. Although participants in direct action groups express plans to continue participating in formal activist groups in the future, participants of educational groups and solidarity groups often plan to foster social change through other means. Specifically, graduates of educational groups plan to open up dialogue on LGBT issues through humanistic careers, and graduates of solidarity groups seek to apply the values of the LGBT movement to their personal family lives.

In the conclusion, I not only reiterate the arguments in the book but also outline the study's broader implications for sociological theory and those working to make colleges and universities more inclusive of LGBT communities. We have much to learn from the brave students who exercise their voice and who dare to be themselves in these challenging environments.

CHAPTER ONE

The Context of Change

LGBT activists at Christian colleges and universities do not mobilize in a vacuum. Although they followed a variety of paths into LGBT activist groups, the students whom I profile in this book all mobilized at a similar historical moment and amidst common sets of structural conditions that made LGBT activism at Christian colleges and universities possible.

In this chapter, I examine the question of why LGBT activist groups began to emerge on Christian college and university campuses at least since the 1980s—but especially by the 1990s and 2000s—from two angles. First, I provide a historical perspective, considering how changes in the political climate for LGBT rights have created a general opportunity for LGBT students and their allies to band together to form LGBT groups and advocate for inclusive nondiscrimination policies at Christian colleges and universities. The goal is not to provide a comprehensive account of the LGBT movement in the United States but rather to highlight key developments in the LGBT rights struggle and to assess how religious communities' responses to those developments either enabled or constrained LGBT activism at Christian colleges and universities.

Second, I provide important statistics bearing on the question of LGBT activist group emergence, explaining why, even at this moment in history, when the political climate for LGBT rights in the United States has never been more favorable, some Christian colleges and universities embrace their LGBT student populations while other Christian schools do not. I especially focus on how certain religious characteristics of each Christian college or university, such as their religious affiliations, have made it more or less likely that a school will approve LGBT groups and adopt inclusive nondiscrimination policies.

My central argument throughout the chapter is that, although the LGBT movement's political gains were necessary for the emergence of LGBT activism on Christian campuses, it was only when an increasing number of religious denominations began to endorse LGBT rights that students at Christian colleges and universities had the cover they needed to seek full inclusion on their campuses.

Historical Opportunities for LGBT Activism at
Christian Colleges and Universities

LGBT activism in the United States, and LGBT student organizing on Christian campuses in particular, has arguably been most visible since activists began mobilizing in favor of same-sex marriage during the 1990s and 2000s.[1] Yet LGBT people have been mobilizing in the United States since at least World War II, and many of the battle lines that people took for granted during the same-sex marriage campaigns—between LGBT people on one side and religious people on the other side—were far from predetermined. To illustrate the historical changes that shaped opportunities for LGBT activism at Christian colleges and universities, then, I begin by reviewing accounts of some of the earliest activism around LGBT issues in the United States.

Following World War II, large cities on the West Coast (such as Los Angeles and San Francisco) and the East Coast (particularly New York City) became notable for their growing gay and lesbian populations and, consequently, became home to some of the earliest gay and lesbian advocacy organizations, which were known as homophile organizations. For example, in 1950, the Mattachine Society, one of the country's first homophile organizations dedicated to promoting the rights of gay men, was founded in Los Angeles,[2] and in 1955, the Daughters of Bilitis, the first homophile organization devoted to lesbian rights, was founded in San Francisco (Armstrong 2002, ch. 2). In the following decade, in 1967, college students formed the first gay rights group on a college campus, the Student Homophile League, at Columbia University in New York City, and in 1968, students established Student Homophile League chapters at Cornell University and New York University (Beemyn 2003).[3] The earliest homophile organizations emphasized discretion and virtue. Few members of these homophile organizations were willing to publicly out themselves, and they often went to great lengths to maintain their secrecy; in the case of the student organizations, gay and lesbian students counted on heterosexual students to sign initial applications and provide cover for closeted students (Beemyn 2003; D'Emilio 1983). Although they approached gay and lesbian advocacy differently than LGBT organizations do today, such organizations provided important foundations for subsequent LGBT organizing in the United States.

This early period of homophile organizing is notable for attracting what people might today consider unlikely allies, particularly people of faith

(H. White 2015). For example, in San Francisco, local ministers took notice of the hardships facing gays and lesbians and began to advocate for gay and lesbian rights. In 1964, sixteen ministers associated with the Methodist, Episcopal, Lutheran, and United Church of Christ faiths met with thirteen leaders of homophile organizations at the Mill Valley Conference. Shortly after the conference, one local church and two leaders of the Daughters of Bilitis formed the Council on Religion and the Homosexual, which was the first organization in the United States to use the word "homosexual" in its title. This council was also responsible for organizing one of the first public events for gays and lesbians in the United States (Armstrong and Crage 2006). When police officers harassed some of the people attending that event, many of these ministers became radicalized and shifted to the front lines of the emerging gay and lesbian rights struggle (H. White 2015, ch. 3). Faith leaders' advocacy extended to the gay and lesbian student organizations on secular college campuses. For example, at Columbia University, school officials nearly revoked the Student Homophile League's charter following a front-page *New York Times* article about the group's approval; although the university was "inundated with outraged letters," and although leaders ranging from the dean to the director of counseling came out in opposition to the group, "the strong support of the league's advisor, the university chaplain, apparently prevented Columbia officials from revoking the group's charter" (Beemyn 2003, 207).

At this point in history, then, it was not obvious that LGBT rights activists would find themselves on the opposite side of a "culture war" (Hunter 1992) with people of faith. Certainly, most religious people in the United States at this time—and most secular people—did not favor gay and lesbian rights; sexual intercourse between two people of the same sex was, in fact, illegal across most of the United States during the early postwar period. But the point is that some prominent Christian ministers did come out in support of gay and lesbian rights during this period, and it is as least possible to imagine those ministers leading their denominations to support gay and lesbian rights and, in turn, facilitating the emergence of LGBT groups at Christian colleges and universities. History, however, took a different turn. Why did so many people of faith turn against the gay and lesbian community in the following decades?

An answer can be found in the social revolution that was taking place in the United States in the late 1960s and, especially, in the vigorous backlash that followed. By the 1960s, many Americans began rebelling against the racial, gender, and economic inequalities that they had often tolerated in the 1950s; students began to mobilize in favor of social and economic equality through civil rights, feminist, and working-class movements.[4] In line with this revolutionary zeitgeist, many gays and lesbians became frustrated with homophile organizations' emphasis on discretion and virtue and established gay liberation and lesbian feminist organizations. These new organizations encouraged homosexuals to come out and pursue sexual liberation and equality through more confrontational means (Armstrong 2002, ch. 3). For example, gay liberationists turned underground gay bars, which were often targeted by police, into sites of political struggle, perhaps best symbolized by the famous Stonewall Inn uprising in New York City's Greenwich Village in 1969 (Armstrong and Crage 2006).

The gay and lesbian movement's radical turn was especially evident on college campuses. Around 1970, Cornell's Student Homophile League changed its name to the Gay Liberation Front and sponsored one of the first gay student sit-ins in the United States at a local bar that had kicked out its gay clientele (Beemyn 2003). Students quickly formed gay liberation groups on other college campuses, and although some secular colleges initially denied these groups recognition, students successfully turned to the courts to secure their right to organize on campus. For example, students at Sacramento State College filed a lawsuit after the school denied recognition to a group known as the Society for Homosexual Freedom (SHF). Republican-appointed Judge William Gallagher's "decision in favor of the SHF was ... the first to use free speech and association grounds to extend legal protection to gay and lesbian student organizations.... That precedent, and the constitutional arguments used, enabled other gay and lesbian student organizations to rebut efforts at preventing their organizing on campus" (Reichard 2010, 633). Overall, the late 1960s and early 1970s were a time of incredible growth for gay and lesbian organizations: while there were only fifty homophile organizations in the United States in 1969, over 800 gay and lesbian organizations existed by 1973 (D'Emilio 1983, 238), including over 175 gay and lesbian college groups (Beemyn 2003).

Where did faith communities find themselves during these struggles? Some Christian denominations certainly joined campaigns on issues such as racial equality (Westhues 1976). Furthermore, the first Christian denomination to welcome lesbians and gays was established during this time period. Specifically, a minister named Troy Perry founded the Metropolitan Community Church (MCC) in Los Angeles in 1968, inspiring an umbrella organization of pro-LGBT churches known as the United Federation of Metropolitan Community Churches in 1970 (Kane 2013b; H. White 2015;

M. M. Wilcox 2001). Perry himself played a significant role in the nation's first gay pride parade, held in 1970, a year after the Stonewall riots (H. White 2015, ch. 5). However, Perry himself founded this denomination only after he was "expelled from two different Pentecostal denominations due to his homosexuality," and most MCC members did not become Christians through MCC churches but rather switched from churches associated with other denominations that were less accepting (Kane 2013b, 138, 142).

Christian colleges and universities themselves were also not immune from the upheavals taking place at many secular colleges and universities during the 1960s. In fact, one of the schools featured in this study, the Catholic University of America, became a veritable "hotbed of activism" (Van Dyke 1998). Specifically, in 1967, the faculty of that school, along with over 2,000 students, led a remarkable five-day strike in protest of the school's decision to fire a tenured professor, Charles E. Curran, who dissented from church doctrine on birth control. Following the strike, the school reinstated Professor Curran, and social justice–minded Catholics began exerting control over the school (Mitchell 2015). Gay and lesbian activists also began targeting Christian colleges and universities during this time period, although those activists came from the outside rather than within. In her book *Reforming Sodom*, Heather White (2015, 147) recounts a remarkable scene at Catholic University:

> In 1971 . . . the *Christian Century* and the more conservative *Christianity Today* reported on a "zap" in Washington, D.C., where gay activists invaded a conference on religion and homosexuality taking place at the Catholic University of America. Both journals presented the theatrics of the demonstration: radicals bearing pink banners marched around the conference hall, seized the microphone, and demanded that conference participants stop examining homosexuality and begin practicing it instead. . . . Neither picture, however, offered a full account. Paul Breton, one of those gay activists, recalled that the "zap" ended in dialogue. Conference speakers ceded the floor to the liberationists, who turned the event into a series of dialogue sessions and a tour of local gay bars intended to introduce the religious leaders to real-life gays and lesbians.

Overall, though, many Christians began to feel like their institutions were under assault in the late 1960s, and they would form the backbone of a major backlash against minority-group movements like the LGBT movement in the decades to come.

Indeed, by the 1970s, as the "Long Sixties" wound down, Christians had seized on homosexuality as a key source of moral concern (Fetner 2008; Stone 2016; D. K. Williams 2010). The Republican Party began campaigning against the perceived excesses of the sixties and won nearly every presidential election from 1968 through 1988. The only exception was the election of 1976, which followed the resignation of Richard Nixon. One reason the Republican Party dominated U.S. presidential elections during this period was the rise of the religious right, a close alliance between faith communities and the political right. For example, Baptist minister Jerry Falwell formed the Moral Majority in 1979, which mobilized churchgoers in support of socially conservative Republican candidates (C. Wilcox 1991). In 1977, former beauty pageant winner and evangelical Christian activist Anita Bryant formed Save Our Children, which sought to overturn local nondiscrimination ordinances inclusive of sexual orientation, beginning in Dade County, Florida. The Save Our Children campaigns inspired the high-profile Briggs Initiative in California in 1978, which sought to bar not only gays and lesbians but also their supporters from employment in public schools, although the ballot proposition failed (Fetner 2008). Finally, the decade of Jerry Falwell and Anita Bryant witnessed the rise of the "ex-gay" movement in the United States, which promised to help gays and lesbians become heterosexual through prayer and other "reparative therapies" (Erzen 2006; Waidzunas 2015). The country's first religious ex-gay organization, Love in Action, formed in a suburb of San Francisco in 1973, followed by Exodus International in the late 1970s (Crockett and Kane 2012; on its recent closure, see Payne 2013).

After bearing the backlash of the religious right in the 1970s, the gay and lesbian movement reached an even lower point in the early- to mid-1980s. Beginning in 1981, gay men in cities such as Los Angeles, San Francisco, and New York City began to fall ill with AIDS. Although activists quickly formed social service organizations to respond to the pandemic once researchers discovered the source of the disease, many politicians either failed to respond or engaged in new attempts to pathologize gay men. President Reagan did not acknowledge the pandemic until well into his second term, and the religious right seized on the epidemic to portray gays and lesbians as harmful to society (Armstrong 2002, ch. 8).

To be sure, the 1970s and 1980s were not completely lost decades for the lesbian and gay movement. Activists consolidated communities and "gayborhoods" (Ghaziani 2014) in many large cities. For example, the ever-present gay subculture in San Francisco became highly visible during the

1970s, and the first openly gay man in public office in California, Harvey Milk, was elected to a seat on the San Francisco Board of Supervisors in 1977 (Armstrong 2002, ch. 6). Furthermore, in the 1980s, some U.S. high schools joined secular colleges and universities in welcoming formal gay and lesbian student groups, with two prestigious high schools in Massachusetts, Concord Academy and Phillips Academy, launching the nation's first Gay-Straight Alliances (GSAs) in the early 1980s (Miceli 2005).

Still, these successes were mostly the exception to the rule: during the 1970s and 1980s, lesbian and gay activists clearly found themselves on the opposite side of a heated "culture war" with people of faith. Although some mainline Protestant pastors sympathized with the lesbian and gay rights movement—and two major Protestant denominations, the Episcopal Church USA (in 1976) and the United Church of Christ (1986), opened themselves to gay and lesbian members during these years (Integrity USA 2011; Open and Affirming Coalition 2014)—most pastors shied away from any public support for lesbian and gay rights. As a result, students attempting to form gay and lesbian organizations on Christian college and university campuses during this time generally came up short. In fact, although the court system had intervened to protect gays' and lesbians' right to organize on secular college and university campuses in the early 1970s, courts provided students at religious colleges and universities no such relief. For example, in 1980, students sued Georgetown University (a Catholic institution) for refusing to recognize their organization, invoking an earlier case in which the Supreme Court ruled that Bob Jones University could not discriminate on the basis of race. Nevertheless, a court ruled that "there is no similar national policy compelling government intervention in matters relating to sexual orientation" (Miceli 2005, 19).

With so much of the public opposed to lesbian and gay rights, how could the lesbian and gay movement recover? And how could LGBT activism at Christian colleges and universities ever become possible? After dominating presidential elections for over two decades, the Republican Party lost the White House in 1992 to Bill Clinton, who encouraged the Democratic Party to turn the page on the heated left versus right debates of the 1960s and adopt a more moderate tone—a "third way." Although he had campaigned in favor of lesbian and gay rights, Clinton continually compromised on such social issues once in office. For example, he approved a Don't Ask, Don't Tell policy that required lesbians and gay men to remained closeted while serving in the military, and he signed the Defense of Marriage Act, which defined marriage as a union between a man and a woman for the purpose of receiving federal benefits. Still, the LGBT movement (as it began calling itself), having already recognized a need to rehabilitate its image following the AIDS crisis, took important lessons from this election and largely followed Clinton's turn toward moderation. Activists shifted their attention to institutional politics and adopted more mainstream goals and tactics, such as pursuing same-sex marriage through litigation (Bernstein and Naples 2015; Zylan 2011). The Human Rights Campaign (HRC), which became the country's largest LGBT organization, was emblematic of this new approach (Armstrong 2002, ch. 9).[5]

The rise of formal LGBT organizations in national politics—and, perhaps just as important, the spread of LGBT groups across secular colleges, high schools, and middle schools—facilitated the slow emergence of LGBT groups at Christian colleges and universities. Initially, only liberal-leaning schools approved such groups, and they established strict rules about the types of events they could hold on campus. Within my sample, the Catholic University of America was the earliest school to authorize a gay and lesbian student organization, the Organization for Gay and Lesbian Rights, in the late 1980s. This approval was, perhaps, natural for a school that had become home to so many on the Catholic Left. However, in the late 1980s, the Congregation for the Doctrine of the Faith, led by future pope Josef Ratzinger, ruled that Professor Charles Curran—the theology professor who had been the subject of the 1967 faculty-led strike—could no longer teach theology at the school, citing his liberal views not only on contraception but also on homosexuality (Curran 2006). As professors like Charles Curran left the school during the 1990s (either involuntarily, through dismissals, or voluntarily, by resigning or retiring), the school replaced them with faculty who held conservative views on sexuality. Catholic University increasingly constrained the Organization for Gay and Lesbian Rights from holding on-campus events, and by 2002, the university shuttered the organization completely. In 1990, Loyola University Chicago decided to approve an organization known as the Gay, Lesbian, and Bisexual Association (GLABA) following at least one earlier rejection of an LGBT organization. However, early on, some students strongly opposed the group, even vandalizing GLABA's office, and the school initially refused to approve an inclusive nondiscrimination policy. Finally, in 1991, students at Goshen College formed an unofficial support group known as the Lesbian, Bisexual, and Gay Alliance. However, although students applied for official status in 1994, the Goshen College Board of Overseers denied the group recognition. It was not until hate crimes against the LGBT community occurred on Goshen's campus in the late 1990s (as described in the introduction) that the school approved two groups, a solidarity group named PRISM and an educational group named Advocates, although Goshen continued to discriminate against LGBT faculty and staff. I found no evidence of LGBT organizing at the more conservative Belmont University during this period.

It was during the 2000s that the LGBT movement really saw its investments in institutional politics begin to pay off and that LGBT students increasingly found allies at Christian colleges and universities. In 2003, following the election of Republican president George W. Bush, the U.S. Supreme Court struck down state laws that had effectively criminalized sexual acts between persons of the same sex (Carpenter 2012). Later that same year, the Massachusetts Supreme Court issued a decision that made Massachusetts the first state in the United States to recognize same-sex marriages (Masci 2008). The initial backlash was swift. In the midst of his 2004 presidential reelection campaign, President Bush campaigned on a Federal Marriage Amendment that would have banned all states from recognizing same-sex marriage. Although that constitutional amendment failed, voters in thirteen states did approve state-level same-sex marriage bans in 2004, followed by ten more states in 2005 and 2006 (Masci 2008). Still, public opinion slowly shifted in favor of LGBT rights, and in 2008, then senator Barack Obama was elected president on a platform that included overturning both the Don't Ask, Don't Tell policy and the Defense of Marriage Act, both of which he achieved during his first term in office. LGBT activists rushed to take advantage of the improved political climate for LGBT rights, and in late 2008 through 2012, several states began to recognize same-sex marriages not only as the result of court rulings (Connecticut, Iowa) but also through legislation (Maine, New Hampshire, New York, Vermont, Washington) (Pew Research Center 2015). President Obama initially walked a fine line on the issue of same-sex marriage itself; in his 2008 campaign, he stated his belief that marriage should be between a man and a woman, but he also encouraged his supporters to vote against same-sex marriage bans in their own states. Furthermore, following his election, he repeatedly told people he was "evolving" on the issue of same-sex marriage, although he did not place himself on one side or the other of the evolution. But during his 2012 reelection bid, as more states legalized same-sex marriage, President Obama came out in full support of same-sex marriage, and by 2013 and 2014, the LGBT movement rapidly tallied up victories. In 2013, the Supreme Court legalized same-sex marriage in California in a narrow procedural ruling. Nine other states quickly joined

California that year, followed by a stunning eighteen states in 2014. Finally, by 2015, the Supreme Court took up the question of same-sex marriage once and for all, and it issued its landmark *Obergefell v. Hodges* decision legalizing same-sex marriage across the entire United States (Pew Research Center 2015).

The years after the election of President Obama were extremely consequential for the LGBT movement, not only because of these important political victories, but also because of the emergence of LGBT religious organizations that worked to shift the debate on LGBT rights within Christianity. One organization, Faith in America, began to counter "religion-based bigotry and prejudice" through books, rapid response e-mails, and media outreach (Faith in America 2014). Another, the Reformation Project, began to hold conferences—movement schools (Isaac et al. 2012)—that trained LGBT people and their allies to advocate for LGBT equality in more conservative churches and communities (Vines 2013). All major Christian denominations, and many smaller ones, have also attracted their own specific LGBT activist groups.[6] As the result of such activism, mainline Protestant denominations slowly moved toward LGBT inclusion. The United Church of Christ and the Episcopal Church USA, which began accepting lesbian, gay, and bisexual members and clergy in earlier decades, formally extended marriage rights to same-sex couples in 2005 and 2009, respectively (Integrity USA 2011; Open and Affirming Coalition 2014). In 2009, the Evangelical Lutheran Church in America voted in favor of the ordination of noncelibate gay, lesbian, and bisexual minsters, although it does not yet officially provide rites for same-sex unions (Kwon 2009); in 2010, the Presbyterian Church USA similarly voted to authorize the ordination of noncelibate gays, lesbians, and bisexuals (Kwon 2010) before authorizing same-sex weddings in 2014 (Kwon 2014); and in 2013, the Christian Church (Disciples of Christ) voted to affirm the "faith, baptism, and spiritual gifts of all Christians regardless of their sexual orientation or gender identity," authorizing churches to ordain LGBT people (Martinez 2013).

Soulforce, an organization that promotes LGBT rights specifically at conservative Christian colleges and universities, was also active during this period. Founded in 1998 by Mel White, a former ghostwriter for religious right leaders such as Jerry Falwell, the organization initially held protests in favor of LGBT rights at meetings of major Christian denominations. However, in the mid- to late 2000s, Soulforce began to organize Equality Rides, modeled after the civil rights–era Freedom Rides, to Christian colleges and universities that discriminated against LGBT students (Powell 2011;

Spencer and Barnett 2013). The organization researched Christian colleges and universities that maintained formal bans on so-called homosexual acts (Wolff and Himes 2010); it then arrived at a list of target schools and notified them of their plans to visit. Some schools, including Belmont University, agreed to allow the organization on campus, sometimes cosponsoring town hall sessions or debates about LGBT issues. Other colleges formally barred the organization from their campuses and arrested members when they attempted to cross onto their property. Regardless, the organization sparked debates over LGBT issues on numerous conservative Christian campuses, sometimes inspiring formal changes in policy (Comer 2007).

Overall, the rapid change in laws concerning LGBT rights, and the rise of LGBT religious organizations, meant that LGBT groups even at more conservative Christian colleges and universities now seemed possible. Indeed, by the late 2000s and early 2010s, new LGBT groups (whether official or unofficial) formed at all of the Christian colleges and universities in my sample, and many of the schools adopted nondiscrimination policies. As recounted in the introductory chapter, in 2009, students formed an unofficial LGBT group known as CUAllies at Catholic University, although the group still lacks official recognition; the GLABA group at Loyola University Chicago changed its name to Advocate in 2005, not long before the school incorporated both sexual orientation and gender identity into its nondiscrimination policy; in 2011, students at Goshen College launched the Open Letter movement to pressure the school into adopting a nondiscrimination policy inclusive of sexual orientation and gender identity, which the school did in 2015; and in 2009, students at Belmont University launched Bridge Builders, which the school approved along with an inclusive nondiscrimination policy in 2011. The following chapters describe the struggle to form these groups and change school policies.

Certainly, LGBT activists did not make unimpeded advances during the Obama years. Although many churches now welcome and affirm LGBT members and clergy (Adler 2012; Whitehead 2013), some mainline Protestant churches continue to discriminate on the basis of sexual orientation and gender identity. Most notably, the largest mainline Protestant denomination in the United States, the United Methodist Church, continues to label homosexuality as a "sin," bars openly gay people (but not transgender people) from ordination, and prevents ministers from performing same-sex unions (Human Rights Campaign 2015). Furthermore, the landscape for LGBT individuals outside mainline Protestant churches remains bleak. Although the Roman Catholic Church officially welcomes celibate gay, lesbian, and bisexual members, a catechism states that "homosexual acts [are] acts of grave depravity," and "under no circumstances can they be approved" (Human Rights Campaign 2015). Accordingly, the church strongly opposes same-sex marriage and adoption rights for same-sex couples. Recent statements by the pope may have softened the church's image on LGBT rights—he told one reporter, "If a person is gay and seeks God and has good will, who am I to judge him?" (Donadio 2013), and he has stated that the church should ask for gay and lesbian people's forgiveness for the way that it has treated them (Pullella 2016)—but the church has not formally changed its doctrine. Evangelical Protestant churches (including the Southern Baptist Convention, the Presbyterian Church in America, the Church of the Nazarene, the Assemblies of God, and most nondenominational churches) remain opposed to any form of LGBT rights (Human Rights Campaign 2015). Finally, historically black Protestant churches (such as the African Methodist Episcopal Church and the Church of God in Christ) and other denominations emerging out of the Christian tradition (including the Church of Jesus Christ of Latter-day Saints [the Mormon Church] and the Seventh-Day Adventist Church) oppose same-sex marriage and ordination for LGBT members (Human Rights Campaign 2015).

Public policy is also not yet on the side of LGBT students at Christian colleges and universities. After coming under pressure from religious leaders and college presidents, the Obama administration announced in 2013 that it would begin to issue nondiscrimination waivers to any Christian colleges and universities that requested them (Anderson 2015). Although none of the colleges and universities that I visited asked for explicit authorization to discriminate against students or faculty on the basis of sexual orientation or gender identity, the U.S. Department of Education disclosed in 2016 that seventy-five colleges and universities had requested the ability to discriminate on the basis of one or both of these characteristics since 2009, and many other colleges and universities had requested exemptions in previous years (Office of Civil Rights 2016). More recently, the Trump administration has withdrawn federal protections for transgender college students at public and private colleges and universities alike (Fain 2017), and it is possible that the Trump administration will be more favorable to some Republican congresspeople's demands for a proposed federal law enshrining Christian colleges and universities' right to discriminate (National Public Radio 2015). Still, Christian colleges and universities' resistance to LGBT inclusion is by no means ironclad, and the next section will explore the political and institutional correlates of LGBT inclusion among Christian colleges and universities.

Explaining the Presence of LGBT Groups at Christian Colleges and Universities

Several historical developments have facilitated opportunities to form LGBT groups at Christian colleges and universities in the United States. LGBT movements have steadily secured civil rights over the past few decades, especially same-sex marriage; LGBT students have won the ability to form groups on secular campuses; and LGBT people have slowly become incorporated into some Christian denominations. Still, although all Christian colleges and universities operate in this new historical terrain, some Christian colleges choose to recognize LGBT student groups and approve inclusive nondiscrimination policies while others resist them. Why?

To address this question, in this section I draw on a comprehensive database of LGBT group presence and inclusive nondiscrimination policy adoption across Christian colleges and universities in the United States—682 in all—to identify the specific political and institutional factors that explain LGBT inclusion across Christian colleges and universities. In constructing this database, I counted only LGBT groups that had been officially approved by their colleges and universities—as evidenced by a listing on the school's website or by some other credible documentation—as well as official policies barring discrimination against LGBT students. The data are from 2013, a time when, as described in the previous section, the LGBT movement was experiencing significant success on the national stage and many mainline Protestant denominations were officially incorporating LGBT members and clergy. I found that 307 of the 682 schools in my database (about 45 percent) had approved officially recognized LGBT groups and that 375 of the 682 schools (about 55 percent) had adopted nondiscrimination statements inclusive of sexual orientation. (I also found that 70 of the 682 schools, just over 10 percent, have approved nondiscrimination statements inclusive of gender identity, although I do not systematically assess the adoption of such policies in this chapter.) Again, why do some schools support these LGBT groups and inclusive nondiscrimination policies while others resist them?

Not only had the broad sociopolitical developments described above created a general opportunity for LGBT students to organize on Christian college and university campuses, but also political opportunities specific to the states in which these schools are located facilitated (or impeded) Christian colleges and universities' inclusivity of LGBT students. The theory of political opportunity in social movement studies suggests that movements for social change are more likely to succeed in contexts that are favorable to their cause.[7] Along these lines, scholars who have attempted to explain the presence of LGBT groups across U.S. high schools, colleges, and universities have argued that schools located in liberal states, outside of the South, and outside of rural areas will be more likely to approve LGBT groups, because residents in these areas express higher approval of LGBT rights (Fetner and Kush 2008; Fine 2012; Kane 2013a).

Table 1.1 assesses the importance of these political opportunity variables to LGBT inclusion at Christian universities. Specifically, the table compares schools with LGBT groups and inclusive nondiscrimination policies to schools without such groups and policies in terms of their likelihood of being in a Democratic-leaning state, a non-Southern state, and a non-rural area. As the table shows, whereas schools with LGBT groups tend to be in states that cast a majority of their votes (51 percent) for President Obama, schools lacking LGBT groups are in states that gave a minority of their votes (47 percent) to President Obama. Furthermore, whereas 78 percent of schools with LGBT groups are outside the South, just over 63 percent of schools lacking LGBT groups are in the non-South. Finally, whereas 80 percent of schools with LGBT groups are outside of rural areas, a lower 70 percent of schools lacking LGBT groups are in non-rural areas. This same pattern applies to schools with inclusive nondiscrimination policies versus schools without them—schools with nondiscrimination statements cast more of their votes for President Obama (50 percent versus 47 percent), are more likely to be outside the South (71 percent versus 68 percent), and are more likely to be outside of rural areas (77 percent versus 72 percent). However, the differences are not as stark and, for the non-South and non-rural variables, not statistically significant—a term social scientists use to mean that an observed difference between two groups actually exists (and is not attributed to chance). Theories of LGBT group approval and nondiscrimination policy adoption that emphasize political opportunity seem incomplete.

Resource mobilization theory in social movement studies alternatively suggests that "communities with more resources—including economic assets, human resources, knowledge, and allies—will be more successful at creating organizations" (Kane 2013a, 834).[8] Specifically, at the institutional level, scholars have argued that schools with higher endowments will

TABLE 1.1 Descriptive statistics for LGBT groups and nondiscrimination policies at Christian universities: Political opportunity variables

	LGBT groups			Nondiscrimination policy		
	Yes	No	Sig.	Yes	No	Sig.
% state vote for Obama (mean)	51.11%	47.07%	***	50.19%	47.31%	***
% non-South	77.52%	63.47%	***	71.47%	67.76%	
% non-rural	80.46%	70.13%	**	77.07%	71.99%	

Note: N=682; * *p* < .05; ** *p* < .01; *** *p* < .001 (two-tailed tests)

be more likely to approve LGBT groups because they have more financial resources to support them, and more selective schools will be more likely to adopt LGBT groups because they draw more liberal faculty and students, who are potential allies (Kane 2013a). Similarly, focusing on student body characteristics, scholars have theorized that schools with larger student bodies (i.e., schools with more human resources), schools with fewer male students or students of color (i.e., given public opinion, schools with a greater number of allies), and schools with fewer low-income students (i.e., schools with more financial resources) will be more likely to approve LGBT groups.

Table 1.2 compares schools with LGBT groups and inclusive nondiscrimination policies to schools without those groups and policies in terms of each of these resource variables. As the table shows, LGBT-inclusive schools are substantially wealthier (in terms of endowment) than non-inclusive schools; specifically, schools with LGBT groups possess over $27,000 more per student than schools without such groups, and schools with inclusive nondiscrimination policies possess over $15,000 more per student compared with schools without such policies. LGBT-inclusive schools are also much larger (in terms of number of students) than schools without LGBT groups and nondiscrimination policies; schools with LGBT groups have over 1,300 more students than schools without such groups, and schools with inclusive nondiscrimination policies have over 900 more students than schools without such policies. As predicted, LGBT-inclusive schools also have lower acceptance rates and are home to fewer minorities and fewer men; however, these differences are not as stark in substantive (and occasionally statistical) terms. Finally, LGBT-inclusive schools are actually more likely to have students on federal loans than schools without

TABLE 1.2 Descriptive statistics for LGBT groups and nondiscrimination policies at Christian universities: Resource variables

	LGBT groups			Nondiscrimination policy		
	Yes	No	Sig.	Yes	No	Sig.
Endowment full-time equivalent (mean)	$44,938.86	$17,816.61	***	$36,813.55	$21,734.13	***
% acceptance (mean)	66.12%	68.99%	*	66.37%	69.32%	*
Number of students (mean)	3,158	1,836	***	2,840	1,932	***
% minorities (mean)	28.88%	34.17%	**	33.35%	29.87%	
% women (mean)	61.65%	57.14%	***	61.88%	55.87%	***
% student loans (mean)	67.80%	66.48%		68.87%	64.87%	*

Note: N=682; * $p < .05$; ** $p < .01$; *** $p < .001$ (two-tailed tests)

LGBT-inclusive policies, a difference that runs against our expectations but is not very significant, at least in substantive terms. Resource variables occasionally provide insights into the differences between schools with LGBT groups and inclusive nondiscrimination policies and schools without them, but they still seem incomplete.

If political opportunities and resource allocations do not adequately explain the presence of LGBT groups and inclusive nondiscrimination policies, how can we explain LGBT inclusion at Christian universities? Much as I argued in the previous section, denominations' stances on LGBT rights ultimately create the opportunities for LGBT students to organize on campus and for schools to adopt inclusive nondiscrimination policies on a broad scale. Religious traditions vary in terms of what I call their *theological orientations*. For example, Kniss (2003) urges attention to *individualist* and *communal* orientations within religion.[9] Some religious traditions exhibit individualist orientations, believing that churches should focus on reforming individuals, such as by opposing practices (including homosexuality) that threaten their moral purity. Other religious traditions exhibit communal orientations, holding that churches should focus on reforming wider communities, including by bringing about a more socially and economically just society. Research within social movement studies[10] and the sociology of religion[11] strongly suggests a link between communal orientations and mobilization in support of social justice.

Might theological orientations explain why some Christian colleges and universities are inclusive of LGBT students while others are not? There are several ways we might assess the role of theological orientations. In terms of the sociopolitical context, we might notice that the religious composition of a Christian college or university's state—the degree to which a state contains adherents to communal or individualist religious traditions—is linked to the presence of LGBT groups and nondiscrimination policies. As private institutions, Christian colleges and universities rely on financial support from local residents and churches; residents also contribute to debates over LGBT rights on Christian campuses by voicing their opinions in the media (e.g., Barton 2014; Coley 2014). The religious composition of a state may also have an indirect effect on campuses' inclusivity of LGBT students, because students looking to form an LGBT group will often consider how welcoming the surrounding community is toward LGBT students. Next, at the institutional level, we might observe that formal affiliation with an individualist or communal religious tradition is associated with the adoption of LGBT groups and nondiscrimination policies at Christian colleges and universities. In many cases, denominations not only provide money to fund Christian colleges and universities' operations but also place their members on these schools' boards of trust; thus, they often exert substantial influence on the policies of these schools. Finally, with regard to student body characteristics, we might notice that the percentage of religion and theology majors at a school is linked to the presence of LGBT groups and nondiscrimination policies at Christian colleges and universities. Students actively participate in campus debates over LGBT rights by voicing their opinions in student newspapers and voting on student groups and campus policies through their student governments (e.g., Coley 2014). When campuses are home to high percentages of religion and theology majors, campus debates may be skewed against LGBT rights, perhaps because students in religion majors are less exposed to social justice issues or perhaps (more likely) because schools specializing in religious studies (e.g., Bible colleges) are more likely to be associated with individualist traditions that shelter students from worldly concerns (e.g., Ringenberg 2006, ch. 5).

Table 1.3 provides descriptive statistics comparing schools with LGBT groups and nondiscrimination policies to schools without such groups and policies in terms of these religion variables. As the table shows, schools with LGBT groups are in states with fewer adherents to individualist religious traditions (17 percent) compared with schools without such groups (22 percent); similarly, schools with inclusive nondiscrimination statements

TABLE 1.3 Descriptive statistics for LGBT groups and nondiscrimination policies at Christian universities: Religion variables

	LGBT groups			Nondiscrimination policy		
	Yes	No	Sig.	Yes	No	Sig.
% state adherents of individualist religious traditions (mean)	16.6	22.41	***	18.06	21.91	***
% affiliated with religious traditions with individualist orientations	4.56	62.13	***	6.67	72.31	***
% religion majors (mean)	1.05	20.68	***	1.85	24.05	***

Note: N=682; * $p < .05$; ** $p < .01$; *** $p < .001$ (two-tailed tests)

are in states with fewer members of individualist religious traditions (18 percent) than schools without such policies (22 percent). These differences are statistically significant. Next, fewer than 5 percent of schools that approve LGBT groups and fewer than 7 percent of schools with inclusive nondiscrimination policies belong to the more discriminatory individualist religious traditions, whereas over 62 percent of schools without LGBT groups and over 72 percent of schools without nondiscrimination policies are associated with individualist religious traditions. These differences are hugely significant in both a substantive and statistical sense. Finally, fewer than 2 percent of students at schools that have approved LGBT groups and fewer than 2 percent of students at schools with nondiscrimination statements major in religion or theology; in comparison, nearly 21 percent of students at schools without LGBT groups and over 24 percent of students at schools with inclusive nondiscrimination statements major in religion or theology. Again, the contrasts here are quite striking in both substantive and statistical terms.

I undertook multivariate analyses to assess whether each of these political opportunity, resource, and religion variables remain significant predictors of LGBT groups and inclusive nondiscrimination policies even when all other variables are held constant (see the online supplement). The percentage of state adherents to an individualist denomination is not a statistically significant predictor of LGBT groups or nondiscrimination statements inclusive of sexual orientation in the multivariate analyses. However, affiliation with an individualist denomination is a consistently strong, significant, and negative predictor of LGBT groups and inclusive nondiscrimination statements. In layperson's terms, this means that schools affiliated with individualist denominations do not approve LGBT groups and inclusive nondiscrimination statements at as high of rates as schools affiliated with communal denominations, even when taking into account all other variables discussed here. Furthermore, the percentage of religion majors at a school was also a significant, negative predictor of both LGBT groups and inclusive nondiscrimination statements, meaning that schools with more religion majors tend to resist LGBT groups and reject inclusive nondiscrimination statements, with the caveat that this is only true at schools affiliated with individualist denominations. The only political opportunity or resource variables that significantly predict both the inclusion of LGBT groups and inclusive nondiscrimination policies at a school—when the effects of all other variables are taken into consideration—are student body size and the state vote for Obama, meaning that larger schools and schools in states that voted for Obama are more LGBT-friendly.

Theological orientations, then, seem to shape (if not completely determine) Christian colleges and universities' decisions to approve LGBT groups and adopt inclusive nondiscrimination policies.[12] Indeed, the individualist versus communal divide may extend to the heart of these schools' missions. Christian schools associated with individualist religious traditions are more likely to see themselves as serving students who identify as Christians, and thus most have no qualms about excluding students who do not agree with their beliefs. Christian schools associated with communal traditions, conversely, view themselves as serving broader communities; although they are generally no less religious in the sense that most will have a chapel, hire campus ministers, require students to take one or more religion classes, and actively promote their religious identification, they do not expect that their students will identify as Christian. Thus, schools associated with communal traditions are more willing to support LGBT groups and adopt nondiscrimination statements even if their religious traditions condemn same-sex relationships.

Conclusion

C. Wright Mills ([1959] 2000) argued that we cannot understand human action without an understanding of history and social structure. LGBT activists who have worked over the past several decades to secure important civil rights for LGBT people, as well as to win over skeptics across the political and religious spectrums, have created a unique historical opportunity for LGBT activism at Christian colleges and universities. However, the growing support for LGBT rights (if not the explicit approval of same-sex relationships) among social justice–oriented (or communal) Christian denominations—contrasted with the continued resistance to LGBT rights by individualist Christian denominations—has made some Christian colleges and universities more willing to approve students' calls for LGBT groups and inclusive nondiscrimination policies than others.

Regardless of whether Christian colleges and universities are predisposed to embrace LGBT rights, most (if not all) Christian colleges and universities are home to students who self-identify as LGBT, and students are mobilizing across all kinds of campuses to create more inclusive communities. In the chapters that follow, I examine LGBT mobilization at schools that vary in terms of their religious tradition (whether communal or individualist) and their presence in a liberal or conservative state, explaining why students join and commit to LGBT groups and how LGBT groups impact their schools and participants.

CHAPTER TWO

Joining an Activist Group

Why and how do people join activist groups? Traditional accounts of activist group participation emphasize a relatively smooth transition between activists' childhood to their coming-of-age, as well as a close link between the current attitudes of activists and the stated beliefs of the activist groups they join. My initial visit to Belmont University in 2010, where I observed protests in favor of an inclusive nondiscrimination statement and talked to members of the then unofficial Bridge Builders group, seemed to confirm this account. LGBT students, most of whom had been raised in accepting families, had become frustrated with the hostile climate toward LGBT people at Belmont and were shocked at the apparent dismissal of a lesbian soccer coach at the school in 2010. Surrounded by friends who affirmed their beliefs in social justice, these students did what they felt was most natural—organize and protest.

Yet when I returned to the school three years later, after Belmont had added sexual orientation to its nondiscrimination statement and officially recognized Bridge Builders, I was surprised to find that many Bridge Builders participants did not fit this profile. Consider the story of Beth, who attended Belmont at the time of the protests in 2010 but did not participate in Bridge Builders until after it was officially approved. Beth's previous involvement in student groups had mostly been limited to conservative Christian ministries at her public high school and now her college campus. Although she was attracted to other women, she was not very open about that fact; indeed, most of her friends were actually opposed to LGBT rights and would not have supported her participation in an LGBT group. She joined the group at the invitation of an acquaintance mostly because she had reached a "very stressful and depressing part of [her] journey" and "was kind of tired of feeling isolated"—"what was going on in [her] life, what was going in [her] head ... was disconnected from most of the people in [her] life," and she wanted to find a place where she could talk about her struggles.

After joining the group, she became one of its most active participants, eventually rising to a position of leadership. But to my surprise, even by the time I met her, Beth believed that same-sex relationships were sinful. She explained, "I don't think that the Bible condones homosexual relationships and homosexual acts. . . . I became a Christian when I was thirteen years old, and the year I became a Christian, I started at the beginning of the Bible and I read through it. . . . I very distinctly remember reading and thinking, oh, I didn't know the Bible said that, I guess that's what I believe. And of course I've heard a lot of discussion on the topic [of homosexuality] from a lot of different sides theologically since then, but . . . I see in the Bible that a covenant relationship of marriage between a man and a woman is not only, like, very explicit in the text regarding humans, but also symbolic, since marriage is not only about human relationships but also a reflection of Christ's relationship with the church body. . . . I believe that as a Christian, God has called me to not act on my feelings . . . toward the same sex."

Although she now openly identifies as queer, this is not because of any left-wing commitments that the term sometimes connotes. Rather, she believes that many people already have preconceived, negative notions about people identifying as gay or lesbian, and the term "queer" provides her an opportunity to explain her beliefs in greater depth. "My life, and my person," she told me, "is an embodiment of that term."

Stories like Beth's beg us to reconsider the question of why and how people join activist groups. The traditional accounts of activist group participation that I have referred to, such as Doug McAdam's (1986, 1988) groundbreaking study of participants in the 1964 Freedom Summer voter registration drives in Jim Crow Mississippi, paint a portrait of a prototypical activist who can be distinguished from a nonactivist on the basis of a single set of characteristics.[1] McAdam, for example, argues that, beginning in childhood, the prototypical activist is *socialized* into beliefs and values conducive to activist group participation[2] and reports *prior participation* in organizations conducive to activist group participation.[3] McAdam also suggests that activists report important characteristics of activists at the time of their *micromobilization*, or recruitment into an activist group—including *attitudinal affinity*, an agreement with the beliefs, values, goals, and tactics of an activist group;[4] *microstructural availability*, an embeddedness in personal networks and organizational networks that affirm one's beliefs and values and provide invitations to join an activist group;[5] and *biographical availability*, a lack of personal constraints that might otherwise increase the costs and risks of participation (as indicated by age, marital status, parental status, and full-time employment).[6]

Yet, although Beth could vocalize important reasons for wanting to be in an LGBT activist group—she believed in promoting LGBT inclusion and in facilitating discussions about religion and sexuality on campus—she does not resemble activist group participants whom scholars usually write about, and she did not resemble the LGBT activists whom I initially met at her school.[7] It might be tempting to consider Beth a mere outlier, whose experiences can be ignored in the interest of constructing a coherent narrative of activist group participation. However, I take seriously the notion that it is "up to the theoretician to unravel" reality, even when it "produces a wealth of the most bizarre combinations," and not "reality which should be expected to conform to the abstract schema" (Gramsci 1971, 159, 200; quoted in Snow and Moss 2014). In other words, I argue that the stories of activists like Beth should inform more nuanced theories of activist group participation.

Specifically, in this chapter, I explore the multiple pathways that students follow into LGBT activist groups at Christian colleges and universities. Analyzing the biographical pathways of my sixty-five respondents, I find that some participants do share the characteristics of activists portrayed in prior studies. However, other participants were socialized into beliefs and values that would not seem conducive to participation in LGBT activist groups, many lack preexisting personal ties to the activist groups, and a few even disagree with the beliefs and goals of their activist groups. As I will show, understanding people's varying identities is key to understanding the multiple ways that people come to join and participate in activist groups.

Not So Typical after All: Pathways of Politicized Participants

To rephrase the questions that opened this chapter: what motivations do students have for joining LGBT groups, and how do students discover opportunities for participating in LGBT groups at their colleges and universities in the first place? I begin by reviewing the stories of a group of activists who do seem to fit the profile of activist group participants whom studies have previously identified, a model of activist group participation that figure 2.1 illustrates. This group of activists had been socialized by families, schools, or churches that support LGBT rights, had reported prior activist group participation, and expressed personal support for (and thus exhibited attitudinal affinity with) the LGBT rights movement. Yet, it is interesting, given that they otherwise reflect the characteristics of activists identified in past literature, that these activists did not seem to require personal ties or biographical availability to initially become involved in their groups. Furthermore, and perhaps most surprising of all, these activists comprise a minority of my overall sample—just 31 percent of my respondents (see the online supplement for details on my analytic strategy).

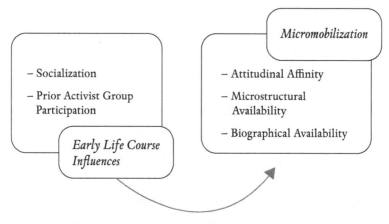

FIGURE 2.1 Traditional model of activist group participation.

A first example of this seemingly prototypical activist is Angela, who participated in the Open Letter movement at Goshen College. Although Angela identifies as straight, she was among the most passionate supporters of LGBT rights whom I met at Goshen; not only did she join the Open Letter movement almost immediately after stepping foot onto Goshen's campus, but when I met with her, she and several other students had recently met with the leadership to ask for even more events and more contentious protests during the semester.

Why was Angela so passionate about LGBT rights? Much as past studies might suggest, Angela's passion partially derived from her socialization, specifically from the influence of her mother, who had been advocating for full LGBT inclusion within the Mennonite Church for years. Angela explained this to me in my interview with her:

JONATHAN: Did you have any previous exposure to or involvement in LGBT activism prior to coming to Goshen?

ANGELA: Oh yeah. So my church . . . is right outside [a liberal city], and we went through a process to discern what our policy on LGBT membership and participation would be in the 1980s, I think, the early 1980s, and since then we've had an official welcoming statement. And about 10 years ago [in the early 2000s] that became an issue with our regional conference, when we sent a delegate who was gay and in a relationship with his [male] partner who goes to our church as well. After a lot of discussion on that, they decided to discipline our congregation and take our voting rights away at the conference level, and that led to a lot of, kind of, frustration, in our church. And my mother is the pastor, and so I was always aware, since age five—I guess she got involved when I was five—about her views and activism on LGBT rights, and I remember going to meetings pre-ordination where they would ask questions to see whether she was fit to be ordained, and one of the questions was, what are your views on LGBT rights? And she was very honest; she said she was for inclusion and that sort of thing. And they did let her be ordained, but it was kind of a tense thing in that process. So I knew about that at the time and since then have known about this, and the dialogue on inclusion is very frequent at my church, especially since this discipline is currently in effect.

Angela indicated that over the past few years, her mother has continued her activism on LGBT issues, officiating weddings for same-sex couples and helping to draft or sign letters in favor of LGBT-inclusive policy changes within the Mennonite Church USA. Although few participants' parents were as actively involved in LGBT activism as Angela's, at least six other participants reported that their straight parents had also been involved in LGBT activism within their religious communities and had encouraged their early participation in LGBT activism.

Kylie, another member of the Open Letter movement at Goshen College, similarly radiated passion for LGBT rights, even though she too identified as straight. As I discovered, her prior participation in LGBT activism contributed to this ongoing passion. Growing up in a family and a church that was strongly supportive of LGBT rights, Kylie had always been at least theoretically supportive of LGBT rights, and indeed she wrote about her support for same-sex marriage as early as her freshman year of high school. However, after one of Kylie's best friends came out as gay, LGBT rights became personal to her, and she subsequently became involved in Pink Menno, an LGBT activist group active at national Mennonite conventions. She recounted giving a speech in favor of LGBT inclusion at one of the convention's delegate meetings:

JONATHAN: When you first got involved with the Open Letter movement, would you say you would have identified as an activist, or is that not a term or word you would have thought of yourself as or referred to yourself as?

KYLIE: Yeah I definitely—well, first off, I'm definitely an ally, and I think you can be an ally and you don't have to be an activist, and I think that's an important distinction. But I'm definitely an activist,

I've always been really passionate about the issue. . . . I was involved in Pink Menno—maybe you heard about that. That was my first Mennonite convention, when that started, and I was already becoming involved in that.

JONATHAN: Why would you say you're so passionate about these issues?

KYLIE: Yeah, well this would be considered my ally story I suppose. . . . My best friend came out my sophomore year—and he came from a more conservative family, not Mennonite, but a more conservative family—he suffered from depression, and he had thoughts of suicide . . . . and it became personal to me. And at the next convention, Pink Menno became a big thing, and I became really passionate, thinking about this friend and how important he was to me. . . . And I remember sitting in a delegate meeting, because I was part of some youth delegate thing where we were allowed to sit at the table for a day. And I was there when they first started talking about the issue of same-sex relationships and everything. And I was there with all of these adults—and I was only seventeen. But I told them my story about my friend, and I said, you know, I understand this is a theological issue and there are these things, but I was like, this is my friend. And it's so important—I don't care what we do, but these people need to know that they're loved. And that was my first time ever speaking out in the Mennonite church about that; it was that moment. And the delegate people talked to me later at my table. And some of them disagreed with the theology but really were receptive to that story. And that's when I started to understand that stories are the key to really driving these things. And I've been telling these stories ever since.

In concluding with "I've been telling these stories ever since," Kylie was not exaggerating; in addition to relaying her story to other people at Goshen and encouraging straight and LGBT students alike to become involved in the struggle for LGBT equality, she has also gone on a speaking circuit of sorts, entering speech contests to relay her story to others.

Past scholars would argue that those who are socialized into inclusive values and who previously participated in activist groups generally exhibit attitudinal affinity with the movement they join, and that was certainly true for these students. But although I will show that participants beyond this group of seemingly prototypical participants similarly reported agreement with the cause of LGBT rights, these participants' attitudinal affinity with LGBT rights was generally steeped in overarching ideologies of social justice. For example, Paul, another straight activist at Goshen, discussed how his LGBT activism fit in with his philosophy of nonviolence:

JONATHAN: Why did you become involved in LGBT advocacy at Goshen?

PAUL: A lot of it stems from my commitment to nonviolence. Even back in high school, I was involved in animal rights activism, because I thought nonviolence should be extended to all life, to animals. I've been a vegetarian for eight years. . . . Abortion is another issue for me—I believe all life is sacred. And while I also believe in individual liberty—take [third] trimester abortions, for instance, I would not be for that. I would say, let's exercise a lot of other options before you consider that. . . . War is another issue. Goshen is very socially conscious and justice oriented; it has a PAX club—the peace club—that I've been involved in. War isn't an answer to our problems. Like with terrorism, we think, if we go and kill terrorists, if we target people and send drones to different countries and bomb houses, that terrorism will deplete. But all of the data shows that, no, with all of the terrorists we hit, we're inciting X number of casualties and creating twenty new terrorists. It's insane. . . . I believe my work on LGBT rights is an extension of my work for nonviolence. As I've listened to stories about people who have been marginalized, especially by the church, I don't—I want to help heal the church. The church should not be causing people to kill themselves, period, no matter what; even if you think people are sinning, you don't want people to kill themselves because of their actions. If I can help counter that, great.

Clearly, some of my respondents do resemble the prototypical activists identified in past studies—specifically, they had been socialized into values conducive to participation, had participated in prior activist groups, and exhibited attitudinal affinity with the LGBT movement—although I did find that they often lacked personal ties to people in the LGBT groups at their Christian colleges or universities, and they were seemingly "biographically unavailable" to participate because they often held outside work or family responsibilities.[8] Still, although nearly a third of my respondents match several characteristics of the prototypical activist, the remaining participants' pathways diverge from this profile in important ways. Why?

I argue that past studies have often overstated the degree to which activists share characteristics like socialization, prior activist group participation, attitudinal affinity, microstructural availability, and biographical availability in part because, methodologically, they were focused on differentiating participants from nonparticipants, a focus that obscures differences among participants themselves (see related critiques by Bosi 2012; Bosi and Della Porta 2012; Isaac et al. 2016; Linden and Klandermans 2007; Viterna 2006). Specifically, although the strategy of comparing participants with nonparticipants is important for demonstrating that certain characteristics are not only possessed by participants but can actually explain their participation—if certain characteristics were widely possessed by both participants and nonparticipants alike, they would not be very helpful in ultimately explaining why some people make the leap to activist group participation—this methodological focus glosses over differences among activists.

Nevertheless, recent studies have pinpointed an additional variable relevant to activist group participation—participants' identities[9]—that is not only a source of real variation among activists but is also important in unpacking some of the differences I observe among activists themselves.[10] Activists carry a number of relevant identities with them into activist groups. First, some participants possess the *activist identity*—or what I prefer to call a *political identity* (Klatch 1999)—that is based on a broad commitment to political, social, or economic justice (Corrigall-Brown 2012; Simon and Klandermans 2001; Valocchi 2013). Other participants hold a salient *value identity* based on a more narrowly defined set of moral commitments, such as moral commitments established by a particular religion (Corrigall-Brown 2012; Gecas 2000). Finally, still other participants possess a salient *solidary identity* that is linked to a specific social location, such as along the lines of race, class, gender, or sexual orientation (Gamson 1991). These identities are not mutually exclusive. For example, a person could identify as an activist (politicized identity), a Christian (a value identity), and a gay person (a solidary identity) simultaneously. However, these identities can be more or less salient in the context of activist group participation (Stryker 2000).

Knowledge of participants' identities might be useful for understanding variations in pathways to activism, because identities, which are often shaped by socialization, have significant implications for people's willingness to participate in prior activist groups, people's political and religious attitudes (given the well-known phenomenon of cleavages in political and religious beliefs), and people's personal networks (given tendencies toward homophily, that is, the tendency to associate with similar others) (Brooks and Manza 1999; Corrigall-Brown 2012; McPherson, Smith-Lovin, and Cook 2001). In other words, variations in participants' most salient identities might help us understand the seeming inconsistencies and contradictions in the characteristics possessed by activists.

A common identity indeed seems to be the ingredient that both ties the aforementioned participants together and distinguishes them from the rest of my sample. Specifically, all of those who followed the pathway of the activists whom I have described in this section—whom I call *politicized participants*—answered "yes" when I asked them whether they initially identified as activists when they first joined their campus organization. They usually also answered "no" when I asked them whether they were persons of faith or members of the LGBT community, or they otherwise emphasized their activist identity above all else when they were telling me why they decided to participate in their campus LGBT group. For example, a student at Catholic University named Jess told me a story of how she began to speak out in favor of LGBT equality and other social justice causes as early as fifth grade. However, she did not realize her own same-sex attractions until late in her college career, meaning that her activist identity was more salient than her sexual identity in her initial desire to participate in CUAllies:

JONATHAN: Why did you become involved in CUAllies [at Catholic]?

JESS: . . . I guess my initial thing as to why I wanted to join, I had just always sort of been fired up about the issue of equality. I still remember debating it with my religion teacher in fifth grade, like that was the first time I had a debate.

JONATHAN: Fifth grade? Wow.

JESS: Yeah, fifth grade, because she brought up how Disney World has gay day and how she refuses to go to Disney World, and I was in fifth grade and I was a precocious little kid [laughs], so I decided to fight with her about it. So it has just always been an issue that I'd been passionate about, and especially, coming here on campus, I was just curious. And then the nature of it [CUAllies] being unofficial kind of made it attractive in a sense as to sort of why, to figure out more about it. I think that was probably my initial desire to want to become a part of the group.

JONATHAN: What made you so passionate about the issue of equality? Especially as early as fifth grade?

JESS: Well—in many ways I've always been passionate about social justice, and I have been involved in various social justice groups, human rights causes. . . . It's one of the reasons I came to D.C.—you know, I went to like three protests my first weekend here just because I could. . . . But I mean, it's a question that I've been reflecting on a lot lately. Because I just got my first girlfriend like six months ago and so, even when I first became involved in CUAllies, it never crossed my mind as to whether or not I was or wasn't, but I guess maybe, I don't know, I guess just the fact that it kind of resounded in me at such a young age, maybe it really was a sign [laughs]. But I think maybe when it comes down to it, again, it's just basic human rights, and that's something that, I don't know, my parents always raised my sisters and I to think for ourselves and to always kind of care for others and to be self-aware as to where we stand in relation to others, so I think just seeing there was a large group of people being persecuted just really pissed me off [laughs]. You know, I may have not understood it all in fifth grade, but I recognized the wrong in it.

Similarly, some politicized students were also active members of their local churches. However, I uncovered clues that these participants' political values were more salient than their religious values, not only in the context of their participation in LGBT activism but also in their day-to-day lives. For example, a few participants who were actively involved in religious communities (particularly Quaker and Mennonite communities) told me that they actually personally identified as atheists or agnostics and that they were involved in these religious communities mostly because they provided outlets for involvement in social justice activism. Even when they identified as LGBT or members of certain religions, then, these students reported that socialization into progressive values and participation in prior activist groups set them on the pathway shared by other politicized participants. It is a shared activist (or political) identity that distinguished those who reported prior activist group participation, socialization into inclusive values, and attitudinal affinity from the activist group participants whom I discuss next.

Influential Outliers: Pathways of Religious Participants

If politicized participants were the only students to closely follow the pathways of the prototypical activists, why and how did students with other salient identities join their LGBT groups? Although politicized participants grew up as "red-diaper babies"—or perhaps, more aptly, "rainbow-diaper babies"—not all participants came from such activist-friendly backgrounds. A second group of participants in LGBT groups at Christian colleges and universities held salient religious identities, generally conservative religious identities that exist in tension with progressive political beliefs or same-sex attractions.[11] Although these *religious participants* comprised only 14 percent of my sample, they were some of the most influential members of their groups, helping to found and serving as some of the most active members of the groups at Catholic University and Belmont University. Thus, it is worth taking their stories seriously.

What kind of upbringing did religious participants report prior to joining LGBT groups at their Christian college and universities? I was surprised to find that none of the religious participants had been socialized by families, schools, or churches that supported LGBT rights and that, in fact, none of the religious participants had previously participated in activist groups. For example, Eric, a student at Catholic University, reported a highly conservative upbringing. Growing up outside the United States, in a largely Catholic country, Eric attended mass nearly every day, and he was taught that homosexuality was a sin:

JONATHAN: How would you have described your religious views?
ERIC: Well, I grew up old school Catholic. One of my [family members] is a bishop in [blinded country], so my family is very super religious, you know, I used to go to daily mass. And as far as what the church teaches, I really do believe that the church—you know, the one that has been around 2,000 years, the Catholic Church—it really moves in the wisdom and tradition of those 2,000 years. I really do believe that the Catholic Church was founded, institutionalized, by Christ, with the keys to the kingdom being given to St. Peter and stuff like that. So you know, I generally considered myself and still do consider myself to be socially conservative, I'm very pro-life. . . . And as far as what the Catholic Church teaches on homosexuality, I was raised to believe homosexuality was a sin. And this is the one issue where I now have a little thing, a small disagreement with the church—but it's the kind of thing where I'm not going to throw away my entire faith over one issue. . . . It's not like the whole thing is spinning on this one point.

In part because he was socialized into such a conservative worldview, Eric reported no prior involvement in activist groups. All other religious participants reported similar stories, and in fact, three told me that they pursued ex-gay therapy prior to their joining an LGBT group. This includes Ashley, a CUAllies member introduced in the introductory chapter, who identified as a "fundamentalist Christian" for much of her life and pursued reparative therapy.

If religious participants had such conservative backgrounds, how did they come to a point where they felt comfortable joining an LGBT group? By the time they arrived at their schools, a small minority of these highly religious participants had experienced a change of attitude toward LGBT rights, generally after they had become aware of their own desires for same-sex relationships. This newfound attitudinal affinity with LGBT rights seems to be the primary reason for their subsequent participation, as these people often lacked personal ties to the group or seemed to be biographically unavailable to participate based on work or family commitments outside of school. However, in contrast to those activists whose commitment to LGBT rights stemmed from an overarching ideology of social justice, these participants rationalized their acceptance of homosexuality within their existing religious belief structures. For example, Eric went on to tell me that he reconciled his own desire for a same-sex relationship within the framework of his Catholic faith by redefining what it means to "procreate" in a relationship. Specifically, rather than defining a sexual relationship as "procreative" because it allows a couple to have children, Eric came to define a same-sex relationship as "procreative" in the sense that it can draw two people closer together in a way that it allows them to raise children (cf. Yip 1997):

JONATHAN: When you first got involved, how would you have articulated your own perspective on the relationship between the Catholic faith and homosexuality?

ERIC: Well, at that time I read a lot. I used to write a lot, just trying to—I like have these idea books, where I write my thoughts out. I got very used to doing that to flesh out my thought processes and the theology behind it. . . . So, you've got to understand, the Catholic Church's take on sexuality is that it's only for procreation, right? So that's why homosexual acts are inherently disorderly. And that's where the whole contraception stuff comes into play too, that when you're using contraception, you're engaging in sexual acts that aren't procreating in that sense. And so it's a disordered use of the human function sort of thing. So with homosexuality, it can't be procreative. Well, that's kind of where my thoughts—at least my own development and search for truths—came into play, that procreation isn't necessarily just procreation in a physical sense; you can be procreative in a sense that a sexual relationship could draw two people closer together in a way that would make them more— well, life-giving is another translation, another term often used in Catholic Church—you can have a sexual relationship that is life-giving that is not, that doesn't physically bring about children but can bring a couple closer to raise children, you know?

Although religious participants like Eric had harmonized their religious faiths with their own sexual orientations or views on LGBT rights by the time they began participating in their LGBT groups, the majority of religious participants had not necessarily come to agree with the values and goals of their LGBT groups at the time that they initially joined. It is interesting to note that this is where factors like personal ties and biographical availability seem to come into play. Specifically, I found that these students began participating because they were directly recruited by another member of the LGBT group who knew about their struggles coming to terms with their sexual identity or who otherwise thought they would benefit from the group. Furthermore, some of these students who were recruited to the group through personal ties happened also to be biographically available, indicating that although biographical availability may not make a difference for people already in agreement on a given issue, it may make the difference for students who are ambivalent about an issue but are being recruited into a cause.

Beth, introduced at the beginning of the chapter, is certainly one example of a student who did not exhibit attitudinal affinity prior to joining the LGBT group (and even after joining), but other examples are available as well. A straight student at Belmont named Isabel, who generally places herself on the right side of the political spectrum, followed this kind of pathway into Belmont's LGBT group, Bridge Builders. Specifically, she told me that she joined the group because she had the time to do so and because she was coaxed by a friend, even though she was ambivalent (at best) regarding LGBT rights:

JONATHAN: How and when did you first learn about the group?
ISABEL: I have, um, a large number of friends who don't really know each other. And I'd heard of the group through many people, not usually in the best context, especially because it met, and meets, in

University Ministries. Many of my friends don't think Bridge Builders should be associated with a Christian ministry. And then a few of my other friends had told me about this group and how cool it was. So I had heard several things about it, but very small, very low on my radar. Then one day one of my friends said, you're coming with me. And I said, oh, I am? Um, okay, I guess! And so I went, and I've been involved ever since then.

By participating in Bridge Builders, Isabel formulated a deeper understanding of LGBT issues, one that she has shared with friends and family. Nevertheless, she still has uncertainty about LGBT-identified people, given a "lasting prejudice" that is difficult to overcome:

JONATHAN: So when you first joined the organization, what did you personally think would come about as a result of your participation?

ISABEL: I had no idea. I was kind of expecting to walk into the room and it would be the weirdest of weirds. Which it is, but in a good way. I was expecting it to be much scarier people, I guess, which is that sort of lasting prejudice that I had and I'll probably continue to hold on to for quite some time, which is what I was taught, which is that if you're gay, you're probably, probably messed up [laughs]. Which is actually pretty hard to let go of and realize that's what you're thinking. Because someone says, I'm bi, and the first thing I go to in my brain is, oh my goodness, something terrible has happened to you. And it still takes me a little bit to sort of walk back.

As another example of a student who followed this kind of pathway into an LGBT group, Timothy, a straight student at Catholic University, first arrived at the school with plans to serve in ministry, and he quickly became involved in a variety of groups affiliated with the school's Campus Ministry. Another student recruited Timothy to be one of the leaders of CUAllies because he believed Timothy could help craft religious messaging. Nevertheless, he had somewhat ambivalent or indifferent views on same-sex relationships and recalls writing an essay in high school about why gays and lesbians should not be allowed to marry. He evolved in his views on LGBT rights only after becoming a leader in the group and experiencing firsthand the difficulties associated with being perceived as gay on campus. I quote his story at length:

TIMOTHY: I first became involved after being approached by [another leader] who knew of my reputation as a leader in other clubs on campus. . . . And then once it became public that I was leading the CUAllies group, I got several Facebook messages congratulating me on coming out. I got an offer from a high school friend whose roommate wanted to be set up with me. I got a reputation on campus as being an openly gay man. And I also got a couple instances where I lost friends who thought I was gay. Like, they just either stopped responding to contact or I had one person who said, I can't be friends with you anymore, because you're a homosexual, and I was, uh, like . . . okay, I don't even know what to do with that.

JONATHAN: Did you respond to them and tell them that you were straight?

TIMOTHY: I did, but then they were like, how can you be in that group? They couldn't understand why some straight guy—they couldn't understand a lot of things, I think. So I got some of the negative things. I had a couple instances on campus where things were yelled at me by drunk people—slurs—and I was just like . . . actually, the first time it took me a while to realize that it was directed toward me, and I sort of looked around, and I was like, man, why would you say that? And then they were looking at me, and I was like, me? And then the other thing that happened, besides the public, is privately people began to share things with me—share their experiences on campus. I got to see—sort of an underworld. [pauses] That's a terrible term. But a subculture of either people who were out and struggling or people who weren't out and thought they couldn't come out on campus. And hearing all these stories, I was like . . . you know, that transformed me. Because first of all, I got the briefest glimpse of what it might be like to be gay on this campus, good and bad. And also, I began to hear all of these personal stories. And I was like, huh, there's a lot here. And there's a lot of people who are also upset about the Catholic Church's stance, and who are allies or whatever they are, who stopped going to Mass and get angry with God and develop all of these other spiritual problems, which is something that really interests me, that prevents them from developing healthy relationships with God and participating in the Catholic community. So sort of those two things ignited me to go, you know, this is a real issue. This is actually a real issue. And one thing that also changed, is for about the first six months, I would go, no no no, I'm straight, don't worry. But I sort of realized the privilege in that comment, or that the inherent message was, I may want the gays to have rights, but I'm not—don't worry, because you can trust me, because I'm a—and then I realized, man, that's a terrible message. Starting then I didn't correct people ever. . . . So part of the becoming receptive to this was also an internal struggle of looking at my own privileges, my own prejudices, the socialized homophobia that I had and had to confront. And once I was really able to—and I still think it's there, it's not like I'm perfect—but it became a lot easier to become receptive to the cause, because I was comfortable challenging myself and being challenged. So that all sort of came together once I began participating in the group.

None of the participants with salient religious identities, then, grew up in families that were particularly accepting of LGBT people, and none of the participants had previously participated in social justice activism. Although some religious participants did exhibit attitudinal affinity by the time they joined their campus LGBT groups, many others lacked attitudinal affinity and needed to be biographically available or to have ties to the group. This kind of participant very much conflicts with the image people normally hold of activists.

The Average Activist: Pathways of LGBT Participants

Some people join LGBT groups already politicized; a few join LGBT groups with conservative religious identities that seem to exist in tension with their new roles as LGBT activist group participants. The majority (55 percent) of participants, however, join their LGBT groups simply because they personally identify as lesbian, gay, bisexual, or transgender. These *LGBT participants* were very active in LGBT groups at their schools, and they generally played some role in founding the LGBT groups at each of the schools, although their pathways also seem to partially contradict people's preconceptions about activists.

In general, I found that the experiences of students with salient LGBT identities fell somewhere between those of politicized participants and those of religiously oriented participants. Specifically, just over half of students with salient LGBT identities had been socialized into values conducive to participation in LGBT activist groups. Nevertheless, this socialization was not as extensive as that reported by politicized participants; for example, none of these students reported having parents who were involved in

LGBT activism. Furthermore, this socialization was usually not accompanied by prior participation in activist groups, and those who had participated in LGBT activism had generally only done so sporadically or for a short period of time. For example, a student at Loyola University Chicago named Elizabeth reported that she was raised by accepting parents and also attended an unusually welcoming church. She did attempt to organize a Day of Silence in recognition of bullied LGBT students at her high school, but her conservative school was resistant to this cause, and she dropped the effort:

JONATHAN: Did you ever attempt to organize an LGBT organization at your high school?

ELIZABETH: No, I went to this strict Opus Dei high school . . . [Opus Dei] is less than 1 percent of the church; they're all Tea Party, pretty much all of them. They're the people in the Da Vinci Code, except they don't go around killing people. . . . It was sort of this weird thing where—you couldn't really come out at my high school or you'd get expelled. There was one girl who was outed, against her intention, and the principal sat her down and said, Okay [blinded], we like boys, and we're friends with girls, or we don't go to this school, okay? And like, basically said you're straight, and okay great, go back to class now. If I hear about this again, you're expelled. So stuff like that. Eventually, I did try to organize a Day of Silence to build support for LGBT students at the school. But I got sent to the principal for doing it, and I said, you really can't take a position to support kids to the point of suicide? You're being ridiculous. So in general, at my high school, I had to keep my mouth shut about everything, and I wasn't allowed to, like, ever tell anyone anything.

The other half of students with salient LGBT identities were more similar to religious participants in that they never reported any kind of prior activist group participation and had usually been socialized into conservative values. Indeed, participation in LGBT activist groups was almost unthinkable for many of these participants, because they had grown up in environments that so heavily repressed sexual or gender minorities. As one example, Sarah, a student at Belmont, was raised by a family who seemed to support her sexual identity, even though she was shy about discussing it with them. However, she had witnessed violence and other bullying behaviors against sexual minorities in her small southern town, which meant she avoided any organized activism on LGBT issues growing up:

JONATHAN: How accepting would you say your high school was of LGBT people?

SARAH: On a scale of 1 to 10, like negative 10. [laughs] . . . I come from [a city in the South]. [This city] is not very—they're still working on some race problems that they have. It's better, but they're not even to that point yet. When it comes to, [sigh], homosexuality doesn't exist, basically. I had a friend who was, he moved into town, and he was, he was bi. He wasn't—he was gender nonconforming, I guess. He, um—it was so bad. He had knives pulled on him. And he got beat up. And one of the worst parts is the principal, they took one of the guys who beat him up, and he shook his hand. He like pretended to get on to him but then shook his hand. So, yeah, it's really bad, it's really bad. And another friend . . . she had to stop going to school because she like came out, and she got bullied so bad that she had to become homeschooled. And it was from the teachers too, not just the students. And the school board told her that she was living in sin, and she shouldn't be rubbing it into everyone's faces. . . . [And] this is the public school board. So that's where I come from.

Similarly, another student at Belmont, Curtis, was raised by parents who were cautious and somewhat concerned about his sexual identity. He reports that he encountered bullying in high school from "friends who told [him] they would support [him] if [he] came out," which led his parents to homeschool him before he entered college. Yet Curtis went on to face the same type of bullying at Belmont before an LGBT group had formed on campus:

JONATHAN: Have you seen or experienced any bullying or harassment at Belmont?

CURTIS: Oh yes, I've experienced firsthand on campus people being really rude and nasty to gay people. I was recipient to that freshman year. The person that lived next door to me harassed me pretty much every day the whole year, calling me a fag and all kinds of other things, drawing penises and other crude pictures on a whiteboard that was on my door, all kinds of things, and it was just . . . you know, it was college, and it was time for people to grow up. And apparently they had not done that.

Although these LGBT participants' pathways were similar to religious participants' pathways, in that they had not previously participated in activist groups, few LGBT participants' backgrounds were as extreme as the religious participants' backgrounds. In particular, none of these students reported pursuing reparative therapy to attempt to change their sexual identity.

Altogether, some students with salient LGBT identities had early life course experiences similar to (if not as politicized as) those of activists; other students with salient LGBT identities had pre-movement experiences not much different from (if not quite as conservative as) those of religiously oriented participants. Nevertheless, all of these students agreed with the goals and tactics of the LGBT rights movement by the time they actually joined their LGBT groups (i.e., they possessed attitudinal affinity). Their agreement with the cause of LGBT rights did not generally stem from an overarching political ideology, such as a commitment to nonviolence, or from any theological framework. Rather, their attitudinal affinity stemmed from a more basic self-interest, such as a desire to make friends or find support in their coming-out processes.[12] For example, Lily, a student at Loyola University Chicago, was one of those LGBT participants socialized into inclusive values, and she expressed her motivation for joining Advocate in terms of her desire to make friends:

JONATHAN: Why did you initially become involved in Advocate?
LILY: I definitely wanted to make new friends—that's something I was really excited about. At my high school, when I came out as bi, it was like—it wasn't like I was shamed for it, but it was a big deal. Not big, but just, people didn't know what to do with it. But I hoped, coming here, that I could find more people in the queer community and generally in the LGBTQIA+—there's too many letters. But yeah, I was hoping to find a social thing and hopefully again become more involved in the community, this was something that never happened at my high school.

Those participants who lacked prior involvement in LGBT groups and who had been socialized into conservative values came to agree with the LGBT movement only after a laborious process of resocialization. However, unlike some participants with salient religious identities, they went through this resocialization process before they actually joined an LGBT organization. For example, Carlisle, a student who attended Loyola as both an undergraduate and graduate student, joined Advocate after rethinking nearly all of his beliefs and after moving from a Catholic to an atheist identity. His story is worth quoting in full:

JONATHAN: You said you were in seminary while you were in undergrad at Loyola—would you have identified as a person of faith? Did you have a Catholic background?

CARLISLE: Well, it began that way. . . . I grew up Roman Catholic and that was a big part of my own development as a child. My mom and my father were Catholic and things like that, so that was a big part of our life growing up. It certainly was in the seminary too, but I started to question a lot of things near the end, about many different things. I had taken a philosophy course on the late Nietzsche. I don't know if you're familiar with him at all, but he was a philosopher, he was very anti-Catholic, anti-Christian, but more importantly he was very anti-dogmatic philosophy. Dogmatic philosophy is very typical, as far as I know, of all religions, or most of them, and it's basically about this unchanging source or fountain of truth; you know, this is it, this is the one thing that's right or correct, you can't question it, you can't alter it. So basically, my thing was, if I'm going to go on to a major graduate-level seminary, my last semester at Loyola, second semester senior year, will be my last chance to take a non-Catholic philosopher, so I wanted to go all out, and I took Nietzsche. And Nietzsche was probably as far away from religion as you could get. So yeah, I read *Beyond Good and Evil*, *Genealogy of Morals*, and a couple others, for the class. And those changed my life. . . . As simple as it sounds, in *Beyond Good and Evil* section nine, he talks about putting your own stamp on this chaos and questioning the world around you and not accepting things as they are, and it sounds very basic and very simple, but that was the first time in my life I felt a true sense of permission to do that . . . and that started me down a path of questioning a lot of things about my faith. And I now actually identify as an atheist. And that also laid the groundwork for me no longer staying in seminary. . . . And I then started significantly questioning everything else. And I mean everything—my taste in music, my political affiliation, my religious views, my sexual orientation, my gender identity; I questioned all of that. And that was the starting point of all that; that's when I first started to discern more closely my own sexual orientation. And after that I came out to myself and fully started to come out to others. And like I said, I started attending Advocate's support group, and that was a huge resource for providing support resources and also finding community.

Although many other LGBT participants describe a similar shift from Christian beliefs to an agnostic or atheist identity prior to joining an LGBT group, this is not to suggest that all LGBT participants completely abandoned a religious identity. Those students who had attended more liberal churches were more likely to retain faith in God even after coming out as LGBT. Furthermore, it was not uncommon for formerly religious students to return to a religious identity after they began to participate in an LGBT group and recognized that LGBT and religious identities could be reconciled (see chapter four). Nevertheless, especially at the time of micromobilization, a self-interest related to sexual identity or gender identity was the primary motivation for these students' participation.

Perhaps the most interesting finding in regards to the participation of LGBT participants is that, although so many of these students joined an LGBT group to find support and build community, the presence of pre-existing social ties was not necessary for any of these participants to join an LGBT group; to the contrary, their lack of pre-existing ties to students in the LGBT group is what seemed to motivate their participation. Most of the students also lacked biographical availability, indicating again that biographical availability may not be necessary for participants already motivated for their cause. Indeed, the vast majority of participants reported that they joined the LGBT group without any personal invitation simply because LGBT issues piqued their interest. For example, Ruth describes examining Belmont's calendar of activities and deciding to go to a Bridge Builders meeting despite not knowing anyone there:

JONATHAN: I'd like you to think back to the first time you joined the organization. Would you tell me when and how you first found out about Bridge Builders?

RUTH: Sure. It was . . . February 2010, I guess, and I was just looking on our school calendar for stuff to do. Like at Belmont we had these things called convocation where we had to go to so many lectures and activities to graduate, so I was looking for stuff to do. And then something caught my eye, it was like, "Bridge Builders Interest Meeting #2," or you know whatever. So I was like, whoa, what's this? So I kind of read the little blurb about it, and it says it was people who are interested in forming a group about sexuality, and at that point I was pretty interested in discussing and exploring this topic, so I was like why not. And I went to the interest meeting.

In summary, attitudinal affinity stemming from basic self-interest is the one attribute that all LGBT participants have in common when they join LGBT groups at Christian colleges and universities. Although some of these students came from accepting backgrounds, they usually lacked characteristics such as prior activist group participation, personal ties to an activist group, and biographical availability.

Conclusion

When people think of "activists," they often think of people whom scholars of activist group participation have long written about. People tend to assume that, prior to joining an activist group, would-be activists are socialized into values conducive to activist group participation by their parents, schools, and other caretakers and perhaps are even brought to a picket line or protest at an early age. People often assume that, by the time they encounter an opportunity to join an activist group, would-be activists have also developed attitudinal affinity with the activist group in question, are surrounded by family and friends who support their participation in an activist group, are members of organizations that pull them into an activist group, and are at a stage in the life course where the costs of participating in an activist group are low.

However, in this chapter, I have criticized a general scholarly tendency to gloss over differences among activists themselves (see also Bosi 2012; Bosi and Della Porta 2012; Isaac et al. 2016; Linden and Klandermans 2007; Viterna 2006). Indeed, in my interviews with LGBT activist group participants, I met a number of activists who were socialized into conservative values, lacked prior movement participation, lacked attitudinal affinity with the LGBT movement, and lacked strong personal or organizational ties to an activist group. Taking a cue from studies that have linked variations in identity to variations in socialization, prior activist group participation, attitudes, and networks (Brooks and Manza 1999; Corrigall-Brown 2012; McPherson, Smith-Lovin, and Cook 2001), I have argued that multiple pathways to activist group participation exist, and these pathways can be linked to students' most salient identities, whether activist (or political) identities, value identities (based on religion), or solidary identities (based on sexual or gender identity).

The point is not that notions of activist group participants held by the public and past scholars alike are completely wrong—scholars have, in fact, identified a number of attributes that can potentially contribute to activist group participation—but that attributes such as pre-movement socialization,

TABLE 2.1 Categories of identity and their associated pathways

Participant identity	Pathways
Activist/political identity based on an ideological commitment to political, social, or economic justice	*Early life course influences:* Socialization into liberal religious and political attitudes and prior participation in activist groups
	Individual attributes at the time of micromobilization: Attitudinal affinity with LGBT movements
Value identity based on a set of moral principles or standards, such as those defined by a particular religion	*Early life course influences:* Socialization into conservative religious and political attitudes and no prior participation in activist groups
	Individual attributes at the time of micromobilization: Attitudinal affinity with LGBT movements, personal ties to other participants, and/or biographical availability
Solidary identity based on a specific social position, such as sexual orientation and/or gender identity	*Early life course influences:* May or may not have been socialized into liberal religious and political attitudes; may or may not have prior participation in activist groups
	Individual attributes at the time of micromobilization: Attitudinal affinity with LGBT movements

prior movement participation, attitudinal affinity, and personal ties play different roles depending on students' most salient identities.[13] Table 2.1 summarizes the key patterns. First, politicized participants were socialized into values conducive to participation in activist groups, participated in prior activist organizations, and exhibited attitudinal affinity with the cause of LGBT rights. However, personal ties to an activist group and biographical availability were not necessary for their involvement in that group. Next, religious participants were socialized into more conservative values by their families, schools, and churches, and they had not participated in prior activist organizations. These participants joined an LGBT group either because they had eventually arrived at attitudinal affinity with the cause of LGBT rights or because they had been recruited into the organization and were perhaps biographically available. Finally, the pre-movement backgrounds of LGBT participants fell somewhere between participants with activist or value identities in that they may have been socialized into values conducive to LGBT activism but often did not have prior participation in activist groups. Nevertheless, these participants are all similar in that they possessed attitudinal affinity by the time they joined an LGBT group, often without (and perhaps because of their lack of) pre-existing personal ties to that group.

Other studies have likely produced this singular portrait of activists not only because of their methodological focus on distinguishing participants from nonparticipants but also because of their overwhelming focus on groups like the Open Letter Movement at Goshen College, which deployed direct action tactics in their effort to effect policy change. In comparison, the few other studies that have shown that people recruited into an activist group may not report prior socialization into the values of the activist group or even attitudinal affinity with the activist group have had a focus on religiously oriented activist groups like the ones I found at Belmont University and Catholic University (e.g., Lofland 1985; Munson 2008; Snow, Rochford, Worden, and Benford 1986); religious movements, of course, have a reputation for attempting to bring converts into their cause, and they sometimes eschew confrontational protest tactics in their attempts to change hearts and minds.[14] Similarly, the few studies that portray participants without deeply rooted political or religious attitudes have studied activist groups like Advocate at Loyola University Chicago, which exist primarily to provide a safe space for students with similar identities and to effect personal change (e.g., Mayberry 2006; Renn 2007).[15]

Attention to variations in the identities of activist group participants, then, will lend useful insights to areas beyond micromobilization. As I will show in the next chapter, variations in the identities of LGBT group participants can be linked to variations in the types of LGBT activist groups that exist in a way that explains commitment to activism. Specifically, I will show that politicized participants are drawn to LGBT groups devoted to direct action, religious participants are drawn to LGBT groups engaged in education, and LGBT participants are drawn to LGBT groups focused on solidarity building; when participants' most salient identities correspond to these varieties of LGBT group ethos, participants are more committed to their groups and thus more willing to devote time and energy to their cause.

CHAPTER THREE

Committing to the Cause

Why do students commit to activist groups? In other words, why do some students devote so much more time and energy to activist groups than others do? Whereas the previous chapter focused on the factors shaping students' initial decisions to join activist groups, and whereas the next chapters will focus on the impacts of LGBT activist groups on their campuses and their participants, this chapter focuses on what happens between those beginning and later points—the process by which students decide to take on leadership responsibilities in a particular group, serve as an active member, or, perhaps, coast along as a sporadic participant.

Consider the story of Erica, a student at Goshen College in Indiana. Having been raised by an anarchist father who read radical literature to her from an early age, Erica began participating in social justice groups focused on issues ranging from homelessness to the Iraq War as early as high school. She eventually came out as a lesbian, but she told me she considered that to be only part of her identity: "Even before then, I would identify myself as an anarchist." Given her strong political commitments, it is perhaps unsurprising that Erica sought out activist groups as soon as she got to Goshen. Indeed, she initially joined all three LGBT groups that were active on Goshen's campus—the Open Letter movement, which organized sit-ins, rallies, and petitions in favor of inclusive nondiscrimination policies at the school; Advocates, which sought to educate students, staff, and faculty about LGBT issues through movie showings and teach-ins; and PRISM, a group designed to assist LGBT students in their coming out processes. Yet she has felt most at home in—and has since devoted the most time and energy to—the Open Letter movement. Furthermore, she has distinguished herself as one of the most active freshmen in the group, and she expresses hopes to join the movement's leadership soon. Why has Erica proved to be so committed to the Open Letter movement, especially compared with many of her peers?

As suggested by Erica's story, the answer to the question of commitment rests partly on one of the concepts introduced in the previous chapter— participants' *identities*. Students carry salient *politicized identities*, *religious identities*, or *LGBT identities* with them into activist groups, and those identities play a role in their decision to commit to activist groups. In Erica's case, she identified as a committed anarchist, and her desire for social change led her to seek out activist groups on campus. But there is also more to the story. If there is one thing we might learn from the small number of studies that take up the question of commitment to activist groups,[1] it is that social psychological characteristics (including identity) seem to play only a small part in processes of commitment. Scholars have offered a range of individual-level explanations for activist commitment, finding mixed support for the role of *rational choice calculations* (e.g., the role of activists' perceptions that an activist group will achieve certain *collective benefits*, such as nondiscrimination protections, or *selective benefits*, such as new skills or new friendships for group members) and almost no role for *biographical availability* (i.e., the likelihood that people could devote substantial time to an activist group given their stage in the life course, as indicated by age, employment status, marital status, and parental status).[2] Regardless, studies that focus on social psychological characteristics fall short of completely explaining activist commitment, because they do not take into account people's experiences in activist groups after they join them, which could in turn influence their participation levels.

To fully understand why students might commit to activist groups, then, we will need to learn more about the dynamics of LGBT activist groups themselves (see other insights on organizational influences on commitment by Baggetta, Han, and Andrews 2013; Dorius and McCarthy 2011; Isaac et al. 2016). Specifically, in this chapter, I introduce a typology (a classification schema) for the kinds of LGBT activist groups organizing on Christian college and university campuses. Just as past treatments of activism have painted a singular picture of what it means to be an activist, past literature has often downplayed differences between activist groups, particularly between activist groups that employ direct action tactics and activist groups that do not employ such tactics (although see exceptions such as Armstrong 2002; Jasper and Nelkin 1991; Rohlinger 2015). As I will show, some LGBT groups, like the Open Letter movement that Erica was drawn to, exhibit a *direct action ethos*, seeking to produce structural or policy changes through more confrontational means. Other LGBT groups, like Goshen's Advocates group, exhibit an *educational ethos*, seeking to raise awareness about LGBT issues and cultivate inclusive values through more conciliatory means. Finally, other LGBT groups, like Goshen's PRISM, exhibit a *solidarity ethos*, carving out a safe space for members of the LGBT community to grow as humans. Although these three types of activist groups pursue different goals through different means, they all seek to bring about social change and are thus all engaged in activism.

Crucially, I will argue that commitment to LGBT activist groups is contingent on the correspondence (or "fit") between a participant's most salient identity and an organization's dominant group ethos; alternatively, a lack of commitment is produced by a mismatch between identity and ethos. Students like Erica who come to their universities with salient politicized identities are especially drawn and committed to direct action groups. However, students with salient religious identities will be committed to educational groups, and students with salient LGBT identities will be committed to solidarity groups. Not all Christian college and university campuses contain all three types of LGBT activist groups, but LGBT activist groups can and do change in their ethos over time, and these changes impact the types of participants who are committed to the groups. I unfold these arguments below through qualitative profiles of direct action groups, educational groups, and solidarity groups that drew in committed politicized participants, religious participants, and LGBT participants, respectively. I then provide summary quantitative evidence showing how the alignment of an organization's dominant group ethos and a participant's most salient identity is linked to commitment levels for all respondents in my interview sample.

Direct Action Groups, Politicized Participants, and Commitment

In both the popular and scholarly imagination, the direct action group perhaps best resembles the prototypical activist group: an activist group willing to put its members' bodies on the line and to disrupt the pace of everyday life in an attempt to bring about certain structural or policy changes. Although other activist groups also attempt to foster social change, perhaps no other type of activist group demands that its members take on so much risk in the process. Perhaps it is unsurprising, then, that direct action groups tend to draw in those with particularly salient politicized identities— identities that are shaped by socialization into the values most conducive to activism and by prior activist group involvement. But how exactly do direct action groups attempt to draw in the kinds of politicized participants that are best suited for their brand of activism? And what does this process have to do with commitment?

The Advocate group at Loyola University Chicago is a great case to begin considering the role of group ethos and identity in processes of commitment, in part because few groups seemed as intentional and reflexive about both the purpose of their group and the type of participant they hoped to recruit. A former vice president named Colin, who was active in the group from 2003 to 2007, reminded me that the LGBT organization now present on Loyola Chicago's campus, Advocate, did not always go by that name. Instead, the organization was first established in 1990 as the Gay, Lesbian, and Bisexual Association (GLABA) and attempted to provide a safe space for gay, lesbian, and bisexual students at Loyola Chicago (similar to the solidarity group model that I discuss later in the chapter). In 2001, the organization changed its name to Rainbow Connection, a name that reflected the growing diversity of members' sexual and gender identities but preserved the group's focus on a supportive atmosphere for socializing.

Around the time that Colin came to the university, the Rainbow Connection was suffering from both internal and external problems—internally from constant infighting, factionalization, and low membership numbers and externally from student skepticism about the actual contribution of the organizations to the campus. In an effort to revitalize the group, in 2004 the group's president began what was called the RainCon Revamp. Specifically, group leaders initiated conversations about the purpose of the group and appropriate activities for the group. Beyond reaching out to more members of the campus community and attempting to boost the group's numbers, the president launched new initiatives such as a Hate Crime Awareness Week, which sought to challenge administrators' response to hate crimes against the LGBT community on campus.

By 2005, with momentum growing behind the organization's renewed purpose and increased presence on campus, the group decided once again to change its name from Rainbow Connection to Advocate. But that is not the entire story. Along with the official name change came a debate over the pronunciation of the organization's name. As Colin explained, "I remember there being a big debate about the difference between Advocate [**ad**-v*uh*-keyt] and Advocate [**ad**-v*uh*-kit], and the president at the time was set on being called Advocate [**ad**-v*uh*-keyt], so it would be much more action oriented, and so we'd be separate from the magazine, which has a more informational focus. I knew that people would eventually just call it whatever they wanted, but the president and other members at the time, including myself, were very set on Advocate [**ad**-v*uh*-keyt]."

Why the big debate over something so seemingly trivial as pronunciation? The debate over the name and pronunciation of the organization can

TABLE 3.1 Categories of identity and their corresponding group ethos

Participant identity		Group ethos
Activist/political identity based on an ideological commitment to political, social, or economic justice	→	*Direct action group* that seeks structural or policy changes through more confrontational and extra-institutional forms of collective action
Value identity based on a set of moral principles or standards, such as those defined by a particular religion	→	*Educational group* that establishes a shared set of values and raises consciousness about those values in a community through more conciliatory and institutional means
Solidary identity based on a specific social position, such as sexual orientation and/or gender identity	→	*Solidarity group* that facilitates personal development and growth by connecting similarly identified students within a safe space

be understood as a debate over the organization's *group ethos*—the nature or character of the group, as communicated through its name, mission statement, and beliefs and as embodied in its practices.[3] The group ethos I saw this 2005 iteration of Advocate embodying was a *direct action ethos*, involving the use of more confrontational forms of collective action (sit-ins, occupations, rallies) as a means to bring about certain structural or policy changes. Indeed, this iteration of Advocate began coordinating with other direct action groups across the city and joined protests, marches, and sit-ins related to HIV/AIDS awareness, employment nondiscrimination, and marriage equality both at Loyola's campus and in the wider city of Chicago.

As I soon discovered, the debate over group ethos was so important to organizational members because of its perceived resonance with current leaders' salient identities.[4] Specifically, Advocate's emerging group ethos seemed to resonate with those who held salient political identities, shaped through past involvement in activist groups and socialization by families, churches, and schools. Table 3.1 models this correspondence, along with the connections between students' other salient identities and the dominant ethos of other groups. As Colin told me, "Our purpose and our drive to accomplish big things and leave a legacy during our time there reflected the social representation of the organization—the interests of the members." Accounting for his own extensive participation and leadership responsibilities in the group, he noted how he had begun involving himself in political groups as early as high school, how he majored in political science, and how he was planning to pursue some type of career in community organizing. He himself was quick to own the label of "activist."

Perhaps just as important, however, Colin added that there was an apparent mismatch between the direct action ethos of this iteration of Advocate and many members' identities, and this seemed to explain why the membership numbers remained lower than the group hoped:

> And actually during the end of our time there, we took a little bit of a row after we were told our group just wasn't much fun, and we were having a lot of drop-off after the beginning of the year from so many students who weren't interested in (a) activism, (b) politics, or (c), you know, intensive discussions. We were falling off on the barbeques and parties and other events that we had when we first started with the organization. So in truth, the mark of a successful organization would probably be one that has a bit of a hybrid status to keep its numbers up but also one that is very specific on what it wants its goals to be. It doesn't have to be one thing, it can be dual track, involved in both . . . politics and culture.

In other words, he pointed out that so many other students similarly did not identify as activists and, instead, desired an organization that would host social events (as a solidarity group would).

A former Advocate president named Franklin, who was involved in the group in the late 2000s and the early 2010s as the group did begin to transition from a sole focus on direct action to an increased emphasis on socializing, largely echoed Colin's arguments. Specifically, he noted that the Advocate group was initially filled with activists who were interested in a "political, activist atmosphere" (i.e., politicized participants who sought a direct action group) and that there were also a few "folks that are deeply religious" who wanted to "rectify their Catholic views with being queer" (i.e., religious participants who sought an educational group). Yet there was a mismatch with the interests of dozens of other Loyola students who were simply "interested in being gay, and in finding a social outlet" (i.e., LGBT participants who sought a solidarity group) and who thus quickly dropped out of the group when this purpose was not being fulfilled:

JONATHAN: How would you describe Advocate, as you experienced it during your time there, to someone who wasn't familiar with it?

FRANKLIN: I would say that it was a group that was mostly focused on activism, the political, but increasingly with an emphasis on community building. I think the constant struggle was that you would get—every year there would be a new group, a new class that would come in, and the first meeting would have 150 to 200 people in it, but then the vast majority of people are there just to see who else is like them, who else identifies as queer or bi or lesbian or trans, if that's how they viewed themselves. And so once they know that, the interest wanes rather quickly, because once they make those connections, and aren't necessarily interested in the political, activist atmosphere, they drop out. So out of 150 new students, only ten to twenty actually stick around and become involved. And I think you have some of those folks who are naturally driven to politics and activism, and then you have some folks that are deeply religious and they're trying to rectify their Catholic views with being queer—those are probably the two biggest demographics we had—we had a very strong Catholic group that was trying to figure out how to be both at the time same time, and then we had the activists that mainly stuck around—but the rest of the time it was just these two groups pleading with those who were only interested in being gay, and in finding a social outlet, to come to the events.

Colin's and Franklin's explanation for why some initial members proved to be more committed than others seemed quite plausible to me for at least two reasons. First, their explanation took into account what happens to students after they join an organization. At colleges and universities, especially progressive universities like Loyola Chicago, many students will express initial interest in joining an LGBT group, but it is only after they begin participating in some of the meetings and begin to understand a group's ethos that they will develop commitment to the group. In other words, a concept like group ethos takes into account what happens after students join an organization—unlike previous concepts emphasized by scholars, such as rational choice calculations and biographical availability— and, along with knowledge of participants' identities, we can gain insights with which to differentiate participants after they join. Second, the explanation seemed quite intuitive. Some of the past explanations of commitment paint a portrait of a rational actor who might draw up a pros and cons list, filled with benefits and costs related to anticipated collective benefits or selective incentives, before deciding to commit to an organization. Yet this image of the rational actor is never one that activists seemed to hold of themselves, or at the very least is never an image that participants communicated to me through interviews. Conversely, Colin and many other respondents I talked with certainly saw themselves as seeking out an organization that resonated with their own identities. Indeed, it is worth noting that nearly every other respondent at Loyola, regardless of the time period in which they participated, repeated this argument that so many people dropped out of the Advocate group each year because the group's purpose did not align with their own identities and desires to meet other LGBT people.

MY INTERVIEWS AT LOYOLA CHICAGO provide important evidence that commitment to LGBT groups is contingent on the fit between one's most salient identity and an organization's dominant group ethos. But most of this evidence focuses on differences in identities between participants in direct action groups that might trigger differences in their commitment levels. Might evidence for this argument also be found in changes within participants themselves? The account that opened this chapter highlighted LGBT activism at Goshen College. Although the school supports three distinct LGBT organizations—the Open Letter movement (a direct action group), Advocates (an educational group), and PRISM (a solidarity group)— the Open Letter movement was by far the largest and most active of the LGBT organizations, at least at the time of my study. In an attempt to challenge the school's discriminatory faculty hiring policy—staff and faculty at the school were being fired or pressured to resign when they came out as gay or lesbian—the Open Letter movement organized weekly t-shirt days (where supporters wear purple shirts asking, "Where's my GLBTQ Prof?"), sing-ins in the university chapel, stand-ins outside board meetings, solidarity protests with Eastern Mennonite University (which was also debating a discriminatory faculty hiring policy), and a large open letter drive directed to the school's board and administrators.

As I found in my interviews, most participants in the Open Letter movement were like Erica, who was profiled in the beginning of the chapter. In other words, even if they did not consider themselves to be anarchists, most students held some type of highly salient political identity and were drawn to the group due to its direct action ethos. Most of these activists also identified as heterosexual, and those like Erica who identified as LGBT had generally developed their political commitments long before they became aware of their sexual orientation. Finally, those politicized participants who attended Mennonite churches generally only did so because of those churches' active promotion of social justice; for example, Erica attended a left-leaning Mennonite church but self-identified as an atheist. Thus, most politicized participants did not possess competing LGBT or religious identities that might have drawn them to a different group.

However, I did meet a Goshen student named Jeremy whose most salient identity did change over time, and this change in identity had implications for his level of commitment to the Open Letter movement. Growing up, Jeremy told me he was "really into activism" and, more specifically, into "pushing for progressive politics." He helped organize protests against the Iraq War and against the Bush administration in high school. Before he came to Goshen, he also joined Pink Menno, an LGBT activist group targeting the larger Mennonite Church USA through protests at the Mennonite Church's general conventions. Following one of those conventions, he came up with the idea of writing an open letter to the regional Mennonite conference along with other young adults in his area calling for full LGBT inclusion within the Mennonite Church. Given his organizing experience and salient activist identity, Jeremy told me it was simply "natural" for him to become involved in LGBT activism, and he helped found the Open Letter movement once he arrived at Goshen College.

It is interesting that although Jeremy reported a "natural" correspondence between his early activism and his involvement in the Open Letter movement at Goshen, Jeremy himself did not openly identify as queer when he helped found the group. When asked why he was so willing to become involved in the Open Letter movement, despite not being open about his sexuality, he said that "it was definitely easier for me, at that point, to become a straight ally activist, that was less of a risk. . . . At that stage of my life, that was easier for me to do, and it made sense with kind of who I was, with my involvement in justice work." However, Jeremy eventually came out as queer while in college, and this queer identity eventually supplanted his activist identity, causing him to step back from a group that was dedicated to activism:

JONATHAN: How many hours each week would you say you spent participating in the Open Letter movement while you were there? Did it vary?

JEREMY: Yeah, it varied. Toward the beginning, toward the very beginning of the movement, it was probably five to ten hours a week, when we were really trying to figure out what to do. . . . But especially as I entered into junior and senior year, I kind of became less actively involved in leadership or in figuring out where to go next. And yeah, that definitely dropped off; I stepped back from active involvement.

JONATHAN: Is there a particular reason you became less involved junior year and after?

JEREMY: I think . . . it was just being a recently "out" person and kind of just needing some time and space to chill a little bit and just to live into that new experience and become more involved in the queer community at Goshen, and less involved in public advocacy stuff; I think that was the biggest part of it for me.

This account of Jeremy's involvement in the Open Letter movement is valuable because so much about Jeremy during his time in college, at least presumably, stayed the same over time—his upbringing, his past experience with activism, his biographical availability, and the college he attended. Thus, explanations that rely on certain background characteristics, knowledge of his life course stage, or structural context cannot explain why his commitment varied over time. However, as he notes in the quote above, his most salient identity did change—now that he had come out as queer, he became less interested in public advocacy and wanted to explore what the queer community had to offer—and this change in identity negatively impacted his level of commitment to the Open Letter movement.

Educational Groups, Religious Participants, and Commitment

The direct action groups described above cultivate commitment by drawing in participants with corresponding salient identities (in their case, activist identities). Does the same dynamic apply to educational groups? Educational groups, as defined here, seek to raise awareness around LGBT issues and cultivate acceptance of LGBT people by holding group discussions about issues facing the LGBT community and by educating their wider campus communities about LGBT issues through lectures, movie showings, and prayer vigils. Thus, although still interested in promoting social change—improving the campus climate for LGBT students, faculty, and staff—educational groups eschew more confrontational tactics such as sit-ins or occupations in favor of more conciliatory tactics. As I found, educational groups indeed drew in a particular type of student, but a different one than direct action groups. Specifically, educational groups tended to draw students with salient religious identities that had been shaped by socialization into (generally conservative) Christian values and beliefs without any prior involvement in social justice activism. Educational groups tended to resonate with them because their more peaceful approach better reflected a Christian approach to social change (at least in their minds) and because the model of holding group discussions and lectures was similar to what they learned growing up in their places of worship (e.g., in Sunday school and church services).[5]

Catholic University's CUAllies group, like Loyola Chicago's Advocate group, has seen its share of changes over the years. The group initially began in the late 2000s as a direct action group that engaged in contentious tactics. In fact, the group in its early stages was perhaps the most radical of all the groups examined here, having regularly organized confrontational events such as unauthorized demonstrations in the student center. However, a few students who arrived at the school after 2010 did not find the group's direct action approach appealing; instead, they sought an educational organization that better aligned with their Catholic identities.

The previous section detailed the many changes that Loyola's Advocate group went through, showing that students can and do exercise their agency to transform the nature of their organizations, but how precisely does that happen? Perhaps paradoxically, the initial approach Catholic University students took to transforming the CUAllies organization from a direct action group to an educational group did involve confrontation. Specifically, in the spring of 2011, rather than waiting for some of the older students to graduate, a few of the newer students initiated what has been described on both sides of the conflict as a *takeover* or *coup*. As one of the incoming leaders, Brent, put it, "I just sort of approached [the current president], and I told her, it was time for a change; it's time for you to step aside."

As Brent went on to describe, the new iteration of CUAllies was very much event-driven. After the takeover, the group started off in that spring of 2011 by bringing in a staff member at a nearby organization that promotes LGBT inclusion within the Catholic Church. During the fall of 2011, the group brought in a lesbian woman who had been denied communion at her mother's funeral because "the priest knew she was a lesbian, stuck his hand over the communion, [said] she couldn't have it." The organization also held a prayer vigil, in which group leaders led a procession from a residence hall to the university student center and concluded with a prayer. Finally, the group brought in a former university campus minister who was now a priest and who specialized in pastoral care for LGBT people. Subsequent semesters have focused on holding similar educational events.

In other words, rather than engaging in contentious protests (as a direct action group would) or focusing on providing a safe space for members of the LGBT community (as a solidarity group would), Brent and the other members of the new iteration of CUAllies wanted an organization that would educate the wider Catholic University community through lectures by Catholic speakers and through "bridging cultural practices" such as prayer vigils (Braunstein, Fulton, and Wood 2014). But why this new approach? When I asked why he was motivated to get involved with this new group, Brent emphasized the perceived fit with one of his most salient identities—his identity "as a Catholic, as someone who wants to participate in church life":

> JONATHAN: So what initially motivated you to get involved with the group and change the nature of the group?
>
> BRENT: Well, that's an interesting question. In the larger context, I felt . . . the university [was] discriminatory in a way [by], one, not allowing a student organization on campus to be officially recognized, and two, not having an organization or something that officially represents the university to the LGBT community on campus, and allies, that they're welcome to attend mass, that they're welcome to attend church functions, that they're welcome to go into Campus Ministries—these sort of things. And I think, for me, *as a Catholic, as someone who wants to participate in church life*, I thought it was important to get involved in CUAllies—and sort of rebrand the organization from what it was, from this very protesty sort of organization, to an organization that was focused on bridging the gap between the Catholic Church and the LGBT community and their allies on campus through more *thoughtful, educational events*. (emphasis added)

What is particularly interesting in this quote is that Brent explicitly links his identity as a Catholic to the approach of providing "thoughtful, educational events" (an educational group), in contrast to those in the former group who sought a "very protesty sort of organization" (a direct action group). Indeed, when I followed up and asked Brent whether he would have characterized himself as an activist in these efforts, he laughed off the label and said that, while the university might apply that label to him, he "would consider myself Catholic, I guess. That's what I considered myself throughout the entire thing." Through his efforts to secure this fit between the CUAllies' group ethos and his own Catholic identity, he came to a place where he was comfortable taking on an extensive leadership role in the organization, and he reported devoting ten to fifteen hours to the group each week—more than nearly all other students in my sample.

Notably, nearly every other student I interviewed from this new iteration of CUAllies agreed that, while the previous iteration of the group did not appeal to them, the new iteration of the group very much resonated with their identities at Catholics. For example, Eric, one of the Catholic students introduced in the previous chapter, who served on the leadership board of the new CUAllies group, noted that he was turned off by the "caustic" tone of the older group that had been focused on "advocating for political things" (as a direct action group would); furthermore, he told me he was happy that the new club was not simply a "gay club meet-up sort of thing" (as one might find in a solidarity group). Rather, he saw the new CUAllies group as one that was "in line with the mission of the school, which was the mission of the Church":

> JONATHAN: So how would you describe the new iteration of CUAllies to someone who wasn't familiar with it? Once you got involved.
> ERIC: ... We wanted to try and work with the administration rather than against it—you know, what are the common grounds, what can we do, *how can we create a group that, I guess, was in line with the mission of the school, which was the mission of the church*, and not start advocating for political things, you know [emphasis added]. Because before it was very, it seemed, my first impression was in freshman year of the CUAllies group, it was kind of caustic—I remember in one of the, like, orientation days, when new students came in, they were doing a big protest, standing on top of tables, throwing flyers in the air, putting tape on their mouths, weird things like that. That kind of steered me away from the whole group.... And—what else was I going to say.... I also did not want us to be a gay club meet-up sort of thing.... But with [the new president], he wanted to take a different tone, and so, that's more why I got more involved with the group I guess.

When I followed up and asked Eric how, precisely, he saw the "mission of the school, which was mission of the church," he told me he believed the appropriate mission is "not to build soldiers to go out and fight battles" (as one might do in a direct action group), but to provide a place "where the church comes to think and think through its theology, its stances." He argued that "we should have scholarly discussions, we should have speakers who can talk through these issues" (as one might do in an educational group) and that this approach resonated with his identity as a conservative Catholic. Brent's and Eric's responses thus provide more evidence that commitment to LGBT groups is contingent on the correspondence between an LGBT group's dominant ethos and a participant's most salient identity.

SIMILAR TO CUALLIES, the Bridge Builders group at Belmont, founded in the late 2000s, also saw a gradual shift from a direct action ethos to an educational ethos. Although Bridge Builders had initially employed direct action tactics—such as sit-ins and rallies at the administrative building—to achieve its status as an officially recognized student organization (see chapter 4), in 2011 the group shifted its focus to educating the Belmont community on issues of faith and sexuality. The new iteration of Bridge Builders embodies the educational ethos so much that the group's weekly meetings resemble a Sunday school class. Beginning at 4:00 P.M. every Friday, students arrive at a room in the University Ministries building, sit in a circle, and introduce themselves to the group (usually by providing their names, preferred gender pronouns, and answers to a random question, such as what animal they would choose to be and why). Then, one of the group leaders provides announcements about upcoming events. Finally, one to three group members give a brief PowerPoint presentation and then lead a group discussion over topics such as LGBT politics, issues facing persons of color in the LGBT community, faith and sexuality, HIV/AIDS issues, and LGBT mental health. The schedule of group meeting topics is set at the beginning of each semester and posted on the organization's Facebook group.

Apart from these weekly meetings, the group also regularly organizes events through which they seek to educate the campus-wide community about issues of faith and sexuality. In a recent semester, for example, the group organized an event called Tell Your Story on National Coming Out Day. Students told stories about reconciling their religious and sexual identities, and the group recorded each of the stories and archived them. The group is aided in their task of organizing events by Belmont's requirement that all students obtain a certain amount of convocation credits—points earned by attending a certain number of university-sanctioned events. For example, Bridge Builders obtained approval to offer convocation credits for students who attended the movie *Saving Face*, about an Asian American lesbian couple.

Given that the group's mission is primarily faith-based—it is sponsored by the school's University Ministries, and it has an official mission of "bridging the gap between the LGBT and Christian communities" through educational events—it is perhaps not surprising that the group draws a number of students who are primarily motivated to participate because of their Christian identities. Although not all students in Bridge Builders actively attended church, almost all of the current students reported that they were raised in Christian households and attended church before they came to Belmont. Furthermore, because even those students who did not attend a church usually reported that they were still spiritual or still believed in God, the group's overarching mission to "bridge the gap between the LGBT and Christian communities" was indeed a draw, as students could discuss issues of faith, sexuality, and gender identity in a way that they could not in church. For example, when asked why he joined the group, an active member named Evan said, "I mainly came because—and this is what it said on the description on BruinLink—Bridge Builders is kind of combining spirituality and sexuality and stuff like that. So I thought, I'm originally Roman Catholic, and I can't really talk about homosexuality in the Catholic Church. So I figured, hey, since I couldn't talk about it there for the first eighteen years of my life, maybe now I can finally talk about it in like a spirituality based way."

The direct influence of a salient religious identity in decisions to commit to an educational group is perhaps best seen, however, in the story of Andrew, whose own identity and commitment level both changed over time. Like Jeremy at Goshen, Andrew initially identified himself as a straight ally and was involved in the initial founding of Bridge Builders. However, by his junior year, Andrew went through a period of significant personal transformation, as he not only came to acknowledge his identity as a gay man but also began to reconnect with his Christian faith. At that point, because of what he saw as a growing mismatch between the more militant nature of Bridge Builders (which at that point was still a direct action group) and his identity as a Christian, he decided to step away from the group:

JONATHAN: How did you initially become involved in Bridge
    Builders?
ANDREW: I was one of the original members of what became Bridge
    Builders back probably in 2009. . . . At that point I wasn't out; I was
    just in the role of an advocate or ally. . . . At that point I was also not
    attending church regularly. . . . But the language they were using was
    very militant—there was a lot of anger there, which I thought was

not the correct way to approach the situation at Belmont. And as I was going through my coming out process and reconnecting with my Christian faith, I—because of that language, I just had to remove myself from that group and I began seeking other ways through just normal—through dialogue, through conversation, to bring about that particular change at Belmont, in a way that would be true with my Christian faith.

Although he withdrew from Bridge Builders and began participating more heavily in the school's University Ministries, a pivotal event at Belmont—the sudden exit of a lesbian soccer coach from the school—prompted him to rejoin the group and attempt to transform the organization to one that would align with his Christian identity. As he continued:

ANDREW: And then [the soccer coach] was let go, or she left, depending on who you ask. It appeared that Belmont was no longer being shy about where they stood on LGBT issues. Because we couldn't get a clear picture, the Bridge Builders leadership decided it was time for action. A lot of those people in leadership in Bridge Builders at the time were not particularly mature in the way they were going to go about challenging the university. A lot of that militant language that was being used previously and in years past was now becoming action. . . . And so it was at that point that I decided I had to do something, to try to take a larger role in the response to [the coach's] firing, to try to shape the message that Bridge Builders was putting out. . . . So I helped lead a prayer walk across campus, because it was very important to me as a person of faith that we affirmed Belmont as a Christian organization, as a Christian institution, and also to show you can be a Christian and be gay and those things are not irreconcilable, which I was learning through my own coming out process as a member of a welcoming and affirming Baptist church in Nashville. And eventually I also began to help lead weekly group discussions, including a Bible study focused on Isaiah.

If the connection between his renewed faith, his preferred purpose for the group, and his level of participation in the group was not clear by that point, he soon made it explicit:

JONATHAN: So would you say your faith played a role in your decision to participate?

ANDREW: It played by far the largest role in my decision to participate and once again take on a leadership role, and it also affected the direction I was trying to steer this group into. In a lot of situations, LGBTQ people have been most discriminated against by the church. And I didn't want—well, I wanted to be available to show that doesn't have to be the case. I am someone who is gay and who is affirmed by faith.

Andrew's story, then, provides more evidence for the idea that the fit between a participant's most salient identity and an LGBT organization's dominant group ethos produces commitment to LGBT activism. Although so much about Andrew remained constant during his college years (e.g., his biographical availability, his college of attendance), his own identity did change over time, initially prompting him to disengage from the group and then prompting him to change the group in a way that would align with his emerging identity.

Solidarity Groups, LGBT Participants, and Commitment

A final group of students came to their universities identifying first and foremost as members of the LGBT community. Generally, such members reported no prior participation in activist groups (with the exception of occasional participation in Gay–Straight Alliance groups in high school), and they often reported being apathetic or agnostic about religion. As I show in this section, these LGBT students were most drawn to and committed to what I call *solidarity groups*, or groups that existed to connect students with *LGBT identities* and affirm these students' LGBT identities within a safe space (cf. Fetner et al. 2012).

As noted in the first section, in the mid- to late 2000s, the Advocate group at Loyola focused its efforts on direct action around issues facing the LGBT community. However, beginning in the early 2010s, Advocate began transitioning to a solidarity group that attempts to create safe spaces for members of the LGBT community. Although some groups change their group ethos through more drastic means such as takeovers or coups, Advocate shifted to its current solidarity form mainly through *cohort replacement* (cf. Whittier 1997)—students who were interested in activism graduated and were no longer present in the group. Indeed, as Illinois became increasingly accepting of LGBT people by prohibiting employment discrimination on the basis of sexual orientation and gender identity and by offering marriage rights to same-sex couples, many incoming students simply no longer saw the need for active mobilization. As part of this shift, students began pronouncing Advocate in its noun form (**ad**-v*uh*-kit) rather than its active verb form (**ad**-v*uh*-keyt), and in fact the most recent students whom I interviewed were not even aware that Advocate was once pronounced as a verb (**ad**-v*uh*-keyt).

Although Advocate is a single organization, the organization carries out two separate functions as part of its solidarity mission. First, Advocate provides support for LGBT students who are beginning to come out to their families and friends—a form of self-help. As an executive board member named Elizabeth explains, the organization provides support through a subcommittee known as Spectrum that meets separately from the main group each week:

> Advocate has a group that it sponsors, which is Spectrum, which is a support group. . . . So they meet as separate groups, but Spectrum is run and sponsored by Advocate. [In Spectrum] we have an open group, and then we have the option for closed group. Open group is, everything is still confidential; we don't reveal number of participants, names of participants, everything that is said is still confidential, but the time and location are publicized throughout campus on flyers. . . . And then we have the option of closed group, which is, people would e-mail us, and we'd set up a special time to meet with them that no one else knows about. But—it's open to anyone in Advocate or anyone else that wants to come and talk, about being on campus as an LGBT student, it's sort of a safe space kind of thing.

Advocate's functions also go beyond self-help; as a solidarity group, Advocate provides opportunities for members of the LGBT community to simply socialize with one another. For example, each year the group sponsors a drag show, which is reportedly the most popular event on Loyola's campus. During a recent school year, the organization partnered with a gay sports league known as the Chicago Metropolitan Sports Association to hold a dodgeball and volleyball night. Finally, the organization also sponsors LGBT trivia nights, Alphabet Soup Bingo nights, ice cream socials, and hot chocolate socials.

Although Advocate carries out two separate functions, all of its activities are focused on building solidarity and community among LGBT students themselves, rather than achieving policy change at the university or educating the broader campus. Although this type of group is often neglected among scholars of social change (though see, e.g., Armstrong 2002), the students themselves do see their group as engaging in a form of activism. As Franklin, who witnessed the change from the direct action focus to a solidarity ethos near the end of his time at Loyola, pointed out, the new iteration of Advocate takes seriously the feminist notion that "everything is political":

JONATHAN: A couple people I talked to who were involved earlier on in the mid-2000s remember the group being more political, and some of the students I talked to during my visit to Loyola say that it's more focused on community building now. So I was going to ask if you experienced a turn in the group?

FRANKLIN: I think that after—there was that lull in trying to get gay marriage passed in Illinois, and during that lull, we focused very internally on the community aspects, and some on how you are queer and Catholic. . . . Yeah, I think that was the initial thing, but also . . . we were much more influenced—we took a lot of our cues maybe from a feminist-political standpoint, from the fact that everything is political, that community is political, building a safe space for students to do identity exploration and be better advocates in everyday life, those things are political actions, and I think we sort of saw the—sort of these efforts by the last leadership to get people involved and galvanized around political issues—everyone would get fired up and go to a march . . . but that would dissipate right away, there was no investment in individuals who then would want to return to the community and then get back. So I think— yes, it was partially outside circumstances. Not only was there the national scene, but then the university really started listening to us in my sophomore and junior year, like the vice president was accessible, the directors of Student Diversity were accessible, so we didn't necessarily have to go off campus to feel like we were doing meaningful work. And I mean, my gut reaction is, if you talked to those early 2000s folks, they may have been—they may have bemoaned that that's the direction we took, but I think our approach is also political.

How did this new solidarity ethos affect students' levels of participation in Advocate? Previous iterations of the Advocate club at Loyola often had trouble maintaining the strong interest it received at the beginning of the school year, because many students who held salient LGBT identities were not interested in direct action. However, a student named Laverne told me that the new solidarity focus of Advocate has been more successful in maintaining an active and committed membership base:

JONATHAN: You said second semester there's usually declining attendance. How many members would you say participate in the first semester versus the second semester?

LAVERNE: We usually have over one hundred people probably at our ice cream social at the very beginning. Last year we definitely had over one hundred; this year we may have had around eighty people. So that's always a big turnout, because people at the very beginning are trying to get a feel for what Advocate is gonna be like, especially all the new freshmen. . . . And then what used to happen sometimes in spring semester is that some events just get the e-board. [laughs] Where we all show up because we have to and then no one else shows up. We had a meeting that was sort of a flop a couple months ago because our president was out of town for ethics bowl and SDMA [Student Diversity and Multicultural Affairs] came to lead a workshop, and we did some theater exercises and stuff and it was like probably half the e-board, so five people plus one or two other people, and there were only five or six of us and that was a pretty depressing one. And that was characteristic of what it was like for most of the second semesters before now—we'd show up, and it'd be like, oh, five to ten people showed up for this meeting, okay, or like, everyone here is on the e-board, awkward. And I think it's because the meetings were a bit too formal, too serious. But this semester has actually been really great—for most events we've had really great turnout, and I think it's because we've been much more intentional about community building. And we're expecting probably at least twenty, thirty people for the dinner this Thursday, hopefully more because we're giving out free food and that always draws people. But yeah we often draw thirty, forty, fifty people now. It used to be a much bigger disparity, so that's progress.

Similarly, when accounting for their own participation in the newest iteration of Advocate, students repeatedly emphasized their own identities as LGBT people. For example, a student named Damon discusses how he became involved in the group because he wanted to make "gay friends," and given his own gay identity, he felt "right at home" in Advocate:

JONATHAN: When you first joined the organization, what did you personally think would come about as a result of your participation; what were your expectations for the group?

DAMON: I was definitely seeking a social outlet. I would say, coming from a high school where there weren't any openly gay people, I was just like, I'm so excited to have gay friends! That's so cool. So it was definitely that social, that feeling that I want to come out of this having a strong sense of community. And I felt right at home in Advocate. . . . The point of it was, we're all out and proud, that's fine, and that enticed me to join. And today I still kind of feel that way, that that's what Advocate wants to celebrate.

As Damon went on to tell me, he served for three consecutive years on Advocate's executive board. Like those in direct action and educational groups, then, students like Damon seem to account for their draw to and commitment to Advocate by emphasizing the close fit between Advocate's group ethos and their most salient identities.

Summary Evidence on Group Ethos, Identity, and Commitment

The qualitative evidence presented above supports the notion that commitment to activist groups is contingent on the correspondence or "fit" between participants' most salient identities and LGBT groups' dominant group ethos. As an additional way to support this theory of commitment, I now turn to quantitative evidence linking identity and group ethos to variations of commitment across my entire interview sample. As described in the introductory chapter, my sample consists of sixty-five student activists and includes a diverse mix of group leaders, active group members, and more sporadic participants who only occasionally attend meetings or who participated in the group for some period of time before dropping out.

To conduct a quantitative analysis, I constructed variables for identity, group ethos, and commitment. To construct the variable for a participant's identity, I first established whether participants responded affirmatively when asked whether they identified as activists, persons of faith, and/or members of the LGBT community. If respondents stated that they identified with more than one of these labels, I then coded their answers to open-ended questions about their motives and expectations for participation to establish which of these identities was most salient. To construct the variable

TABLE 3.2 Percentage of respondents who assumed leadership responsibilities, by identity and group ethos

	Dominant group ethos		
Salient Identity	Direct action group	Educational group	Solidarity group
Activist identity	**63%**	0	0
Religious identity	0	**67%**	0
LGBT identity	30%	30%	**73%**

for group ethos, I inductively coded respondents' answers to an open-ended question that asked, "How would you describe [your organization] to someone who wasn't familiar with it?" I found that organizations tended to exhibit one of three group ethoses on the basis of their stated missions and the nature of their activities: a direct action ethos, an educational ethos, or a solidarity ethos. In those cases where groups took on multiple functions, I drew on data from questions that asked respondents to list specific activities that their group had been engaged in, which allowed me to assess the groups' priorities and emphases. Finally, I constructed a variable, as one way to measure commitment, indicating whether respondents took on leadership responsibilities in their LGBT organization (based on a direct question about respondents' leadership positions). For organizations that had adopted a nonhierarchical leadership structure, I simply considered whether respondents had taken on responsibilities (such as organizing events, leading meetings) not shared by most of the general membership.

Table 3.2 indicates the percentage of respondents who had taken on leadership responsibilities across two variables of interest, identity and group ethos. This table provides consistent evidence that students' willingness to serve in leadership is contingent on the correspondence between a student's most salient identity and an organization's dominant group ethos. Specifically, a high percentage of politicized participants involved in direct action groups (63 percent) served as leaders of direct action groups. An even higher percentage of religious participants involved in educational groups (67 percent) served as leaders, and a similarly high percentage of LGBT participants involved in solidarity groups (73 percent) took on leadership responsibilities. Those students whose identities do not seem to correspond with their groups' ethos seldom (if ever) served as leaders.

Looking for another way to examine whether a correspondence between identity and group ethos produces commitment to an LGBT organization, I constructed a variable based on a question that asked students how many

TABLE 3.3 Mean hours per week respondents participated in organization, by identity and group ethos

Salient Identity	Dominant group ethos		
	Direct action group	Educational group	Solidarity group
Activist identity	6	2	1
Religious identity	1	6	1
LGBT identity	3	3	5

hours per week they participated in an organization during the past year (or their last year in the organization). Certainly, these data should be viewed with some degree of caution; time use data are less reliable when the data are based on students' recall rather than official records or time use diaries (e.g., Brenner 2014; Hadaway, Marler, and Chaves 1993). Nevertheless, as an indicator of how much students perceived themselves to have participated in the organization, the variable is still instructive.

Table 3.3 provides the number of hours students claim to have participated in their organization by identity and group ethos. Once again, students' perceptions of their time commitment to the organization seem to be contingent on the correspondence between identity and group ethos. Specifically, students with activist identities claimed to spend six hours per week in direct action groups but only two hours in educational groups and one hour in solidarity groups. In contrast, students with salient religious identities seemed to devote six hours per week in educational groups but one hour in direct action groups and one hour in solidarity groups. Finally, respondents with salient LGBT identities said they participated five hours per week in solidarity groups but three hours in educational groups or direct action groups.

In multivariate analyses—that is, analyses that consider whether these patterns related to identity, group ethos, and commitment hold even when accounting for the potential impact of factors such as collective benefit expectations, biographical availability, group meetings, student demographics (race, sex, and sexual orientation), and organizational context—I found that these patterns continue to strongly hold (see the online supplement). In short, quantitative analyses further bolster the idea that commitment to activist groups relies on the correspondence between participants' most salient identities and LGBT organizations' dominant group ethos.

Conclusion

College is a time of rapid personal development for most young adults. With increasing physical, emotional, and sometimes financial distance from their parents, and with emerging understandings of their own political commitments, religious beliefs, sexual identities, and gender identities, many young adults feel that college is the first time that they have the opportunity to join groups devoted to LGBT rights. However, although so many students express initial interest in LGBT activist groups, only some commit to group leadership or even active membership. Why do some people commit to activist groups while others do not?

In this chapter, I have worked to address this question of activist commitment to activist groups and shed light on what Cohn, Barkan, and Halteman (2003, 311) have called a "black box in the social-movement and voluntary-association literatures." Specifically, I have argued that commitment to activist groups is contingent on the correspondence (or "fit") between a participant's most salient identity and an LGBT organization's group ethos. LGBT organizations are often reflexive in drawing in like-minded people, signaling their group ethos through their branding efforts and their choices of activities. Nevertheless, potential participants also retain agency and can transform the nature of their organizations by gradually replacing previous cohorts or by attempting to take over the organization.

It is true that considerations related to identity and group ethos likely do not exhaust all variation in participants' commitment to LGBT groups. I did not find that the individual-level characteristics emphasized in past scholarship, such as rational choice calculations about collective benefits and selective incentives or biographical availability, influenced commitment levels in any meaningful way here.[6] A few recent studies have also identified organizational-level factors potentially related to commitment, such as the amount of time people spend in meetings or the level of bureaucratization and centralization in an organization, but I similarly did not find that those played a major role here.[7] However, none of this is to suggest that there are no other factors impinging on activist commitment. In response to open-ended questions asking members whether they might consider becoming leaders, a few students responded that they preferred to remain general members rather than leaders because they were heterosexual. Similarly, I also found that some students with salient LGBT identities exhibited a greater willingness to join direct action groups or educational groups than other students whose identities did not correspond with an organization's group ethos (see tables 3.2 and 3.3). This was especially true at colleges and universities like Catholic or Belmont where only one LGBT group was present, and as these students reasoned, they felt like they should play a part in any effort that would ultimately benefit students like them, even if the group did not function in the way they preferred. This points to a small role for a general LGBT organizational identity (rather than a more specific group ethos). Nevertheless, these students' levels of participation are still not as high as those LGBT-identified students whose identities aligned with a group ethos (see tables 3.2 and 3.3).

The chapter holds implications for other areas of study on activist groups beyond commitment. As I will argue in the next chapters, concepts like group ethos hold implications for understanding the impacts of activist groups. As I will show in chapter four, knowledge of a group's ethos provides insight into why some groups are more successful than others in facilitating changes in policy and campus climate. Furthermore, as I will show in chapter five, knowledge of a group's ethos can enlarge our understanding of the ways in which activist groups impact participants. Prior research on biographical consequences has previously been focused on activist groups of the 1960s—groups overwhelmingly engaged in direct action campaigns— and has shown that direct action groups produce activists who engage in direct action across the life course. However, I explore whether activist groups with very different group ethoses, including activist organizations focused on educating others or on carving out a safe space, might produce different kinds of activists—for example, activists who forgo future social movement activity to focus on applying their group's values through humanistic careers or intentional family lives.

CHAPTER FOUR

Creating Change

Katie, a student at Belmont University, was a member of Bridge Builders during the time it organized protests against the school's discriminatory policies toward LGBT people. As a core member of the organization, she had deep insight into the group's strategies and tactics, and as she told me about the group's approach to the protests, she repeatedly emphasized the group's messaging to Christians: "I knew going into these protests [in 2010] that we weren't likely to change many minds overnight. We didn't necessarily expect people to see our signs and say, 'Oh, all of a sudden we agree with them.' It wasn't about changing people's personal beliefs. It was more, *we just wanted to show that the Christian community at Belmont means including and accepting and encouraging everyone*, not just tolerating some people and brushing them off, but really respecting them and trying to have a conversation. So even if people didn't agree with us, I would hope they could agree we at least deserve to be included and heard. . . . I mean, *can we at least be Christian enough to welcome and care for everyone?* If we could at least get people to agree with that, we thought we had a chance of winning" (emphasis added).

Katie's remarks were both insightful and prescient. They were insightful because they revealed an important and common approach to challenging Christian colleges and universities' policies on LGBT issues—namely, challenging people's preconceptions about what it means to be a Christian university. They were also prescient, because they foreshadowed larger changes at Belmont that followed our interview. By the time we talked, Katie knew that Belmont had undergone a significant change in its policies, adding sexual orientation to its nondiscrimination statement and officially approving Bridge Builders as a student organization. Yet, perhaps even she did not realize then how drastically Belmont would evolve in its Christian identity over the next few years and how those changes would affect the campus climate for LGBT students.

The previous chapters examined the factors facilitating the formation of LGBT activist groups at Christian colleges and universities and the processes of joining and committing to LGBT activist groups at these universities. But how do LGBT activist groups impact their campuses? In this chapter, I analyze the impacts of LGBT activist groups on campus policies and climates. By *campus policies*, I mostly refer to official nondiscrimination policies that prohibit discrimination on the basis of sexual orientation and/or gender identity, although groups occasionally attempted to challenge other policies, such as rules regarding the types of weddings that could be held on campus. The term *campus climate* is widely used in scholarship on LGBT-inclusive schools and refers not only to campus policies but also to "lived oppressive experiences" (such as the experience of bullying or harassment) and "perceptions of anti-GLBT oppression on campus" (Rankin 2003, 4). For this chapter, I use the term *campus climate* in these latter senses, focusing on the degree to which respondents experience anti-LGBT oppression on campus and feel that they can be open about their sexuality and/or gender identity on campus. Finally, I briefly consider the impacts of LGBT activist groups on their members, especially members' relationships with family and friends, although I leave a full exploration of activist groups' impacts on members' political, work, and family plans to chapter five.

I focus especially on the case of Bridge Builders, because it is the case for which I have the most complete data about the impacts of LGBT activism on a Christian university. Not only has Bridge Builders attempted to transform both campus policy and climate—targeting campus policy during its iteration as a direct action group before fostering change in the climate for LGBT people during its educational group phase—and not only has Bridge Builders effected real changes in the lives of its members, but Bridge Builders had also successfully completed many of its campaigns and goals by the time I spoke to students during my two waves of interviews (in 2011 and during the 2013–14 school year). In comparison, LGBT groups at Catholic University, Goshen College, and Loyola University Chicago were still in the middle of at least some of their campaigns during the time I visited the schools. As of this writing, the CUAllies group at Catholic University is still pursuing official recognition and making slow progress in transforming its campus, and the Advocate group at Loyola Chicago has for the time being dropped its challenge to its school's marriage policy; the Open Letter movement at Goshen College was also still ongoing at the time I visited the school, although it did achieve its goal of an inclusive nondiscrimination statement in 2015. Still, although I focus on the case of Bridge Builders, I also provide tentative insights into these groups' impacts.

The chapter contributes both to the literature on the impacts of activist groups in general and to the literature on activist groups and cultural change in particular. Scholars who study the impacts of activist groups overwhelmingly focus on activist groups targeting the government, although there is an increasing focus on activist groups mobilizing within a business or corporate context. This chapter contributes to a small but growing literature on activist groups mobilizing within higher education.[1] I do so with a particular focus on how activist groups transform culture. Cultural transformation is sometimes assumed to be secondary to, or even a distraction from, the so-called real work of activist groups. For example, in some cases, activist groups produce books, songs, artwork, and plays as resources that are mere means to the real ends of policy change.[2] If those artistic products have some lasting impact on a cultural field, such cultural impacts are often understood as unintended consequences of activism. In other cases, activist groups may spend significant time forming their own subcultures, with attending identities, symbols, worldviews, and frames of reference, that can buoy them through hard times; this kind of cultural change may be an end in itself (rather than a means to an end), as well as an intentional outcome of activism, but it is still often criticized for being separate from the work of policy change.[3]

In this chapter, I show how activist groups can intentionally pursue cultural change in the form of shared meanings or understandings and at the same time effect other desired changes (see the online supplement for more on this theoretical approach).[4] For example, in the case of Bridge Builders, I show how a strategy of engaging in conversations about Christianity, and subsequently transforming people's understandings about what it means to be a Christian university, a Christian community, and an LGBT Christian, has been central to Bridge Builders' successes in transforming campus policy, climate, and their members' growth. In other words, I show that cultural work can, in fact, be central to many goals of activist groups. I thus turn now to a discussion of LGBT activist groups' work in transforming cultural understandings of Christianity and, in so doing, propelling changes on their campuses.

Changing Campus Policies

At one point or another, all four of the Christian colleges and universities I visited were home to LGBT activist groups that exhibited a direct action ethos, typically waging campaigns to add sexual orientation and sometimes gender identity to their schools' official nondiscrimination policies. Such policies not only protect openly LGBT students and faculty from discrimination in admissions and hiring but also send an important message to prospective students and faculty that the school is accepting of LGBT people. At Belmont University, Bridge Builders was successful in transforming the school's nondiscrimination policy through direct action, and as I will show, central to their success was their ability to simultaneously challenge prevailing understandings of what it meant to be a Christian university.

To understand how drastically Belmont changed due to Bridge Builders' campaigns, it is helpful to first understand what Belmont was like as LGBT and allied students initially began to organize on campus. Belmont affiliated itself with the Tennessee Baptist Convention (TBC) starting in 1951, and the funding that Belmont University received from the TBC was conditioned on its adherence to several strict rules. First, the TBC required that any person who joined the Board of Trustees be an active member of and leader in a Baptist church (Baptist Press 2006). In practice, this meant that the Board of Trustees consisted mostly of conservative white men, who would no doubt hold the line on the school's discriminatory policies against LGBT people. Second, the TBC required that all faculty and staff identify as Christians, actively participate in local churches, and live up to certain "biblical standards," such as marital fidelity (fidelity within marriage being impossible for same-sex couples in Tennessee until same-sex marriage was legalized in 2015). To this day, Belmont's faculty handbook states that "a personal alignment with the institutional mission is an important condition of ongoing employment" (Belmont University 2015, 19). Finally, the TBC pressured Belmont to maintain a prohibition on "homosexual behavior" in both its student and faculty handbooks (Selden 2009). According to my interviews, if Belmont had revised its rules to remove the prohibition on "homosexual behavior" and ban discrimination on the basis of sexual orientation while it was affiliated with the TBC, it would have almost certainly forfeited an important source of funding.

In 2007, shortly before LGBT and allied students began to organize at the school, Belmont severed its ties with the TBC after a few religious yet non-Baptist donors asked to join its Board of Trustees and promised that they could bring in new funding for the school (Baptist Press 2006). What did this decision mean for LGBT students, faculty, and staff at the school? At least at first, very little. Belmont maintained strong commitments to its Christian identity, with the strong implication of a more conservative brand of Christianity; indeed, the school continued to receive funding from individual Baptist churches, most of Belmont's trustees were still Baptist, and staff and faculty were still judged according to the alignment between their values and those of the institution. As late as 2009, just one year before the protests, Belmont maintained the prohibition on "homosexual behavior" in its student handbook (Selden 2009).

Signs that change at Belmont could be possible were certainly on the horizon. Specifically, Belmont was rapidly establishing itself as a more progressive, nationally recognized university: during the 2000s, the school nearly doubled in size, grew its high-profile music business school, and leaped onto the national stage with a 2008 presidential debate between Barack Obama and John McCain (Robertson 2010). More than a few observers argued that Belmont was in the midst of an identity crisis, torn between its identity as a growing nationally recognized university with a highly visible music business school, which placed it in a league of universities that generally embraced LGBT students, and its identity as a Christian university in the South, which placed it in a group of universities that generally discriminated against LGBT students. As Robertson (2010, A10) framed the identity crisis in the *New York Times*: "Some see a continuing identity crisis—on the one hand, the university has a long reputation as conservative and Christian; on the other hand, Belmont has aggressively earned a reputation as a progressive, artsy place to study the music business." Similarly, Nashville's alternative weekly newspaper the *Nashville Scene* asked, "can Belmont be both a progressive university and a fundamentalist scold?" (Caress 2010, 1), and an influential donor at Belmont named Mike Curb stated simply, "Belmont has to decide whether they want to be a national, recognized university, particularly with their school of music business, or they want to be a church" (Robertson 2010, A10).

Still, even as students began organizing, the Belmont administration gave strong indications that Belmont would hew to a conservative understanding of its Christian identity, which implied alliance with universities that discriminated against sexual minorities. For example, on Sunday, December 5, 2010, the *Tennessean* published a story about Belmont that quoted the chair of the Board of Trustees, Marty Dickens:

> Belmont University may not be Baptist-affiliated anymore, but it's still Christian.
>
> So faculty and staff must do what the Good Book tells them to do. And at Belmont it's telling them no sex outside of marriage.
>
> "We do adhere to our values as Christ-centered, and we don't want to make apologies for that," said Marty Dickens, chairman of Belmont's board of trustees.
>
> . . . .
>
> [Belmont has] retained a written policy for students, faculty, and staff that forbids any sexual relations outside of marriage.

Dickens said the expectations for faculty are clear. . . . Belmont won't apologize for its Christian values.

"We expect people to commit themselves to high moral and ethical standards within a Christian context," he said. "That includes members of the board, faculty, and administration." (Smietana 2010, A1)

In other words, as late as December 2010, Belmont's leadership seemed to interpret its "Christ-centered" values and Christian moral and ethical standards as necessitating discrimination against lesbian and gay people, who were unable to marry at that time.[5]

What did all of this mean for the possibility that an emerging LGBT group, Bridge Builders, could transform Belmont's policies toward LGBT people? In part, it meant that Bridge Builders would need to deploy the kinds of direct action tactics that would draw the attention of community members, donors, and the media. But to ultimately convince the administration to add the words "sexual orientation" to a nondiscrimination policy, it meant that Bridge Builders would also have to change the administration's—and the wider Belmont community's—understanding of what it meant be a Christian university, and thus change preconceived notions about Belmont's obligations to the LGBT community.

An opportunity to pressure the school to change its policies toward LGBT people arose by the end of 2010 when a soccer coach, who had just revealed to her soccer team that she and her same-sex partner were having a baby, suddenly left the school.[6] Bridge Builders members believed the school had forced her out because of her sexual orientation, and they engaged in direct action through protests and sit-ins during the final week of the semester in December 2010, throughout which Christian messaging would play a central role.

Forty students and alumni attended a first rally on a street adjacent to Belmont's campus on Sunday, December 5, 2010. Although snow kept some people away, a retired Methodist bishop made a surprise visit and delivered a positive speech. Especially after reading Marty Dickens's comments to the *Tennessean*, the students realized that one of their most important tasks would be to frame LGBT inclusion as a Christian value, and so pro-LGBT religious signs emerged as an early theme of the protests, with students holding up signs such as "WWJD?" (What Would Jesus Do?), "Jesus Loves [the coach]," "God is Love, 1 John 4:8," "Belmont, Love Thy Neighbor as Thyself," and "Jesus Had 2 Dads and He Turned Out Just Fine."[7] The protest was covered by Nashville's newspapers and local news stations.

Next, students held a sit-in outside the office of the school president on Monday, December 6, 2010, drawing about fifty students (Heim 2010). Several local newspapers and news stations were present. The school's president was out of town but issued an e-mail to the Belmont community, subsequently reported by the media, containing his first public statement in response to the protests: "We support every individual's right to share their opinion. I would ask that respect, patience and thoughtfulness drive our actions and conversations as a Belmont community now and in the coming days" (Heim 2010).

Over a hundred students, alumni, and members of the Nashville community then attended a second rally outside the school's main administrative building on Wednesday, December 8, 2010, a university-designated reading day in which no classes were held. Protesters again held up a variety of religiously themed signs, such as "Jesus Was Born to a Nontraditional Mother, Would Belmont Fire Her Too?", "There is Neither Male nor Female, Slave nor Free, Jew nor Greek, Yet All are One in Christ's Love (Galatians 3:28)," "All I Want for Christmas is Equality," and "CHRIST=LOVE." Furthermore, on the way to this rally, students held a prayer walk drawing over fifty students. This protest was widely covered by local and national media outlets, including the Associated Press, *New York Times, Los Angeles Times, Huffington Post, Sports Illustrated,* ESPN, and CNN.

As students and alumni engaged in protests, others in the Belmont community joined the students in opposition to the school's actions. For example, over four hundred people sent e-mails to the school's president, nearly all opposing the dismissal of the soccer coach (Belmont University 2010). The school's faculty senate passed a unanimous resolution encouraging the school to engage in open dialogue about religion and sexuality, although it tabled a more strongly worded resolution (Caress 2010). Most significantly, the major Belmont donor and former trustee named Mike Curb, who founded the record label Curb Records, released statements saying, "It's time for Belmont to change" (Robertson 2010); "'I promise you, if the matter is not resolved, I will continue speaking out about this the rest of my life'" (Nashville Scene Staff 2011).

Reflecting on the role of religion in the protests, students continually noted that they saw a strategic opportunity to reframe Belmont's Christian mission. For example, a student named Perry told me that he saw the Christian admonition to love others and treat others as one would want to be treated as central to the mission of a Christian university: "The fact that Belmont is a Christian university affected how we approached the protest and also how we responded to the media. For example, we wanted to say, we love Belmont because it's supposed to be a Christian school, and we just feel like what they're doing right now has kind of strayed from the path of a Christian. You're supposed to love others and treat others as they want to be treated. So Belmont right now isn't acting like a Christian university."

Bridge Builders' effort to frame LGBT inclusion as a Christian value and the duty to love and welcome everyone as a core mission of a Christian university turned out to be quite successful. On Wednesday, December 8, 2010, immediately after students held their second rally outside the school, Belmont's president, Bob Fisher, held a press conference at which he announced a new nondiscrimination statement inclusive of sexual orientation (Belmont University 2010), which was officially approved by the Board of Trustees in January 2011 (Belmont University 2011). As he stated, "*Because of Belmont's aspirations to demonstrate Christian character*, it is a safe and welcoming place for all" (Belmont University 2010, emphasis added). Furthermore, after the Board of Trustees officially voted to add sexual orientation to the school's nondiscrimination statement in January 2011, Belmont's president released the following statement on behalf of the board:

> Today our Board of Trustees met and affirmed officially who we are and who we will continue to be. *We are a Christian community that is welcoming, loving, and inclusive of everyone.* To reflect the unique character of Belmont University, the Board added a preamble to our existing non-discrimination statement. The language in this preamble was inspired by our existing mission statement and our current employment handbooks. It states that Belmont is a Christian community, and the university's faculty, administration and staff uphold Jesus as the Christ and as the measure of all things. In addition, the Board voted today to amend the university's written anti-discrimination policy to reflect our long-standing practice of non-discrimination as it relates to sexual orientation. (Belmont University 2011, emphasis added)

In other words, Belmont's president invoked the same Christian values that board chair Marty Dickens had previously cited as a reason to discriminate against sexual minorities as requiring the school to be "welcoming, loving, and inclusive of everyone." It seems that Bridge Builders' protests facilitated a redefinition of what it meant to be a Christian community, allowing the university to defend adding sexual orientation to its nondiscrimination policy.

Certainly, Bridge Builders' efforts to reframe Belmont's Christian mission through its direct actions were not the only factors at play in Belmont's decision to revise its nondiscrimination policies, along with later policies, such as a decision to offer benefits to married same-sex couples (Zylstra, Lee, and Smietana 2015). For example, Bridge Builders benefited from rapid advances in political opportunities for sexual minorities: whereas only a third of Americans expressed support for rights such as same-sex marriage a decade before the protests occurred, a majority of Americans reported that they approved of same-sex marriage by 2011 (Public Religion Research Institute 2014). Similarly, Bridge Builders benefited from structural opportunities for the advancement of LGBT rights at Belmont, especially Belmont's break from the TBC, a denomination with a highly individualistic theological orientation (see chapter one). Still, there is little doubt that Bridge Builders was central to adding LGBT inclusion to Belmont's agenda once these structural opportunities opened.

HOW DID BRIDGE BUILDERS' efforts to transform campus policies on sexual orientation compare with those of other schools? In many ways, the efforts by the Open Letter movement to change Goshen College's nondiscrimination policy beginning in 2011 mirror those of Bridge Builders. Although Goshen College had long recognized official LGBT student organizations on campus, it had resisted adding sexual orientation as well as gender identity to its nondiscrimination policy because it saw such a policy as contrary to (or, at minimum, not necessitated by) the values of the Mennonite Church USA. The Open Letter movement challenged the exclusionary policy in part by pointing out that it contradicted Goshen College's identity as a social justice college. Furthermore, after the Mennonite Church USA inaugurated a "listening period" to seek out members' perspectives on same-sex relationships, the Open Letter movement saw an opportunity to make religious arguments in favor of an inclusive nondiscrimination policy. For example, Paul, introduced in chapter two, described a pitch he would give to Goshen administrators: "I'm pro-LGBTQ inclusion and rights. It primarily comes from my faith as a Christian and my commitment to nonviolence. I think Christ's model calls us to inclusion and to reach out to society's marginalized and oppressed. I see the fruit that those people who identify as LGBTQ bring to congregations where it's accepted, and it's phenomenal. I want to support their full inclusion at Goshen." In its protests on campus, the leaders of the Open Letter movement invited its members to sing Christian hymns and partake of communion.

In July 2015, the Open Letter movement's efforts bore fruit. The Goshen College Board of Directors added both sexual orientation and gender identity to the school's nondiscrimination policy, and like at Belmont, Goshen College's president defended the action by invoking its "Christ-centered" values:

> As an institution rooted in the Anabaptist tradition, we reaffirm our strong relationship to Mennonite Church USA, and recognize the diversity of interpretation of Scripture on this issue within our denomination and the broader Christian church, a diversity reflected within the board of directors and on our campus as well. . . . As a liberal arts college, we strive for an educational environment that encourages critical thinking, loving and respectful dialogue, and continual pursuit of living into our Christ-centered core values. We affirm the equal value and worth of each unique member of our community as a beloved child of God, and *we seek to be a hospitable community for all*—including those who disagree with this decision—*as Christ modeled to us.* (Goshen College 2015, emphasis added)

Again, the Open Letter movement's religious arguments in favor of LGBT inclusion were not the only factors shaping Goshen's decision to revise its nondiscrimination policy. Goshen was similarly aided by political opportunities in favor of LGBT rights and structural opportunities for dialogue within the communalistic Mennonite Church. The more conservative Eastern Mennonite University revised its nondiscrimination policy at the same time, providing Goshen College cover from inevitable pushback. Still, the similarities between Goshen's and Belmont's rationales for adopting an inclusive nondiscrimination policy in light of Christian values are striking, illustrating how policy changes are tightly coupled with cultural change.

At the same time, CUAllies' early efforts to transform Catholic University's policies toward LGBT people in the late 2000s provide a striking contrast with the efforts of both Bridge Builders at Belmont and the Open Letter movement at Goshen. To challenge the school's inaction on LGBT issues, CUAllies not only e-mailed stories about harassment against LGBT students to administrators, faculty, and staff on campus but also engaged in direct action through unauthorized protests at the university's student center. However, even though one of the group founders was a theology student, some group leaders expressed antagonistic attitudes toward religion, and thus the group avoided using religious arguments in favor of LGBT-inclusive policy change. This allowed administrators to paint the CUAllies group as antagonistic toward the university's mission, and as discussed in chapter three, the group ultimately alienated even many LGBT students on campus who were committed to the Catholic faith, students who would eventually take over the reins of the group. Although it was at least plausible that Catholic University could have revised its policies on LGBT issues—it had supported an LGBT group in the 1980s—the group failed to change nondiscrimination policies at Catholic.

Efforts by students at Loyola University Chicago to challenge the school's ban on weddings of same-sex couples in 2014 also fell short. After Illinois legalized same-sex marriage and a student requested that she be able to marry her same-sex partner in one of Loyola Chicago's chapels, Loyola Chicago quickly revised its policies about on-campus weddings to state that only "Catholic weddings" (between opposite-sex couples) would be allowed. However, statements issued by Advocate leaders generally conceded the idea that same-sex weddings would be contrary to Catholic values—acknowledging that "many find a ban of this nature unsurprising for a Catholic campus"—and advanced an argument in favor of holding same-sex weddings from a general human rights perspective (Kubicki 2014). Although such arguments may have resonated with the student body, which was the least religious of the four campuses I visited, they failed to challenge prevailing understandings of what it meant to be a Catholic university. This, combined with a mismatch between the group's solidarity ethos and the goal of policy change, may explain why the group's campaign was short-lived and ultimately a failure.

Changing Campus Climates

LGBT activist groups work not only to change official policies toward LGBT people, often through direct action, but also to make their communities more welcoming toward LGBT people, most effectively through education. After successfully challenging Belmont University's official nondiscrimination policy in the fall of 2010, Bridge Builders began to shed its direct action ethos in favor of an educational ethos in the spring of 2011, and it shifted from targeting official policies to changing community members' hearts, minds, and behaviors. The organization pursued this goal through educational efforts that brought LGBT students and religiously oriented students (along with those who identified as both LGBT and religious) together to discuss issues of religion, sexuality, and gender identity.

Again, to appreciate Bridge Builders' role in transforming Belmont's campus climate, it is helpful to understand what Belmont was like on the eve of Bridge Builders' emergence. Given Belmont's history as a conservative Baptist university, it is perhaps not surprising that many people at the school believed that a Christian university is one that must necessarily exclude LGBT people; thus, most students and faculty members whom I interviewed initially described Belmont as an isolating environment for sexual and gender minorities. When official discussions about LGBT issues ensued, they were usually from a conservative perspective. For example, the school's University Ministries occasionally invited speakers that preached abstinence before marriage for heterosexual students and the sinfulness of all non-heterosexual behaviors. Otherwise, students, faculty, and staff either shied away from open discussions about gender and sexuality at the school or broached issues about LGBT issues at their own risk. For example, one faculty member said that a student who wanted to do research on sexuality was treated harshly by administrators at the school. Another faculty member reported receiving an e-mail from one of the many "incredibly vocal, evangelical, the-Bible-is-the-direct-word-of-God" students on campus when students were first trying to establish Bridge Builders. Among other things, the student told the faculty member that Bridge Builders was "building a bridge to sin." Finally, one student named Georgia, who later became a leader in Bridge Builders, described the reaction she received when she asked whether the school had a Gay–Straight Alliance: "I have this very long involvement with searching for LGBT rights at Belmont, starting from the first time I ever set foot on orientation. I went to an orientation session and asked if there was a Gay–Straight Alliance or anything like that. I got completely shot down—they told me, there will never be anything like that at Belmont, that is completely against our Christian morals. I was like, okay, a little bit shell-shocked."

Thus, my respondents, especially the staff and faculty who had been at the school for many years, reported that the climate for LGBT people at the school was quite chilly prior to the formation of Bridge Builders. Indeed, many of the eventual participants in Bridge Builders had been personally discriminated against or harassed by their peers at the school, with some students relating situations in which their roommates switched rooms after finding out they were gay, and with other students reporting being called names such as "dyke" or "fag" by their peers. Students reported that they longed for greater dialogue on LGBT and religious issues on campus, especially with the increasing number of openly LGBT students on campus. Perry told me, "I felt like . . . [homosexuality] was not talked about a lot in the general Belmont community. Religious people claim we don't have that 'problem' here, whereas in reality there are tons of people who have that 'problem' here." He said that he hoped Bridge Builders would "promote a discussion about these issues, about LGBT people and Christianity. And whether or not people were going around campus saying 'oh my gosh, I hate those Bridge Builders'—they will still be talking about us, and hopefully that will promote discussion with other students."

To address the often chilly climate for sexual minorities at their school—which seemed to be rooted in the understanding that a Christian community is one that excludes LGBT people—a group of students asked Belmont to officially approve Bridge Builders so that they could openly promote dialogue about faith and sexuality issues at their school through group discussions and convocation events. Yet, an application to establish the student organization was denied by the school's administration in the spring of 2010. The administration instead proposed a compromise group known as Difficult Dialogues that began to meet in March 2010. The group was not open to the entire university community—rather, only students, staff, and faculty who were invited could attend. Furthermore, any materials the group discussed had to be approved by the administration, with the goal of providing a "balanced perspective" on homosexuality.

Most students felt that the Difficult Dialogues model was too limiting and thus initiated petition drives in favor of official recognition in the fall of 2010, along with the December 2010 protests described previously. Although the protests were primarily intended to question the departure of a lesbian soccer coach from the school and to ask for a nondiscrimination policy inclusive of sexual orientation, the protests convinced the administration of the need to approve Bridge Builders as an officially recognized student organization. By the spring of 2011, Bridge Builders was thus able to shift back to the educational form that students perhaps originally intended, meeting each week to discuss topics relevant to the LGBT community.

Given the apparent role of religion in silencing and excluding LGBT students at this Christian school, the students recognized they would need to address issues of religion and LGBT inclusion head-on if they were to truly change the climate for LGBT people at the school. As part of the negotiations to approve the group, students agreed to have their group sponsored by the school's University Ministries, which would thus take on, as part of its official, university-sanctioned mission, the goal of "bridging the gap between the LGBT and religious communities." Although the decision by University Ministries to sponsor the group raised some fears of co-optation

(McAdam 1982; Piven and Cloward 1977), the decision meant that the new organization would not simply be an isolated group of LGBT-identified students and allies who remained walled off from religiously oriented students on campus. Instead, Bridge Builders began to draw a diverse mix of LGBT- and religious-identified students to its meetings. University Ministries also assigned one of its supportive full-time ministers as its adviser, and he would serve as a liaison on issues of faith and sexuality to the broader campus community.

As described in chapter three, the group held weekly meetings covering a range of topics relevant to the LGBT community, including "GLBT History," "Biology of Gender/Homosexuality," "How to Be a Good Ally," "Heteronormativity/Bullying in Schools," "AIDS and Its Impact in the GLBT Community," "Deconstructing the Binary," "Media Representation of the LGBTIQA Community," "Deconstructing Trans-Phobia," "Reclaiming Words," "Recognizing and Addressing Relationship Violence," "Famous Gays & Allies," "International Rights," and "Drag, Camp, and Gender." At least once a year, and usually once a semester, the group focused on "Faith and Sexuality."

Furthermore, during its first year, one of the more religious students, Andrew (introduced in the previous chapter), volunteered to lead Bible studies for the Bridge Builders students. According to Andrew, he did not focus the Bible study on LGBT issues; rather, he recalled, "I think I talked about Isaiah [a book in the Old Testament], because I love Isaiah. I mean—it was a normal Bible study, but it was intended for students who were gay [and] who had been rejected by their churches to come and just be Christians and not have to focus solely on their sexual orientation. I wanted to show the people who came that they could be people of faith. I wanted to provide a space at Belmont where people were comfortable with exploring that. Not everyone is comfortable coming into the church, especially if in your mind it represents a space of discrimination. And so I wanted to start the process of bridging that divide for some people."

Finally, as an official University Ministries organization, Bridge Builders was able to hold convocation events on campus promoting dialogue on faith, sexuality, and gender identity. Whereas University Ministries once promoted talks critical of homosexuality, by the spring of 2012 University Ministries organized a "Sex & the Soul" week that featured talks on open and affirming congregations by local ministers supportive of the LGBT community. Such events provided convocation credits that students were required to accumulate before their graduation and thus drew a diverse group of students.

In the years that followed, Bridge Builders facilitated positive transformations in the campus climate toward LGBT students. Specifically, students now felt that they could talk freely about LGBT issues on campus, and none relayed stories of bullying and harassment, which were more common in previous years. These changes seemed to stem in part from a changing understanding of what it meant to be a Christian community; specifically, through their educational work, Bridge Builders had also convinced many Christians at the school that a Christian community was one that loved and accepted everyone. I had the opportunity to talk to four Bridge Builders students both shortly after their freshmen or sophomore years (in 2011) and then again either shortly before or after their graduations (in 2014). Their comments allowed me to gauge the impacts of Bridge Builders on the campus climate toward LGBT people. For example, Curtis, introduced in chapter two, had reported being bullied because of his sexual orientation during his freshman year. When I spoke to him in 2011, he was hesitant as to whether some of the changes Bridge Builders seemed to be facilitating would be permanent:

JONATHAN: Have you noticed any changes at Belmont in terms of the campus culture?

CURTIS: To an extent. I do think that the whole protest thing made people on campus more aware of the fact that there are people who are not being treated nicely on campus and there is something they could do to help those people and that they could help raise awareness of gay rights and other things on campus. I'm still not sure it's a place where people can be comfortably, fully out.

In 2014, he was more sanguine about the campus climate, noting the support the group has received from students in general and the religious community in particular:

JONATHAN: How do you think Bridge Builders has impacted your school, if at all?

CURTIS: I think it's become a more welcoming place. The student body for the most part has been really supportive of us. Maybe it's just generational change, but we don't get the kind of pushback we received before. To a large extent the student body is supportive, even if they aren't maybe vocal about it or even if they aren't involved. . . .

JONATHAN: Has the University Ministries been supportive of your group?

CURTIS: They are our official sponsors. And [Blinded] is our staff sponsor, and he is extremely supportive, much more so than [a previous staff member]; he was more hostile when were first getting started. I've noticed—*there is a lot more acceptance of the LGBT community among people in the religious community at Belmont now.* (emphasis added)

Another student, Ruth, describes the transformation she witnessed from the time she was a freshman (in 2011), when the protests occurred, to the time that she was a senior (in 2014). Specifically, in 2011, she remarked on the positive changes she was already witnessing during the group's petition drives in favor of recognizing Bridge Builders, with fewer people claiming that Christianity prohibited them from supporting such a group and with many religious students being open to dialogue with LGBT students:

JONATHAN: Have you noticed any changes in the culture or atmosphere at Belmont [this semester]?

RUTH: I would say yes, because . . . this sort of slipped my mind . . . we set up tables on campus and we talked to passing students. . . . And people would come and talk to us, and we had so many more students sign up. . . . Students would say, yeah, I support that. . . . And then we even had several faculty members that would say, yes I'm in support. . . .

JONATHAN: Did you get any rejection [in previous semesters]?

RUTH: Yeah, we had quite a few . . . *many people would say, oh I don't support that, I'm a Christian.* . . . But after the protests we had so much more support and much less rejection, so that was actually surprising, it was really, really good. (emphasis added)

Then, in 2014, she remarked at how people were moving from mere passive support of LGBT rights—which was already a step forward for Belmont—to an increased willingness to actively participate in Bridge Builders or at least partner with Bridge Builders for its events:

JONATHAN: What kinds of changes do you think the organization has helped bring about at your school, if at all? How have you seen the school change since you've been at Belmont, and do you think those have been driven by Bridge Builders?

RUTH: I think—from the beginning of my freshman year, when there were barely whispers about LGBT issues, to the very end, when we had a stable presence on campus, it was very much a—I saw a transformation in people, oh yeah, I support LGBT rights, to oh yeah, I really enjoyed going to Bridge Builders last week, thanks for, you know whatever. . . . I remember in the very beginning when we were sort of getting people to sign petitions to support us, people would be like, yeah I guess I'll support that, and they may not have wanted to be an active member but they supported our presence on campus. . . . But now we—I mean, not everyone is going to be a member of Bridge Builders, of course, but we see a lot of student groups, *even groups in University Ministries, come to us and say, oh, we'd like to help plan an event with you.* I mean, everyone for the most part has been very great. (emphasis added)

Overall, Bridge Builders has seemed to achieve some success in making the campus more welcoming toward LGBT people, a place where people felt that they could openly discuss LGBT issues. The group has done so through educational efforts that have brought the LGBT and religious communities together both symbolically (through the formal recognition of Bridge Builders by the University Ministries) and physically (by holding meetings in the University Ministries space and inviting members of other religious groups to join), promoting the idea that a Christian university is one that is loving toward and accepting of everyone.

HOW DO BRIDGE BUILDERS' efforts to change the climate for LGBT people at Belmont compare with the work of groups at other schools? Although Bridge Builders has changed in its ethos over time, Goshen College was home to three separate LGBT groups at the time of my visit; at the same time that the Open Letter movement was challenging Goshen's nondiscrimination policy, an organization called Advocates was carrying out its work to promote dialogue around LGBT issues on campus in keeping with an educational ethos. As discussed in the introductory chapter, such dialogue was sorely needed, because the campus had garnered headlines for acts of hate committed against the LGBT community on campus; for example, someone set a bulletin board on fire after other students posted pro-LGBT messages on it.

To create a more inclusive campus climate, the Advocates group regularly showed movies and organized lectures about LGBT issues. The group also facilitated Safe Zone trainings on campus, in which students, staff, and faculty were taught how to be an ally—how to provide a listening ear—to students who were going through a coming out process or who felt marginalized as a member of the LGBT community on Goshen's campus. Importantly, in this latter endeavor, the Advocates group entered into a remarkable partnership with the school's Campus Ministries. Specifically, Campus Ministries trained several student ministry leaders to live in various dorms across campus and provide spiritual support to students. The Campus Ministries required that all of these ministry leaders attend Safe Zone trainings and learn how to be an ally to LGBT students in their dorms. The students whom I interviewed believed such trainings have been instrumental in creating a climate of inclusion, particularly among the religious community on Goshen's campus. Mennonite students in particular have been the most vocal supporters of LGBT rights on Goshen's campus.

After transitioning to its current educational form, the CUAllies group at Catholic University began to facilitate some change in attitudes toward LGBT students on campus. The students who took over the organization made a concerted effort to change the group's image on campus, from one that was widely seen as antagonistic toward religion to one that was, in the group president's words, "focused on bridging the gap between the Catholic Church and the LGBT community and their allies on campus," quite similarly to Bridge Builders at Belmont. The group has organized lectures by Catholic priests who were favorable to the LGBT community, a discussion with the head of an LGBT Catholic organization, and a prayer vigil. At one point, the CUAllies members began attending mass together.

Whereas the previous iteration of CUAllies was mostly shunned by administrators, the school entered into formal dialogue with the CUAllies group after it shifted into its educational form. In one of its most significant achievements, the CUAllies president—through a direct e-mail exchange with the school's president—convinced the school to address issues of sexual orientation as part of a new community pledge it was asking incoming freshmen and other members of the Catholic University community to sign. The pledge states:

> Founded by the United States Catholic bishops in 1887, under the papal charter issued by Pope Leo XIII, the University is an academic community faithful to the Church's teaching that every person is a son or daughter of God, created in the image and likeness of His Son, Jesus Christ. *Our relationships are governed by the two great commandments: "Love the Lord, your God, with all your heart, your mind and your strength and love your neighbor as yourself." Mindful of these teachings, The Catholic University of America calls upon her sons and daughters to create a*

culture of light and love on our campus and in our lives. As a member of
The Catholic University of America community, I promise: ... To
reject and witness against bullying and violence toward women or
men of any race, creed, ethnicity, sexual orientation, or socio-
economic status, or persons with disabilities. (Catholic University
2016, emphasis added)

The pledge, which frames the need to "create a culture of light and love on
our campus" (including toward LGBT people) in light of Christian values,
is mostly symbolic and does not yet reflect any official policy commitment
to nondiscrimination (although, as I have shown above, changes in cultural
commitments can provide the basis for official policy changes). However,
the students whom I interviewed told me they did believe the community
pledge was indicative of an improved climate for LGBT and allied undergraduates; the CUAllies' various events that informed the Catholic community about issues of religion, sexuality, and gender identity were well
attended, and students told me they had not recently heard of the kind of
harassment and bullying against LGBT people that seemed to be common-
place in the late 2000s.

The organization can hardly be called a complete success. At the time of
my visit, CUAllies leaders had applied for but were denied official recognition, and without such official approval the organization is completely de-
pendent on the energy of students, who come and go every four years, to
keep going in the face of rejection and burnout. But at the time of this writing, a large, energetic, new group of students has taken the reins of the
CUAllies group and is again applying for official approval; it is possible such
change is around the corner.

Finally, Loyola University Chicago supported the most welcoming and
inclusive climate for LGBT people out of the four schools studied here, but
to the extent that there was work to do in terms of challenging conservative views or behaviors such as discrimination and harassment toward LGBT
people, a strategy of embracing conversations about religion, sexuality, and
gender identity also seemed to hold promise. Whenever Advocate met resistance, group members usually attributed it to some of the highly religious
students within the Loyola community, whether resistance took the form
of clashes over the drag show on campus (described in the introduction)
or rare cases of harassment (one lesbian student told me that her room was
vandalized and that she had evidence that this was due to her participation
in Advocate). For its part, in both its direct action and solidarity forms, Ad-

vocate has had a reputation of being dismissive toward religion, leaving some religious members feeling like they had to be silent about their faith.

In an effort to facilitate dialogue about LGBT issues among the religious community at Loyola Chicago, one of the Advocate leaders signed up to lead one of the small groups through the school's Campus Ministry, which Campus Ministry calls Christian Life Communities (or CLCs), that was devoted to exploring issues surrounding faith and sexuality. Although the group is not huge—the Campus Ministry caps these groups at a dozen people—it drew several members from Advocate as well as several people more closely associated with the Campus Ministry. An Advocate member named Samantha said that, prior to the formation of this LGBT CLC, a person just had to hope that "by chance, the group would be okay talking about LGBT issues, and if it wasn't, you were out of luck." However, this CLC has provided a crucial space for students to talk about the integration of faith and sexuality on campus. Samantha reports that the Campus Ministry has been very supportive of this CLC and highly supportive of Advocate and the LGBT community at Loyola Chicago in general; for example, she told me that she had recently noticed that several staff members in Campus Ministry had posted Safe Zone stickers on their doors (which she thought was unusual, in a positive way, because the Safe Zone program is not particularly visible at Loyola). For Advocate's part, she observed that "Advocate has come a long way" in its approach to religion: "We had a queer theology discussion a couple weeks ago, and we are finding that people in Advocate want that." Several members whom I spoke to were encouraged by this turn in the Advocate group, because it ultimately means that more members of the LGBT community at Loyola feel like they are being supported. It is difficult to pinpoint precise changes in the campus climate at this early stage, but a precedent for engaging in conversations about faith and sexuality is now in place.

Changing Students

Because the next chapter focuses on the biographical consequences of activist groups—impacts that each type of activist group produces, whether intentionally (in the case of solidarity and educational groups) or unintentionally (in the case of direct action groups)—I do not provide a comprehensive discussion of the impacts of LGBT activist groups on their members here. However, it is worth briefly considering whether the strategy of embracing conversations about religion and LGBT issues can similarly explain these groups' success in changing their members. The answer, I find, is yes, but with an important caveat—engaging in conversations about religion, sexuality, and gender identity is important only to the extent that activist groups' members see themselves as being conflicted about their own religious and sexual or gender identities.[8] Specifically, although a Christian institutional identity is common to all four of the colleges and universities, and although sizable Christian communities can be found at all four of these schools, LGBT groups at Belmont University and Catholic University contained more conservative religious participants than groups at Loyola Chicago and Goshen College; engaging in discussions about religion, sexuality, and gender identity seemed to be important for members' personal growth only at Belmont and Catholic.

To highlight again the case of Belmont, many members joined Bridge Builders either as students with highly salient religious identities or as students who had once been religious but had abandoned their faith once they found out they were gay, lesbian, or bisexual. Rachel, who began her participation in Bridge Builders as a student and then continued as an alumna, attended a conservative church in Nashville because she was paid to sing there. Yet, she had personally pulled away from religion because she found it to be unsupportive, and she was brought back to religion only as Bridge Builders helped her reconcile her sexual identity with her faith:

> At the time [of the protests] I was working for [blinded] Presbyterian Church. I do sort of—I'm a paid singer at various churches, for extra money on top of my job. They were a pretty gay-negative group. And while I loved them very much, I realized that I wasn't going to be able to stay there very much longer if I was to be comfortable with myself and deal with my own religious issues surrounding sexuality. [After participating in Bridge Builders] I put in my notice there and got a job at [blinded] United Methodist Church. . . . And the Methodist church has been a lot better for me than—I was raised Southern Baptist, and they were very gay-negative. They just don't deal with that at all. There were kids I grew up with who I found out later had killed themselves just because their families were seminary people who were pastors or whatever and kicked them out of the family, et cetera. So it did make me move around a little bit, and in doing so I was able to get over some of my own personal issues with religion. Basically, I had pulled back from religion because of being in an unsupportive and hurtful environment, and Bridge Builders brought me back.

When I asked what about Bridge Builders brought her back to religion, Rachel then continued:

Well, there were a lot of allies involved, as well as—one of the women in Bridge Builders . . . is a religion major and she is very passionate about the fact that it was okay for her to be a pastor and to be gay, and that was totally fine, and that everyone should just get the fuck over it. And she is one of the most religious and theological and spiritual people that I've ever known. So in just talking to her, in getting to know her . . . sort of made me feel like there didn't have to be this divide, I didn't have to stick with the views that had been espoused to me since I was a child about gay people in religion.

Another student, Molly, described a similar and common story of having attended a conservative church most of her life and having soured on religion. However, she came to understand alternative religious perspectives on LGBT issues through her participation in Bridge Builders, which helped her grow in her faith:

I think there were some really strong spiritual leaders that were part of Bridge Builders. And that still are. Many of these people felt like someone needed to pray over our meetings, and they did. I learned that—my home church is very exclusive and not very open, and every week I'd hear at least one homophobic or racist statement made. Generally unintentionally racist and intentionally homophobic. And there were a lot of really sexist statements too—I stopped counting those a couple years ago. And I knew deep down that wasn't right, but I didn't know anything else, so I just kind of sat there, and I had begun to pull away from religion. But after seeing these people that firmly held this conviction that homosexuality was okay and having someone sit down and teach me and showed me in the Bible where it talks about it and how it talks about it and the verbiage that's used, having someone sit down with me and teach me was very helpful. So I think I've become stronger in my faith.

Bridge Builders thus helped many of these participants make sense of their identities, including moving some from an understanding of their sexual identity and religious convictions as oppositional or contradictory to an understanding of their sexual identity and religious beliefs as compatible. Although the next chapter will focus explicitly on the impacts of LGBT activism on participants, it is worth quoting from the stories of a couple members who said that, after reconciling religion with their sexuality through the group, they were able to come out to their own friends and families, a type of impact that is common to each type of LGBT activist group. One student, named Michelle, told me she was outed to her father as a result of participating in the group; however, she began to relay the things she learned about religion and sexuality, such as through a Tell Your Story event in which participants relayed narratives of coming to reconcile religion and sexuality, and her parents have now become much more accepting of her: "I came out to—well, I was outed to my dad after I began participating in Bridge Builders. And I began to share my own story with my parents, as well as other stories I heard at Tell Your Story. And they both became fired up and recognized the importance of the group, and maybe through hearing these stories, they realized what it's like to be LGBT and how it affects every aspect of your life. So I think they've changed as a result of my participation in Bridge Builders. They've become really supportive."

Another student named Evan, who came from a traditional Catholic household, similarly said that he became much "cooler" talking about sexuality through the group and has since communicated his perspective on faith and sexuality back to his family. His family, in turn, has gone so far as to stop attending their local church (which preached against homosexuality) and informing their own friends about LGBT issues:

JONATHAN: Do you think you've personally been changed as a result of your participation?

EVAN: For one, I'm so much cooler about talking about homosexuality. I probably like, if it weren't for Bridge Builders, I probably couldn't have this interview to be completely honest. I would be like really nervous about what I could and could not tell you. Now I just don't care—I'm cool with talking about everything, because I know there are people out there who are gonna wanna listen to me. And also I've have had a lot of opportunities to talk about faith and sexuality with people in the group. I've found ways to take what I've learned in Catholicism and kind of mend that with my own thoughts about sexuality.

JONATHAN: You said you've become more comfortable talking about sexuality. Have you talked to your friends and family members about the things you've learned through the group, and have any of your friends or family members changed their views on LGBT issues since you started participating in the organization?

EVAN: Definitely, I mean all the stuff that I learn about faith and sexuality, I relay back to my family, and they've learned a lot through me, which is great, and they've even kinda started implementing it into their lives, which I think is incredible, like they started telling other people about it, like the word is spreading through Bridge Builders.

JONATHAN: How would you say they've implemented it into their lives? Just what you said, by telling people, or are there other ways?

EVAN: My parents don't go to our local church anymore. Yeah, as a result of me coming out to them—that's something else I did after joining the group. I mean they're still Catholics, they still believe in all the tenets and stuff, but they just can't go to mass and listen to all that hate, and like I said before, I don't want to bash the Catholic Church, because there's so many Catholic churches out there that are accepting of LGBTQ people and stuff like that, I've even heard of this one organization, Dignity USA, a Catholic organization supporting LGBT; no, there are definitely people finding ways to implement those two areas. But I told my family about it, and they're doing research on it.

Although I met numerous Bridge Builders members with stories like these, on rare occasions I met students who insisted that the groups had no impact on them. A common thread through their stories is that they came into the group believing that homosexuality was sinful, and they still maintain that belief to this day (or at least when I last talked to them). For example, Beth, the student introduced in chapter two who rose to a position of leadership despite believing that God did not want her to marry someone of the same sex, told me this about why the group did not significantly shape her personally:

JONATHAN: Would you say that you personally have been changed as a result of your participation in Bridge Builders?

BETH: I guess I would say I value the relationships I've made through the organization. I don't know that the group has changed me, but I value the people whom I've met.

JONATHAN: . . . Have your views on religion, politics, or LGBT issues changed as a result of your participation, in any ways? And have you talked to your friends and family members about any things you've learned through the group?

BETH: No. No, not really. [laughs] I said earlier I kind of believe the same things. I think—well I do feel like I can administer more grace now though, and have more compassion and mercy on other people. But I believe the same things as I did going in.

Because Beth still views her Christian faith as incompatible with her proclivity for a same-sex relationship, she did not see the group shaping her relationships with friends and family.

Students at Belmont, as well as Catholic, commonly related stories about how the group helped them develop a fuller appreciation of how their religious and sexual identities fit together. However, at schools like Goshen and Loyola, although students commonly reported that their groups shaped their postgraduation activist, work, and family trajectories, their groups' impacts on their own religious views and identities had little to do with this process because, with few exceptions, most participants did not hold conservative religious beliefs that might have prevented them from being shaped by their participation in LGBT activism.

Conclusion

Students who participate in LGBT activist groups at Christian colleges and universities often have many goals in mind, but a common one is to make some lasting impact on their campus, whether that be through an official change to a school's nondiscrimination policy or through a shift in the campus climate for LGBT students. Students also hope that they will be personally changed. Why are some groups more successful in achieving their goals than others? The inroads that the LGBT movement has made in terms of transforming public opinion toward same-sex couples, as well as challenging state and federal laws on LGBT rights, certainly cannot be ignored (see chapter one). Simply put, LGBT activist groups would not have been able to impact any of these campuses so successfully in, for example, the 1950s; beyond the problem of self-definition—the category of LGBT people did not exist then—hostile attitudes toward those who engaged in same-sex relationships or who attempted gender transitions would have ensured that students participating in any LGBT activist groups were swiftly expelled from their schools. The key roles of denominational affiliation—particularly affiliation with a communal or individualist denomination (see chapter one)—and, relatedly, the religious composition of a school's administration also must be taken into account. The conservative takeover of Catholic University, for example, has for the time being ensured that challenges to the school's official nondiscrimination policies (if not the campus climate) are met with resistance.

Still, in this age of changing attitudes toward LGBT rights, at schools where administrators or donors could plausibly approve changes in campus policy toward LGBT people, some LGBT groups achieved more success in transforming the policies of Christian colleges and universities than others. Why? This chapter emphasizes not only the role of group ethos—the idea that certain activist groups are more effective in achieving certain kinds of change—but also the key role of cultural change. Specifically, direct action groups that attempt to reframe discussions about religion and LGBT rights— and that transform prevailing understandings about Christian universities' obligations to their LGBT students—have been more successful in achieving inclusive nondiscrimination policies. At Belmont, students invoked the school's Christian mission to call for the school to be more loving and accepting of LGBT students. Whereas on the weekend prior to Bridge Builders' protests, the chair of the Board of Trustees invoked the school's "Christ-centered values" to defend the dismissal of LGBT people, directly following the protests, the school's president announced the school's intentions to be a "Christian community that is welcoming, loving, and inclusive of everyone." At Goshen, where the Open Letter movement held vigils and even communions in support of an inclusive nondiscrimination policy, school administrators announced their intentions to become "a hospitable community for all . . . as Christ modeled to us." In comparison, student mobilization at Catholic and Loyola Chicago was not characterized by any sustained dialogue over Christian values, and perhaps as a result, school administrators mostly shrugged off their calls for inclusive nondiscrimination policies or marriage policies as antithetical to their Christian missions.

Whether or not official changes to campus policies were truly possible at each of these schools, students did commonly say that their educational groups had achieved at least some successes in transforming campus climates for LGBT students, and these gains also seemed to stem in part from a strategy of embracing conversations about religion and LGBT rights. In the years leading up to Bridge Builders' approval, detractors—including those on the University Ministries staff—invoked Belmont's Christian identity to push back or mock the idea of an LGBT group on campus. Now, because of leaders' decision to brand themselves as an organization that seeks to "bridge the gap between the LGBT and Christian communities," the University Ministries has gone so far as to sponsor the Bridge Builders as one of its official student organizations. Belmont has gone from a campus that generally shied away from discussions about LGBT issues and where students who dared to be open about their sexuality or gender identity were bullied to a campus that brings in pro-LGBT speakers during University Ministries–sponsored "Sex & the Soul" weeks and where students feel comfortable coming out as lesbian, gay, bisexual, and even (within the past few years) transgender. Goshen was once an inhospitable place for LGBT students—as evidenced by the reports of hate crimes discussed in the introductory chapter—but because of a new Safe Zone program, which all ministry leaders at the school are required to attend, LGBT students now have people in their residence halls whom they can talk to about issues they are facing on campus. The previous chapters detailed many instances of hate crimes, bullying, and harassment of Catholic University's underground LGBT community, but in part because the school has invoked "the Church's teaching that every person is a son or daughter of God, created in the image and likeness of His Son, Jesus Christ" to require that incoming students "reject and witness against bullying and violence toward women or men of any race, creed, ethnicity, sexual orientation, or socio-economic status, or persons with disabilities" (Catholic University 2016), the newest members of the unofficial CUAllies group say that such acts are now uncommon, even if there is much more work to do in creating a campus that truly embraces its LGBT student population. Finally, the relatively little pushback that LGBT students at Loyola received to their events—such as the campus drag show—came from religious students, but with a new LGBT Christian Life Community, students hope that a precedent of respectful dialogue about religion, sexuality, and gender identity is now in place.

Students join LGBT groups not only with the mission of changing campus policies and climates. Many join for much more personal reasons. As I have argued, a strategy of embracing conversations about religion, sexuality, and gender identity also pays dividends for their members. When students at schools like Belmont University or Catholic University come to feel that their own religious and sexual identities are compatible, they are much more likely to come out to others or start conversations about LGBT issues with their friends and family members. In the next chapter, I will explore more fully both the intended and unintended impacts of LGBT groups on their participants, not only on their participants' relationships with others, but also on their participants' postgraduation political, work, and family plans and trajectories.

CHAPTER FIVE

Becoming an Activist

Participants in LGBT activist groups come from a variety of backgrounds— some from highly politicized households, others from more conservative, religious families, and still others from relatively apolitical upbringings. Nevertheless, nearly all participants in LGBT activist groups share a remarkable willingness to accept risk, to reexamine old values and beliefs, and to face potential backlash from their families, friends, and universities. Given the remarkable journeys many of these participants take over just four years—at a period in their lives when young adults often experience rapid growth (Mannheim [1928] 1952)—it would not be surprising if these LGBT activist groups had a significant impact on participants' lives. But what exactly are these impacts? What precisely explains these impacts, and how might impacts vary across participants?

Dustin, a student at Catholic University, told me that, for as long as he could remember, he identified as a Democrat, albeit one who did not agree with Democrats on some issues like abortion. Although he believed his political values taught him to "treat everyone the same," he admitted to me that, "as a heterosexual male, [he] hadn't really [had] to deal with the experience of coming out and discovering [him]self and all that." Thus, initially he did not give the CUAllies group much thought. Still, after one of his friends recruited Dustin to the group after it had transitioned into its educational form, he was willing to give the group a try.

How did participating in CUAllies impact Dustin? Although he said that "before, I really did want to get involved with the nitty gritty of political issues and political campaigns, the stuff I've done in Allies really drove home that the biggest issues can't be addressed in the current climate of partisan rancor." Specifically, he said that as a result of "trying to get Allies granted recognition, and interacting with people with so many different viewpoints"—people of different religious views, political views, and sexual orientations—he has now arrived at his new calling in life: "I am now looking for a job focused on nonpartisan redistricting." He wants to reform the political system to make respectful dialogue between people of different viewpoints more possible, just like what he experienced in CUAllies.

Related to his desire to make respectful dialogue between people of opposing viewpoints possible, he says he has learned how to talk with his family and friends back home about LGBT issues. "When I was in high school and involved with my church, I got told by the deacon that Obama is a piece of shit, and why the hell am I voting for him, that I should really be careful. . . . And people were telling me that homosexuality is a mental illness, that gay people are not to raise children, and that it's a scientific fact that gay people are bad at raising children. And my gut reaction was to react with anger and disgust in those scenarios, and it didn't get me anywhere—it doesn't make any progress, it doesn't make that person any more likely to be accepting and loving. But through CUAllies I learned how to tailor my arguments to someone who doesn't think they are wrong, who doesn't think they are homophobic, just sort of learning how, for lack of a better phrase, to open these peoples' eyes at least a little bit, in a more respectful manner."

As we see in this account, although Dustin was initially interested in joining issue-based political campaigns following graduation, his experience in CUAllies has made him more interested in reforming existing institutions to promote more respectful dialogue; he has also now learned how to engage in more respectful dialogue with friends and family himself. What is particularly interesting here is how he links the educational ethos of CUAllies to the changes he experienced—because the group was focused on promoting respectful dialogue about LGBT issues, he learned a specific set of skills that he can apply to his expressed work plans and in his interactions with others. Might group ethos provide insights into the reasons why activist groups impact participants, and might variations in group ethos explain variations in these impacts?

In raising such questions about how LGBT activist groups impact their participants, I join scholars who have sought to identify the biographical consequences of activist groups ranging from the 1960s movements to more contemporary movements.[1] Although they often diverge in their methodological approaches, studies on the biographical impacts of activist groups all produce remarkably similar portraits of activists, showing that activist groups make people more willing to continue participating in formal activist organizations, enter into humanistic occupations, and alter their family plans.

My own respondents similarly reported that their participation in activist groups led to changes in their plans to participate or their approaches to participation in social movements (45 percent of respondents), changes in their choices of or approaches to future careers (75 percent of respondents), and changes in their decisions to form families or approaches to relating to families (49 percent of respondents). I also found that respondents commonly reported changes in their relationships with others (91 percent of respondents). However, I generally found that past studies could not help me understand at least two important things about my findings. First, past studies have generally failed to provide robust theories as to why activist groups impact participants. The majority of the studies on biographical impacts of activist groups reference Mannheim's ([1928] 1952) theory of generations to explain the effects of activist groups—namely, that experiences shared by people during young adulthood powerfully shape their political views and behaviors (see critique by Sherkat and Blocker 1997). But as Klatch (1999) points out, although people of the same age may share certain experiences, they often interpret them and act upon them quite differently; thus, we need a more fine-grained theory for why activist groups impact their participants. Second, most studies have focused on demonstrating differences between activists and nonactivists, meaning that these scholars have said little about potential differences in the biographical consequences of activism among activists themselves.[2] Especially because most literature is focused on direct action-oriented movements of the 1960s, it is particularly unclear whether the biographical consequences that scholars have identified apply to activists involved in educational or solidarity groups.

With this chapter, I innovate within the literature on biographical consequences of social movements by examining not only whether LGBT groups impact their participants' political, work, and family lives, but also why LGBT groups have such impacts and whether these impacts vary across activists. As hinted through the story of Dustin, I will show that the concept of group ethos provides a perfect conceptual tool for theorizing the impacts of activist groups on their participants, not only allowing us to understand the diverse mechanisms by which LGBT groups impact their participants, but also allowing us to unpack variation in the biographical consequences of activist groups. Specifically, because direct action groups, educational groups, and solidarity groups provide participants with different sets of *skills*, *values*, and *social ties*, it would make sense that they impact their participants in distinct ways. I will show that, because direct action groups provide participants with concrete extra-institutional organizing skills, a refined philosophy of social change, and ties to other direct action groups, graduates of direct action groups are most likely to pursue subsequent involvement in social movements. Because educational groups often provide participants with skills for working inside institutions, expanded humanistic values, and ties to nonprofit organizations, graduates of educational groups are most likely to enter into humanistic careers. Finally, because solidarity groups provide participants with improved relational skills, clarified personal values, and ties to new role models, graduates of solidarity groups are most likely to reconsider their future family plans.

To be clear, the biographical consequences of LGBT activist groups that I identify in this chapter are immediate or short-term in nature. Given the short time horizon of my interviews—which were conducted in 2011 through 2014, not only with current students but also with alumni who had graduated up to ten years prior—I cannot speak to the enduring consequences of LGBT activist groups over participants' entire life courses.[3] Nevertheless, some of the consequences I identify—such as gaining courage to come out to one's family members and friends—are no less significant in their biographical impacts. In addition, it is important to note that, because I do not have a sample of nonparticipants with which to compare my sample of LGBT activists, and because my interview data are retrospective in nature, I cannot make conclusive causal claims about the impact of LGBT activist groups on participants' life trajectories (as in some quasi-experimental studies such as McAdam [1988]). Nevertheless, wherever possible, I bring in participants' claims regarding their political, work, and family plans prior to joining an LGBT activist group to demonstrate that participants' postgraduation plans were likely not predetermined. I show that my respondents indeed believed their experiences in LGBT activist groups to be transformational.

Social Movement and Political Activism as Biographical Trajectory

Studies consistently find that activist groups inspire future participation in protests and other organized political activities across the life course.[4] As a result of their participation in LGBT activist groups, 49 percent of my respondents did continue to be involved—or express intentions to continue involvement—in social movements and other political organizations, and they reported that their groups shaped their approaches to these future social movement campaigns. Yet, this group fell just short of a majority; why? As I found, respondents who planned to continue their activism through participation in social movements were disproportionately involved in LGBT activist groups exhibiting a direct action ethos (see table 5.1). Direct action groups were most likely to produce this sort of trajectory because these groups provided respondents with concrete organizing skills, transformed respondents' philosophy of social change, and gave participants ties to other activist groups in which they could participate (see table 5.2).

TABLE 5.1 Self-reported biographical impacts, by group ethos

	Biographical impact			
Group ethos	Political impact	Career impact	Family impact	Relational impact
Direct action group	72.41% (21 of 29)	75.86% (22 of 29)	48.28% (14 of 29)	82.76% (24 of 29)
Educational group	22.73% (5 of 22)	86.36% (19 of 22)	50.00% (11 of 22)	95.45% (21 of 22)
Solidarity group	21.43% (3 of 14)	42.86% (6 of 14)	85.71% (12 of 14)	100.00% (14 of 14)

TABLE 5.2 Categories of group ethos and their associated biographical impacts

Group ethos		Mechanisms	Biographical impact
Direct action group that seeks structural or policy changes through more confrontational and extra-institutional forms of collective action	→	Extra-institutional organizing skills, refined philosophy of social change, inter-movement ties	Future social movement or political participation, such as continued involvement in LGBT activist groups or participation in marriage equality ballot campaigns
Educational group that establishes a shared set of values and raises consciousness about those values in a broader community through more conciliatory and institutional means	→	Intra-institutional leadership skills, expanded humanistic values, employer ties	Pursuit of humanistic careers, such as jobs with church reform organizations or careers in LGBT social services
Solidarity group that facilitates personal development and growth by connecting similarly identified students with one another within a safe space	→	Relational skills, clarified personal values, ties to role models	Revised family plans, such as intentions to enter into more equitable martial partnerships or plans to raise tolerant and accepting children

Perhaps no group better embodies the direct action ethos than the CU-Allies group of 2009–11. As profiled in the introduction, students at Catholic University decided to form CUAllies after an incident of vandalism committed against an LGBT student at Catholic and after a heated exchange over LGBT rights in the campus newspaper. Inspired in part by anarchist theory and practice, the students formed an LGBT group that was nonhierarchical in structure, although a core group of students did take on most of the responsibilities. Furthermore, inspired by a more radical queer strand of politics, the students in this iteration of CUAllies deployed direct action tactics to challenge the university's response to violence and discrimination against LGBT students, including demonstrations and banner drops in the student center. Finally, the group held off-campus meetings that were devoted not only to planning the group's actions but also to socializing students into a more radical approach to social change.

Such commitment to direct action on LGBT issues required an enormous amount of dedication by student members. Not only did participation in the group require a willingness to engage in a certain amount of rule breaking—an application for the group's official approval was denied by the administration, and the group was not formally allowed to hold meetings and events on campus—but participation in the group also placed members in the national spotlight—the group was profiled in several national and local newspapers, which in some cases "outed" participants to their families. Given the intensity of the campaign and the lessons the respondents learned through its successes and failures, it is perhaps not surprising that the CUAllies group had a direct impact on the participants' biographical trajectories, beginning first and foremost with the participants' future social movement and political activities.

One example of how CUAllies shaped a participant's postgraduation political trajectory can be seen in the story of Neil, whose story was first shared in the introduction. Neil was one of the students who had pushed for CUAllies' nonhierarchical organizing structure, so that rather than having one student or a group of students dominate the organization, responsibilities for running the group would be shared among all of the members. However, after participating in the group, Neil told me that he learned a new approach to organizing, coming away with a better appreciation for the need to cultivate diverse leadership that could outlive a campaign. Specifically, although he said CUAllies' structure worked well enough, if they had critiqued it to make it more sustainable, the group might have built leadership development into everything they did. As he now argues, "What we should have done is pick five freshmen and say, we're going to do the first five [meetings], and then you five do the next five, and doing it that way, being much more intentional about it. That would have been smart." He continued by saying that this lesson "has influenced the way I organize—I have mentees [whom] I've brought into this work and I very much put out a program for them, and said this is what you have to do. . . . In direct action campaigns, building alternative structures often allows you to win even if your target doesn't concede, because you've developed leaders who can outlive a campaign." Indeed, following graduation, he dropped plans to go to law school and now works full-time at an organization that coordinates direct action campaigns, where he has implemented this revised approach to organizing.

Although Neil's story demonstrates how participation in an LGBT group can transform one's approach to activism, Neil had previously been involved in leftist activism prior to participating in CUAllies, so we cannot be certain that his participation in CUAllies group led to his subsequent participation in other activist groups. The story of another Catholic student named Ashley is more insightful in this regard. As discussed in the introduction, Ashley had come from a very conservative background (she reported that she had been a fundamentalist Christian) with no prior involvement in activism. However, Ashley noted that her participation led her to adopt a new philosophy of social change—one that did not see the world as naturally moving toward justice but as being pushed toward justice by the concerted efforts of humans—which subsequently inspired her involvement in a campaign for marriage equality in her state:

JONATHAN: How would you have described your political leanings going into the group, and did the group have any impact on your political views or political development in any way?

ASHLEY: Yeah. Probably the biggest impact that it had—and not even like a discussion about, oh, I used to be right of center and now I'm left of center, which is true—but I think I had previously just thought the world moved toward justice. Like, the arc of human history bends toward justice, and all of those well-known sayings, and that it just naturally happens. And I think getting involved in a group like this made me realize that the only reason why that stuff happens is because people work to make it happen, you know? We don't just become more accepting of people of other races because we just realize at one point that it's bad—we become accepting because we realize at one point that people stood up and said, you can't treat me like this, I'm a human being, you know? And then they worked, and they worked hard. And I think this realization led me to become involved in working for marriage equality in [blinded state]. There were so many of my friends that were like, oh, no, it'll pass . . . why do you have to work so hard, it's not that big of a deal. It'll pass, everyone's becoming more accepting now. And I'm like, yes, that is true, but they're becoming more accepting because we're picking up phones every single night and calling people, we're going places and talking about these issues. Stuff just doesn't happen—so I think the biggest effect that it had is recognizing that if people want shit to change, they need to go and try to change it, and that's what I've tried to do.

Other students who were involved in this early CUAllies campaign at Catholic similarly reported that their participation in the organization influenced their decision to become involved in future political activity. This includes Julie, who despite having no prior involvement in activist groups before CUAllies, became involved in activism around marriage equality in her state—she not only donated to a marriage equality campaign but also knocked on doors throughout the state. She reported that her participation in CUAllies helped her become comfortable "knocking on a door and not knowing if that person is gay themselves or not knowing if that person is a right-wing pastor, being able to converse with those people in respectful ways . . . and also to get across this idea of human rights and equal rights and what we all want—we all want the same thing, we all want to go home to a loving family, and these type of things—that CUAllies really emphasized, that bottom line that we focused on." As another example, a student named Sonja, who described herself as an "activist without a cause" before joining CUAllies, said her participation in CUAllies "moved [her] to change [her] perception of acceptable risk." Indeed, she subsequently took on the challenge of moving to a developing country and working full-time on efforts to alleviate poverty there, and she says that once she returns to the United States she hopes to focus her studies and activism on intersectional campaigns.

COMBINED, THE STORIES of CUAllies students inform us of two crucial ways by which direct action groups influence future social movement participation: giving students concrete organizing skills—for example, by giving them experience with leadership development or talking about LGBT issues with people who were different from themselves—and by influencing students' approach to social change—whether by convincing them of the need for social movements or by moving their perceptions of acceptable risk. The experience of students at Goshen College highlights a third mechanism by which direct action groups shape future activist group participation—by directly linking them with other activist groups in which they can participate.

The Open Letter movement at Goshen coordinated a campaign to change Goshen's faculty hiring policy. Although the movement began small, with an open letter to the school that students were invited to sign, the campaign quickly grew to involve weekly actions, including sing-ins in the chapel, vigils on the campus lawn, and solidarity protests with Goshen's sister school, Eastern Mennonite University. Unlike some of the other LGBT groups studied here, which took on multiple functions or changed focus over time, the Open Letter movement was completely focused on this protest campaign, given the existence of other LGBT groups that focused on other functions (e.g., Advocates, an educational group, and PRISM, a solidarity group).

Once again, such immersion in a direct action campaign had a profound effect on participants' lives, and many participants in the Open Letter movement reported that their involvement in the campaign directly led to their involvement in future direct action groups. This can perhaps best be seen in the story of Roger, one of the founders of the Open Letter movement. Unlike many of his peers at Goshen, Roger had no history of involvement in social justice groups prior to college; in fact, when I asked him whether he had been involved in LGBT groups growing up, he said, "Definitely not. My high school was pretty conservative, so that would be completely out of the question." Furthermore, unlike some other Goshen students, Roger did not join an array of activist groups once he got to Goshen; rather, he dove headfirst into Goshen's lively music and theater scene. However, near the end of his time at Goshen, he began searching for a student teaching internship outside of Goshen, only to discover that local schools were discriminating against him due to his sexual orientation. He began to feel solidarity with LGBT faculty and staff at Goshen, who had to hide their own sexual orientation or gender identity if they wished to be employed at the school, and he worried that, if he ever wished to return to Goshen as a faculty or staff member himself (something that was very common at this tight-knit school), he might be prohibited from doing so because he was gay.

Roger was actively involved in the Open Letter movement near the end of his time at Goshen, but his work did not cease once he graduated; rather, he stayed close to the Goshen area and worked to expand the campaign through more outreach to Goshen alumni, staff, and faculty. Importantly, he also worked to connect the Open Letter campaign with like-minded organizations within the Mennonite Church, including LGBT groups at other Mennonite schools; the Brethren Mennonite Council, a group that has worked to promote awareness about LGBT people within the church since 1976; and Pink Menno, a direct action group that has organized protest actions at Mennonite Church conventions since 2009. Although he had begun to step back from the Open Letter campaign by the time we talked, Roger told me that he had recently become a leader in the Pink Menno campaign:

JONATHAN: So how have you been involved with the movement since you graduated?

ROGER: Now I'm in kind of a different position, where I'm off campus. It's been about—yeah, building more of an online presence, connecting with alumni, even staff and faculty now, and connecting with the other larger Mennonite groups. . . . EMU Safe Space is a group that's pretty active at their college, and the other Mennonite Colleges there are about five or six that have their own groups, and trying to support them, too, to be more active. And BMC [the Brethren Mennonite Council] . . . [who are] the initial people, the pioneers, in the LGBTQ movement in the church. So yeah, connecting with them as well, and trying to get all these groups on the same page so we can all work toward a common goal. And really, if the church were to pass anything to be more inclusive, then all of these colleges would follow suit.

JONATHAN: Have you become involved in any of these organizations yourself?

ROGER: Yes, especially Pink Menno—I've become a leader there, since connecting with them through the Open Letter movement. So Pink Menno has been vying more for queer people in leadership and in ministry positions in the Mennonite Church, membership isn't officially okay for the denomination, and of course like marriage covenants. And Pink Menno shows up especially at the Conference, for example we have had signs and have had a demonstration at a delegate session of the [Mennonite Church USA] Board. And it's just incredible—the people you meet there are just incredible. They have an incredible amount of energy for this kind of advocacy work, they are very invested in the church, because I mean they wouldn't be doing this unless they wanted to be part of the church. So, yeah, just incredible people and . . . some of my closest friends have come out of this kind of work.

Although so many of the Goshen students I talked to had not yet graduated from the college, nearly every student I interviewed did express interest in becoming involved (or becoming further involved) in Pink Menno's campaign. It is true that, as noted in chapter three, most of the Goshen students in my sample had participated in social movement campaigns prior to coming to Goshen, and thus their intentions to continue participation in social movement campaigns might not be surprising. For example, Kylie, who described her pre-college participation in Pink Menno in chapter two, reported that she planned to become more involved in Pink Menno following graduation. Nevertheless, in addition to Roger, my sample did contain other students who had not previously been involved in any social movement activity and who intended to become involved in LGBT activism following graduation. For example, Tyra, who came from a deeply "red" state where Pink Menno was not active, told me that she hoped to join Pink Menno's campaign after she graduated.

Combined, the stories of Goshen students demonstrate not only that participation in LGBT groups gives many students their first hands-on experiences with organizing but also that participation in groups like the Open Letter movement can directly link students to other LGBT activist groups, providing them with a natural outlet for subsequent social movement activism.

Humanistic Careers as Biographical Trajectory

Studies on biographical consequences of social movements also show that activist groups have a significant impact on participants' careers.[5] Seventy-five percent of participants in LGBT groups at Christian colleges and universities have, indeed, pursued—or expressed plans to pursue—careers that reflect the values of their group, especially humanistic careers that involve the reform of existing institutions. Although this includes the majority of those who participated in direct action groups,[6] the group ethos that seems most tightly linked to the pursuit of humanistic careers is the educational ethos. Educational groups inspired this kind of occupational trajectory by giving participants leadership skills useful for working within institutions, providing students with a set of humanistic values that they would use to guide their selection of careers, and directly linking participants to new employers.

Catholic University's CUAllies shed its direct action ethos and adopted an educational ethos beginning in 2011. Rather than organizing confrontational protests, the group began to focus on events that would educate the Catholic University community about matters of faith and sexuality, including through guest talks by Catholic priests or leaders of Catholic reform organizations. Although such activism required no less dedication on the part of CUAllies' members, such activism placed members in a dramatically different mind-set that eschewed confrontational protest tactics in favor of conciliatory bridge-building tactics (Coley 2014).

After graduation, several dedicated members of the CUAllies group at Catholic entered into careers focused on reforming the Catholic Church through outreach and education on LGBT issues. And in the case of members like Timothy, who was first introduced in chapter two, this kind of career path is dramatically different than the career they had initially planned to pursue upon entering college. Timothy had little exposure to LGBT issues prior to his time in CUAllies and indeed had argued against full equality for LGBT students before college. However, after being recruited to the CUAllies group because of his demonstrated leadership skills on campus, and learning about the many issues LGBT people faced on the campus, Timothy quickly became passionate about the cause of LGBT rights.

Following graduation, Timothy abandoned initial plans to enter seminary and successfully applied for a job at a Catholic LGBT organization. Timothy's time in CUAllies prepared him for this job in at least three ways. First, Timothy gained leadership skills that were ideal for working in this kind of organization. As he explained, in the Catholic world there are several groups that do church reform, and among those groups, his organization specializes in education: "We publish stuff—like, we wrote a book . . . that's like a Q&A of how Catholics support marriage and how to talk about things. We do educational workshops, [and] we help with parish ministry development." Because CUAllies had similarly specialized in educational tasks, Timothy's skill set was easily transferable to this organization. Second, although he previously knew little about LGBT issues, Timothy's time in CUAllies provided him with humanistic values that helped him see the importance of this kind of career, even though many of its day-to-day tasks are monotonous: specifically, he said that CUAllies "open[ed] my eyes and [gave] me personal experience with some of the issues at play. . . . Just to have that as sort of a background has been—it keeps me grounded, right, when I'm in this nonprofit industrial complex, this mentality right, and I'm like what am I doing? Oh, it's because of that student I had a conversation with. So that's helpful." Finally, Timothy's work in CUAllies had put him in direct contact with the leaders of this LGBT organization—the organization's leader was among the first speakers brought in by this new iteration of CU-Allies. Without this contact, Timothy may have not even known about this organization.

Another Catholic student named Jess, also introduced in chapter two, similarly changed her career plans as a result of her time in CUAllies. Unlike Timothy, Jess had long been committed to the cause of LGBT rights—she recalled speaking out in favor of LGBT equality as early as the fifth grade. Furthermore, she initially exhibited a proclivity toward direct action—she reported that she went to "three protests my first weekend here just because I could." However, following several years of participation in CU-Allies, Jess reported that although she was still fully committed to LGBT rights, she no longer participated in protests. Specifically, she is "not the kind of activist who's tying myself to a building"; rather, she told me that "I think I'm always looking for opportunities to engage in conversations . . . and sort of never shying away from, you know, if I hear someone say 'that's so gay' or 'you're a fag,' just sort of saying, do you understand the implications of saying that?" Indeed, she has sought such conversations head-on by pursuing a career with an organization dedicated to outreach to faith communities, and she notes that certain skills she gained (such as the ability to talk to people in authority) and specific faith values she internalized through her time in CUAllies have proven useful in this career:

JONATHAN: Do you think you were personally changed by your participation in the organization—in CUAllies—and if so how?
JESS: Yeah, I think I'd definitely say, having the opportunity to sit down with the president [of the school], I don't think I would have had the guts to do that earlier on, just sort of seeing the shape of the organization and seeing what everyone else put into it—having that confidence, to sit down and have this conversation, and to be this proud representative, I think it definitely shaped me in that way. And I think it's—I have discovered what I want to be active for. It's helped

me find my voice. Like now I have an internship with the [blinded LGBT organization], and I guess in that sense, it's sort of—like, I'm aligning myself with a group that I know will be a voice for change and stuff like that. So I guess I'm finding more constructive ways to be—you know, I'm not going to protests all the time anymore.

JONATHAN: What is that internship in [blinded organization]—what's your involvement with that?

JESS: I'm actually focused on religion and faith, so again it's a lot of this intersection and stuff with faith traditions and sexual and gender identity. And so what the program—what the actual religion and faith program does is that they reach out to different faith communities and faith leaders and engaging in those dialogues. And they publish resources in how to implement acceptance in your own faith community. And they have, you know, different programs— like, one I really love focuses on Latino Catholicism and how to like cope with sort of sexual orientation in that sort of household or cultural identity. . . . So a lot of it is about open dialogue and really creating these resources to implement acceptance.

JONATHAN: Do you see [any other] link between your involvement in CUAllies and that internship? And is this something you would like to pursue as a career?

JESS: Oh, absolutely. I think—I think especially, just sort of preparing myself with the rhetoric and understanding of what LGBT acceptance in a faith tradition means—definitely has equipped me to want to be in that department. And I think I would absolutely love to have the opportunity to work for, you know, [blinded LGBT organization] or something like that. I think that would be beneficial, especially as I'm finding my own sexual identity; I'm sort of recognizing the implications of this on my future and that I sort of need to work for this change if I actually want to be able to live in an environment where I'm not judged differently and stuff. So I think definitely after graduation, I would like to sort of work for a nonprofit organization; it's just kind of a matter of where I can kind of do my part. So I think that's absolutely on the agenda.

The remaining CUAllies respondents similarly entered into careers in which they could apply skills and values that they learned in the group. This includes Eric, a conservative participant with strong religious convictions. Although he reported that his decision to enroll in medical school was primarily a response to "this Christian call to care for people who are sick and ill," he believes he can effect change in what he calls a "very conservative field" by being open about his sexual orientation and joining a new LGBT health issues organization.

Combined, the stories of these Catholic University students demonstrate that participation in LGBT groups with an educational ethos can provide students with a specific skill set for reforming institutions—for example, Jess's ability to sit down and discuss LGBT issues with faith-minded people; a greater immersion in values of diversity and inclusion, which could keep students like Timothy grounded in nonprofit work; and connections to organizations where students could later find employment, which directly led Timothy to his new career.

BRIDGE BUILDERS AT BELMONT similarly adopted an educational ethos around 2011, focusing on facilitating group discussions and holding community events about issues facing the LGBT community. Given their involvement in these types of educational and outreach events, participants were able to envision future careers involving outreach to LGBT communities.

The effect of Bridge Builders on its participants' postmovement career trajectories can be best illustrated through the story of Sarah, first introduced in chapter two. Sarah reported that she always had a passion for social justice, and indeed as soon as she stepped foot on campus during her first year, she joined a campus organization devoted to international human rights. Accordingly, she initially envisioned working for a human rights organization like Amnesty International following graduation. Nevertheless, her involvement in the human rights group was generally restricted to behind-the-scenes work, such as writing letters to legislators, because she reported that she was "very, very shy," an attribute that actually led her to become involved in Bridge Builders:

> JONATHAN: So when you first joined Bridge Builders, what did you
> personally think would come about as a result of your participation?
> SARAH: Um, well, for me I just wanted, I guess, at that time I was very,
> very shy. Like I was pathologically shy almost. Like I couldn't—
> talking to someone, it was very bad. So I just kind of wanted to be
> in a space where I felt safe and—well actually more than that,
> because I wasn't talking, I wanted other people to have a space to be
> themselves. And that's what I wanted to come out of it more than
> anything. I just kind of wanted to see other people be themselves.

Despite her initial shyness, she reported, "Bridge Builders helped me throughout that, to become a more open person. . . . I was just able to talk more. I was like an instant extrovert." When asked what about Bridge Builders made her less shy, she said that being asked to lead some of the group discussions on topics such as mental health helped her break out of her "shell." This personal transformation helped her envision a shift in careers to social work, a career that would require intense interpersonal skills and also allow her to work with LGBT youths:

JONATHAN: Before you joined the organization, what had your postgraduation plans been? Are they still the same, or if not, what are they now?

SARAH: Oh no, they're different. Before joining, I wanted to—well, before college, I wanted to definitely work with Amnesty International. Like, that was hands-down what I wanted to do with my life; there was no other option for me. I wanted to either work for Amnesty or—work with an organization like it. When I became a part of Bridge Builders, that's when I started thinking, I think I could see myself working with the LGBT community, that's awesome, I love what I'm doing. I could be like a child advocate, like, teens in juvy. Our criminal justice system, social services, they aren't always set up to work with LGBT youth. And that's why I began taking sociology classes, because I was interested in social work. And . . . in the future I would love to work with LGBT youth.

JONATHAN: And would you say that's influenced by your participation in Bridge Builders?

SARAH: Oh, definitely. I mean, I wouldn't have even thought of that before. Yeah. And I wouldn't have wanted to do something that required me to work that closely with people.

Other students at Belmont reported similar shifts in career plans after participating in Bridge Builders. Ruth, who was initially interested in pursuing a career in journalism, has since joined a social services organization catering to low-income youths (including LGBT youths), and she reported that she chose this career path because "Bridge Builders definitely gave me a love and a passion for helping people and serving." In addition, a student named Michelle said that, despite her initial plans to "play and write music and tour and record" following graduation, and despite initially joining the group just to "meet other gay people," she is now interested in working full-time at an LGBT community organization following graduation. She went on to say she changed her career plans after she witnessed so many other "graduates of Bridge Builders who participate in the community now, doing outreach to the LGBT community, and at least one of them as his job." Bridge Builders participants thus picked up specific skills (e.g., the ability to speak up and work with other people) and values (e.g., a love and passion for helping people), along with connections to people working in LGBT community groups, that will quite possibly ease their entrance into humanistic careers.

Intentional Relationships as Biographical Trajectory

Finally, scholars examining the biographical consequences of activism have shown that activist groups shape participants' subsequent relationships and family lives.[7] I identified at least two of these kinds of personal impacts. First, nearly all respondents reported some type of changes in their relationships with other family members and friends. This is perhaps not surprising, given that the very act of participating in an LGBT group is something that could alter their relationships with others (such as if they subsequently came out to—or were outed to—family members). Second, 49 percent of respondents reported that their participation in LGBT groups changed the way they related to their partners and envisioned raising their future children. LGBT groups with a solidarity ethos were most likely to produce this kind of change, given that they imparted participants with improved relational skills, clarified personal values, and new ties to potential role models. I discuss such relational and family changes below, with a focus on the Loyola Advocate group after 2010.

Of all of the LGBT groups studied here, the Loyola Advocate group after 2010 perhaps best exemplifies an LGBT group with a solidarity ethos. As discussed in chapter three, the group has now mostly moved away from direct action campaigns and other organized political activity. Instead, the group offers weekly social events, from ice cream socials to trivia games to dodgeball nights. The organization also sponsors Spectrum, which provides a safe space for students who are early on in their coming out process or who are otherwise facing stressors related to their sexual orientation or gender identity.

Given this focus on social events, most participants certainly expected to have fun and develop friendships with LGBT-identified students, but rarely did they anticipate the other changes that would follow. For example, Damon, introduced in chapter three, reported that he first joined Advocate "because [he] thought the social aspect of it was really important." He had never been involved in any LGBT group or other social justice group before and certainly had no prior reason to think of himself as an activist. In fact, he reported that he "never thought that [his] opinions" were "valid" before.

However, after years of participating in Advocate, Damon told me he had gained confidence in talking to his family and friends back home about LGBT issues. Specifically, he had both gained practice talking about LGBT issues in the group and come to a better understanding of his own values. Not only does he now consider himself to be an activist, but his friends and family also call him an activist. His story is worth quoting in full:

JONATHAN: Coming into the organization, would you say that you would have identified as an activist, or was that not really a term you would have thought of yourself as or applied to yourself?

DAMON: Yeah, I didn't consider myself an activist at all.

JONATHAN: Do you now?

DAMON: I do now, and it's funny, when I go back home, and all of our friends go back home for Christmas or whatever, my friends always make the comment of, oh, [Damon], you're an activist now, you're so—because I come back home with my "Loyola Supports Love" t-shirt or I have my pride wristbands, and they're like, this is who you are now, you're an activist. And yeah, I had never thought of myself as one before this, just because I've never—I guess I never thought that my opinions were, like, valid, you know? I never valued my opinions, I guess. I'm very nonconfrontational, so I'm just like, yeah, I'll agree with you, that's fine. But definitely coming to Loyola and becoming involved in Advocate, it helped me develop a sense of what is—not necessarily what is right and wrong, but what I feel should be right and what I feel should be wrong. And especially being in Loyola and in a Jesuit institution, since they do value social justice so much, I feel like—yeah, I would call myself an activist. Yeah. I'd never thought of myself as one until Advocate, definitely.

JONATHAN: Is that just—are you an activist . . . when talking to friends or family about LGBT issues, or are you involved at all in protests?

DAMON: I would say it's shaped more of my daily life. I feel like I make active choices now where my choices reflect the morals and standards that I've set up for myself because of how much I know now. And definitely it helps me kind of—it helps me direct certain kind of conversations I have with friends and family now, especially with my family too. I feel like they've just noticed it. You know, my family doesn't talk to each other about feelings or whatever. They're very much a family of, like, they can take cues from you. But I feel like now that they know I'm a member of Advocate, they've kind of softened up what they talk about, or they're very careful about what they say; they try to make sure they carefully word things. They've been very gender neutral, which is nice; they're just very vague. So yeah, I would say that. And especially with friends too, the roommates I have now are in the same way. We could be like watching episodes of *Medium* or whatever but in the middle have a long, deep conversation about queer theory or whatever, something like that. So it's kind of helped how I relate with others, and kind of helped me see what I value in other people, too.

Another Loyola student named Franklin, who participated in Advocate at the time it was transitioning into a solidarity group, told me that he gained a greater appreciation for diversity and inclusion through the group that he has related to friends and even romantic partners:

JONATHAN: Have any of your friends or family members changed their views on LGBT issues since you got involved in Advocate? For example, did [your participation] spur on conversations with friends or family members? Does anything like that come to mind?

FRANKLIN: I mean one thing that I—I think another thing that is, that we haven't talked a lot about—it's something that was very true about my involvement—is that one of the difficulties about having a bunch of young people and organizing around sexuality and gender is that there are romantic relationships involved, obviously. And it's just a normal part of the process. So when I was involved, one of my ex-boyfriends—he later became president of the group—[blinded leader] and I dated, and on our first date we had a conversation about trans issues, something I learned a lot about in the group. And I remember him saying something along the lines of—just not being very accepting and not feeling comfortable with that identity. And he will never admit that conversation to people, but now that he became president, he is so incredibly progressive on everything when it comes to LGBT issues, so I think—I'm not going to take 100 percent credit for that transformation, but I think that's just one example of someone who went from a bigoted view to being a huge ally and advocate for a specific subpopulation of the community.

I think that . . . a lot of the people I've dated, if they're not willing to have an openness to new issues, those relationships haven't lasted long. So I think that's one thing I've seen in my personal life and partnerships in general—I want to be around people who want to learn with me, and I think the learning and change of attitudes happens.

Franklin concluded his response by saying that the things he has learned in Advocate have influenced the kind of partner he is looking for, which leads to a second kind of impact that solidarity groups in particular have on their participants—LGBT groups can help students plan out or envision their own future family lives. For example, Damon from Loyola went on to say that he is now also able to envision himself having a husband and raising a family. As he puts it, despite initially feeling that he "wasn't allowed to have" certain things such as a family or a marriage, he now feels that he is not only "allowed to have those feelings" and "allowed to have those plans," but that he indeed "deserve[s] to have those" feelings and plans:

> JONATHAN: You talked about the impact of the group on your friends and family members. Has your participation in Advocate, if not shaped or changed your family plans, like a decision to get married or have children in the future, has it shaped the way you might raise children or relate to a partner? Or would you say that it has not really had that kind of effect?
>
> DAMON: Yes, I think it has, definitely. I think—the biggest thing that's affected that is that I feel like I'm allowed to have those feelings now—I feel like I'm now allowed to have those plans. That it's valid for me to want a family and want things I always thought I wasn't allowed to have, whether that's have a family, be married, stuff like that. . . . And like, specifically with raising children, now I feel like I can have children or that I'm allowed to—that I can do that—to be able to raise children. And I can help them see that things in the world of being gay are valid, and like, tell a child and teach a child that it doesn't matter, if your parents are gay, it doesn't have to be—you're a child of gay parents! It's, you're a child of parents, it doesn't have to be so specific sometimes. And it's opened up to me that possibility, that I deserve to have those things, that's one of the biggest things that I'm going to take away from Advocate.

Finally, another Loyola student named Samantha reports that she is now able to envision marrying someone of the same sex and raising children of her own one day. Samantha was raised in a somewhat traditional, religious household, one that long expected her to marry someone of the opposite sex and have children of her own one day. Samantha was initially afraid that she would let her family down because of her desire to have a partner of the same sex. However, given the presence of LGBT role models within the group, Samantha reports that her participation in Advocate has now given her an "understanding [of] how a same-sex partnership works," and indeed a partnership in which she might raise children of her own:

JONATHAN: Has your participation in Advocate directly shaped or changed your future family plans, like a decision to have children or whether to marry? Or if it hasn't directly impacted plans in that way, has it shaped the way you might raise children or relate to a partner or anything like that?

SAMANTHA: Yeah, yeah. Meeting people in Advocate who are partnered has sort of helped me understand sort of the dynamics of a same-sex partnership. That hasn't been an experience I've had in college, but yeah, understanding how a same-sex partnership works. In terms of children—my family wants me to have children, because it's like, oh, we want grandchildren. And it's like, okay, we'll figure that out somehow. I can now envision raising children of my own, and raising my kids with an understanding that there are different people in the world and that's okay. You know, if I had a daughter who—it's not expected you'll be a housewife or necessarily submissive in any way to your husband and wife in terms of explorations of gender. My son probably wouldn't wear blue all the time or my daughter wouldn't wear pink all the time. Son, you can grow to a ballerina, and my daughter, you can grow up to be an engineer. Both of those things are fine. Or son you can grow up to be a fire fighter and daughter you can grow up to be a ballerina, that's fine too. Yeah, so I think my understanding of same-sex partnerships has matured, and in terms of raising children, just in terms of, there are different people in the world, and it's okay to expose young children to the fact that there are different people in the world. The argument that, oh, what am I going to tell my kids if two men can get married? It's like, that two men can get married! The problem is not that you have to explain it to your kids, it's that you don't want to explain it to your kids. Kids can handle it. It's like, oh, so-and-so doesn't go to church on Sunday, they go to a mosque. And they're like, okay, that's fine. So-and-so doesn't eat pork because their religion is different. That's fine. So-and-so has two moms—like I have a mom and a dad or whatever.

Other students in Loyola's Advocate group similarly reported that their participation in the group spurred on changes in their personal life. Beyond inspiring conversations with friends and family or altering their future family plans, these changes include developing a better sense of their own sexual or gender identity, something that will certainly influence their future relationships. Since arriving at Loyola and becoming involved in multiple LGBT groups, a student named Jordan reported becoming more comfortable breaking rigid gender norms (e.g., norms about gender-appropriate clothing) and has since adopted a "gender fluid" identity. Lily, who is bisexual, reported that her involvement in the group has "opened [her] up to the idea of being in a relationship with a woman." And Elizabeth notes that the group exposed her to diversity in the LGBT spectrum, and she has moved from a bisexual identity to a pansexual identity.

Respondents' demonstrated ability to talk about LGBT issues with their friends and families seems to stem from the practice they gained every week in discussing LGBT issues with their peers, as in the case of Damon and Franklin, who communicate their values about LGBT inclusion to friends, family members, and potential partners. Furthermore, their plans to marry a same-sex partner and potentially raise children of their own seem to arise from the values they gained through their organization, such as Damon's sense that his desire for a family is valid. Participation in LGBT groups like the Advocate organization at Loyola even put respondents in direct contact with same-sex couples, which allowed students like Samantha to observe the dynamics of a same-sex partnership.

Conclusion

In this chapter I have sought to show that LGBT activist groups profoundly affect their participants' political, work, and family lives. The body of literature on biographical consequences of social movements has long shown that activist groups produce activists who become more active citizens, enter into more humanistic careers, and alter their family plans. Nevertheless, studies mostly focused on differences between activists and nonactivists and also ignored high-risk activism that eschewed direct action; thus, scholars assumed that certain outcomes of activist group participation (such as subsequent involvement in political campaigns) were shared by all participants. Here, I have used the concept of group ethos to show that different types of LGBT groups produce different kinds of activists. Although most participants in LGBT direct action groups do pursue future involvement in social movements, participants in other types of LGBT groups seldom report this impact. Rather, graduates of educational groups (along with veterans of direct action groups) go on to pursue humanistic careers, and graduates of solidarity groups (much more so than veterans of other types of groups) experience changes in their family plans. Finally, graduates of all of the LGBT groups studied here commonly undergo transformations in their relationships with family and friends.

Attention to group ethos not only provides insights into a potential source of variation in the biographical impacts of activist groups but also the mechanisms by which activist groups impact their participants. Graduates of direct action groups are especially likely to report plans to participate in subsequent social movements or organized political campaigns because they are especially equipped with the organizing skills that facilitate such participation; socialized into a praxis that inspires their future participation; and provided with direct connections to other social movements in which they could subsequently be involved. Veterans of educational groups are the most likely to enter into humanistic careers because they have gained skills more useful for working within (rather than outside of) institutions; internalized values that they could use in selecting such careers; and been put in contact with appropriate employers over the course of their participation in such groups. Finally, graduates of solidarity groups most commonly report changes in family plans because solidarity groups provide safe, confidential spaces through which participants can improve in their relational skills; clarify their own personal goals and values; and form ties with others that provide support.

Although the chapter demonstrates affirmatively that participants in LGBT groups at Christian colleges and universities become change agents in a variety of social spheres, readers may still wonder the extent to which these participants see themselves as activists. Indeed, past research on LGBT groups specifically has produced somewhat mixed findings on this question.[8] Importantly, however, I found that participation in LGBT groups did lead to a greater willingness to identify as an activist. Specifically, I found that, prior to their participation in an LGBT group, 43 percent of students self-identified as activists.[9] However, following their participation in LGBT groups, 78 percent of student self-identified as activists.[10]

The findings thus speak to the potential for LGBT groups to mobilize and empower a broad cross-section of LGBT and allied students at religious colleges and universities. Many of the respondents in this study had at one time held views quite contrary to the missions and purposes of the LGBT groups they joined; others reported that they had faced bullying, harassment, and physical violence in their schools, leading them to be silent or soft-spoken about their views. Although not all of the respondents in this study intend to pursue future involvement in social movements, most respondents did say they now considered themselves to be activists or advocates. Nearly all participants expressed more confidence in talking with their friends and family about LGBT issues and in standing up for their beliefs at work. Many respondents will indeed desist from future, organized political activity, but if their plans come to fruition, they will all be change agents by living out fuller, more purposeful lives.

Conclusion

Growing up, Damon did not consider himself to be an activist. Having been raised in a traditional Catholic household, and having attended a Catholic high school, Damon had never been involved in an LGBT group, and he had certainly never participated in any protests. He attended Loyola University Chicago in part because of the allure of a big city and in part because of the school's Catholic identity, but he never stepped foot on the campus before he moved there, and he knew very little about the campus climate for LGBT students.

Once he arrived at Loyola, Damon immediately became involved in the school's theater department and began pursuing his lifelong dream of being an actor. But when he attended Loyola's student clubs fair, he saw the booth for Advocate, the campus LGBT group, and decided to become involved in that group as well—mostly because he was excited to have the opportunity to make gay friends. As it turns out, alongside theater, Advocate would become one of his biggest commitments and passions at Loyola; he participated in the group starting at the beginning of his freshman year and all the way through the end of his senior year.

In chapter five, I began to discuss Damon's slow transformation into an activist. It began with a gradual immersion into queer theory and philosophy that he was exposed to in the Advocate group. He could be doing something as arbitrary as watching a TV show when, in the middle, he would suddenly engage in "a long, deep conversation about queer theory" with friends. He also found himself speaking out more in his classes when issues related to sexuality or gender identity were brought up. In turn, his family, friends, and classmates began to tease him: "oh, [Damon], you're an activist now." His slow realization that he was an activist took even Damon by surprise—he had "never thought that [his] opinions were . . . valid," before, but he had now developed a strong sense of "right" and "wrong."

Damon's emerging activist commitments led him to question many of his prior beliefs and commitments. For example, although Damon grew up Catholic, he made the decision to begin attending an LGBT-friendly Protestant church with his boyfriend. He says it felt much different attending a church that on paper had many of the same rituals and beliefs as a Catholic church but that openly accepted members of the LGBT community. Damon feels that he has grown both in his faith and in his relationship as a result.

His newfound activist identity also influenced his work life. Advocate sometimes partnered with other groups to hold events such as Queer Shakespeare, where a Loyola professor talked about queer themes in Shakespeare, and Damon became more curious about how his queer politics might influence his professional life. As he told me, "As time went on, my involvement became more and more about . . . finding a way to be an activist in my life as a theater-artist and performer, figuring out how I can meet those two worlds."

For example, at Loyola itself, the theater department put on a production of Shakespeare's *Twelfth Night*. Although the play is not about LGBT issues specifically, he viewed the characters in the play as being "very ambiguous" in that they "embraced queer-ness and did not exist in specific binaries." He and the production team made a point to draw out some of these queer themes. One summer during college, he also decided to intern for a queer theater company, where he was excited by the opportunity to act in plays that were specifically focused on LGBT issues. As Damon told me, he has been able to "take what I've become really passionate about and what I've learned more and more about in Advocate, and put that into practice. . . . I feel like I now look for projects that have a strong sense of meaning, or that say something about society or about LGBT issues, and I directly relate that to my activism in Advocate."

Finally, going forward, Damon expressed to me a strong desire to become involved in other LGBT groups, likely groups that focus on providing cultural opportunities or safe spaces for LGBT people. Although not involved in direct action campaigns—traditional social movement activity— he views these kinds of LGBT groups as important agents of social change.

Damon is an excellent example of the potential for LGBT groups to produce activists, those who consciously seek to foster changes in policies on LGBT rights or attitudes and behaviors toward LGBT people. Such participants are indeed succeeding in transforming not only the policies of their institutions but also the hearts and minds of fellow students, churchgoers, coworkers, policymakers, family members, and friends. And although my data are limited in temporal scope, if past movements are any indication, the graduates of these LGBT groups may very well be agents of change in their communities for decades to come.

Key Findings

In this book, I have sought to support the idea that there is more than one way that a person can be an activist. Although LGBT groups are filled with participants like Damon, who have little background in activist groups, the very word "activist" often conjures to mind those whom I have called politicized participants—people who have been socialized into political ideologies and who have participated in activist groups from an early age. Such people are generally embedded in personal and organizational networks that support their activist endeavors.

It is indeed true that many LGBT groups are filled with such politicized participants, even if many of them fall short of the ideal type as portrayed in previous studies. Nevertheless, the assumption that LGBT groups mostly consist of politicized participants rests on an additional faulty assumption about the nature of activist groups. Specifically, many people assume that activist groups take the form of direct action groups, or organizations that deploy extra-institutional protest tactics in support of their goals. Although these kinds of activists and LGBT activist groups are present at Christian universities, they do not exhaust the meaning of activism.

As I have argued here, it is important to consider the possibility of other kinds of activists—those who participate in activist groups because of specific other-oriented values (such as the religious participants studied here) and those who participate because they stand to directly benefit from an activist group's efforts (such as the LGBT participants studied here). Religious participants, as I have shown, had not been socialized into leftist ideologies that are often presumed to precede activism. These religious participants had also not been involved in activist groups prior to coming to their university. Rather, many actively opposed LGBT rights before coming to college, or at least attempted to hide their own sexual orientation or gender identity.

Those participants in LGBT groups whose sexual or gender identities were particularly salient had also not been extensively socialized into political ideologies that might facilitate early involvement in activist groups. Rather, many of these students reported experiences with bullying or harassment that made them think twice about speaking up in favor of LGBT rights in their classrooms or at their dinner tables.

Despite these sometimes complicated biographies, people with salient religious identities, and people who identify as LGBT but lack firm religious and political convictions could also be found in LGBT groups at their

Christian universities. Many of those religious participants who were thoughtful about identifying some set of beliefs and values that might guide their lives were attracted to activist groups that I have referred to as educational groups, groups that similarly try to hammer out a collective set of values and share them with their wider communities. These educational groups often hosted weekly group discussions about matters of faith and sexuality and hosted university-wide events that they hoped would facilitate change in campus climates.

LGBT participants, more than any other type of participant, were open to involvement in a range of LGBT groups, but they felt most at home in what I have called solidarity groups, activist groups that facilitate connections between students who share a sexual or gender identity and that provide a safe space for students to discuss issues related to their own identities.

If one doubts the possibility for these types of groups to facilitate social change on their campuses and beyond, one should look no farther than the stories of students like Damon. We have long known that the organizations that I have called direct action groups have lasting consequences on participants' lives, with participants pursuing involvement in other direct action groups and making work and family choices that are unlike those of the general population. However, because the group in which Damon participated was not engaged in direct action, he has not expressed an interest in joining direct action groups in the future.

Still, Damon's is a life transformed in so many ways. As discussed above, Damon plans to pursue his career in such a way that facilitates cultural change—by raising awareness and changing beliefs and attitudes about LGBT issues through theater. Furthermore, Damon is making choices in his personal life that are fostering social change as well—broaching difficult conversations about LGBT issues with his friends and family and classmates, being honest about his sexuality in church, and otherwise being open about his sexual identity in day-to-day life. Scholars may sometimes overlook this kind of "everyday activism" (Mansbridge 2013), but the point is not missed on Damon's friends and family, who now recognize Damon to be a change agent in the area of LGBT rights.

Theoretical Implications

The book's findings speak most closely to theories of activist group participation. In terms of literature on micromobilization, chapter two joins a few other recent studies that show that multiple paths to activism exist (e.g., Bosi 2012; Bosi and Della Porta 2012; Isaac et al. 2016; Linden and Klandermans 2007; Viterna 2006). Previous scholarship had often assumed that participants could be distinguished from nonparticipants on the basis of a single set of characteristics, and when this assumption was combined with a focus on a single type of movement (such as direct action movements that target the state), they produced overly narrow explanations of why and how people join activist groups. However, by focusing on differences among activists, this book reveals substantial variation in paths to participation, and innovating within the micromobilization literature, the book links these divergent pathways to variations in participants' most salient identities.

How might this book's insights on micromobilization inform future theories and scholarship on activist group participation? Although the specific identities I focus on here—politicized identities, religious identities, and LGBT identities—are particularly useful for understanding participation in LGBT activist groups at Christian colleges and universities, these specific identities exemplify broader categories of identity—activist identities, value identities, and solidary identities—that might well prove generalizable to other kinds of activist groups. For example, to take a favorite example of the micromobilization literature, one might consider participants in activist groups addressing racial inequality, such as the Southern civil rights movement. The civil rights movement certainly drew battle-hardened activists, but it also drew those who held salient value identities (Christian identities) that aligned with the religious tone of part of that movement, and it also drew many African Americans who participated because they stood to benefit from the movement given their solidary (racial) identity (see Fendrich 1993).

In addressing issues of activist commitment, chapter three takes up a question that has seldom been addressed by the social movement literature, again because past literature mostly focuses on differences between participants and nonparticipants and ignores variations among participants themselves. Those few past studies that have addressed the question of activist commitment fall short in various ways; for example, studies that focus on participants' rational choice calculations do not take into account how emerging group dynamics may alter participants' willingness to participate and perhaps paint a picture of a rational activist that participants do not themselves hold. Contributing to theories of commitment, chapter three argues that commitment to activist groups is contingent on the correspondence (or "fit") between a group's dominant ethos and a participant's salient identity. Students not possessing a corresponding identity often drop out or take a backseat, although participants do possess agency to transform the nature of LGBT organizations, either through takeovers or gradual cohort replacements.

The field of activist organizations I have mapped out in this book—direct action, educational, and solidarity groups—may similarly prove generalizable to other movement fields. For example, again taking up the example of race relations, one might imagine a field of organizations including direct action groups (e.g., civil rights movement groups), educational groups (e.g., racial reconciliation groups), and solidarity groups (e.g., black student associations). Those people who would be most expected to commit to these groups would be those holding salient identities as civil rights activists, persons of faith, and African Americans, respectively. Beyond analyzing the link between identity, ethos, and commitment, future research might also systematically compare these types of organizations to identify potential differences in the issues they mobilize around (Coley 2013; Fetner 2008), their strategies and tactics, and so on.

The book's finding that graduates of LGBT activist groups sometimes enter into humanistic careers or more intentional relationships rather than other activist organizations challenges past literature that has implied that all participants of activist organizations will experience a greater likelihood of future social movement involvement. The finding about the effects of activist group involvement on career and relationship choices also adds to the growing research on the consequences of Gay–Straight Alliances, which heretofore has mostly focused on the effect of LGBT student groups on mental health outcomes, student safety, and academic achievement.

These findings should encourage future research on the divergent biographical consequences of activist groups. To take up the example of race relations a final time, those who study the biographical consequences of civil rights movements will likely find that participants continue to participate in social movement groups throughout their lives; but they might also find that participants in racial reconciliation organizations gain skills in conflict management that they can apply in corporations (e.g., by facilitating diversity training) or that graduates of black student associations gain an increased confidence in their own identity and views that lead them to speak up when they experience microaggressions in their everyday lives.

Finally, in engaging with theories on activist group participation, this book also makes the case that scholars should broaden their conception of what it means to engage in activism itself (for another perspective, see

Brown 2016). In sociology, literature on activist groups is concentrated within the subfield of social movement studies; yet, most social movement scholars agree that a defining characteristic of social movements is their reliance on extra-institutional protest tactics (Snow et al. 2004), and the field has long privileged social movements pursuing policy and other political changes (see critiques by Armstrong and Bernstein 2008; Yukich 2013). As I have argued, activist groups defined broadly deploy a range of tactics—from the more contentious protest tactics to the more conciliatory consciousness-raising or solidarity-building tactics—in pursuit of multiple kinds of changes, with some groups seeking changes in policy, other groups fostering changes in campus climate, and still other groups facilitating personal development. Regardless, participants in all of these activist groups are taking on real risk, banding with others in pursuit of their goals, and seeking to facilitate changes at their institutions. They are all in some sense activists.

Broader Implications

On a Thursday afternoon in the middle of exam season, I met a Belmont student named Byron. My interviews with participants of LGBT groups at Christian colleges and universities had thus far exposed me to a wide range of students—from straight allies to LGBT students, from group leaders to dropouts, from alumni to current students. But most of these participants had at least a few semesters of college experience under their belts and had usually participated in an LGBT group at their school for over a year. So I was particularly interested in meeting with Byron, who had only participated in the Bridge Builders group for a few weeks and who was wrapping up his first semester as a college freshman.

As it turned out, Byron was not only new to his Bridge Builders group but also a newly out member of the LGBT community; he had come out as bisexual via a Facebook post to all of his friends only a few days before our meeting. He was soft-spoken, and at times my tape recorder had difficulty picking his voice up. As he told me, he was similarly shy in other social settings, including at his family dinner table, where he found himself sitting out political debates between his family members. "I just kind of avoid everything political," he told me. "Because everything just gets—it always starts arguments or fights. Like my family is very loudmouth, and I just try to, like, stay out of it."

In most of my interviews, I concluded with a series of questions about how participation in the LGBT group at their school has impacted my respondents' lives. In Byron's case, he could not yet report much of an impact; in fact, one of the biggest biographical consequences of Bridge Builders on Byron's life to date was his willingness to participate in my interview—something he said he would not have done even a few weeks earlier. I thanked him for having the courage to speak with me, and I told him I would love to follow up with him further into his college career.

Given his seemingly shy nature—and his tendency to avoid arguments and fights—it was to my surprise when, two years later, Byron's name came up in news stories about a new, unofficial activist group at Belmont that was initially named Bridge Burners but was later renamed the Queer Straight Student Organization (pronounced "Queso" for short). After participating in LGBT events at Vanderbilt University, which is located nearby Belmont University, Byron decided he wanted to help break off the ties (bridges) that LGBT students had made with the school's University Ministries and to become a more secular LGBT group. Byron said that some students felt uncomfortable talking about issues such as sex in a religious setting.

Because Byron told me that he was not religious, it is perhaps not surprising that he did not feel he fit in with Bridge Builders' more religious, educational nature, where meetings could sometimes feel like queer Sunday school. What is perhaps more surprising is that, given his starting point as a soft-spoken, newly out member of the LGBT community, Byron was able to so quickly find his voice and become a (potential) force for social change on campus.

Byron's story hints at broader implications for this book. Beyond contributing to sociological theories on activist group participation, the book speaks to the potential for LGBT groups to create change agents—to empower often vulnerable, marginalized student populations and to foster feelings of resiliency and agency. For example, the book shows that LGBT groups often draw students who were raised in conservative environments, who hold religious beliefs that may seem counter to LGBT activism, and who have often faced bullying, discrimination, and harassment in their educational environments. Because LGBT young adults raised in conservative religious environments often face rejection from family members and peers and experience higher suicide rates than their straight counterparts, LGBT groups that effectively bring in these students may have important roles to play in creating healthier, safer student bodies. The results point to several outlets for recruiting such students: not only from the ranks of other activist groups, but also from the population of religious students who are open to dialogue on LGBT issues and from the population of LGBT students with no firm ideologies.

The book further shows that not all students who initially join or participate in an LGBT group will ultimately commit to that group—rather, they must feel that they belong, that their own identity resonates with the ethos of the group. As Byron's story illustrates, students may not settle for organizations that do not align with their own identity. The results thus suggest potential design implications for LGBT groups seeking to retain the students who join them. Specifically, to draw in the highest number of committed participants, LGBT groups might consider how best to cater to the sometimes disparate interests of the students (e.g., politicized participants, religious participants, and LGBT participants) who join them. This might mean that activists should form separate organizations (e.g., distinct direct action organizations, educational organizations, and solidarity organizations) to cater to these different interests, although future evaluative research might consider whether the competition between those organizations has a deleterious effect on overall participation and commitment levels. Alternatively, an organization might consider providing subgroups or at least distinct activities catering to the different interests represented within the organization, although future evaluative research might also consider whether this boundary spanning might muddy an overall organizational identity and thus also weaken overall participation and commitment levels.

The book also powerfully attests to the ability of LGBT organizations to change their campuses and transform participants into change agents. Although students often self-select into LGBT groups that align with their identities, they can still grow after participating in such groups—these activist groups help them refine their own approaches to social change, gain concrete organizing and leadership skills, forge new social and organizational connections, and come to terms with their own identities as activists. Practically, the results suggest specific activities that LGBT groups should focus on, depending on their goals for participants' lives: if LGBT groups seek to produce future political activists, they should directly expose participants to political philosophies, task participants with organizing direct action campaigns, and connect participants with other social justice organizations. If LGBT groups seek to influence participants' future careers, they might encourage students to gain skills organizing activities inside (rather than outside of) their educational institutions, and they might host career workshops that link participants with potential employers. Finally, if LGBT groups seek to influence participants' future family lives and personal relationships, they should cultivate safe spaces that allow students to reflect on their own issues with families and relationships and allow students to form social connections presaged on values of tolerance, acceptance, and openness.

Finally, the findings of the book certainly suggest that LGBT organizations can play a major role in transforming not only the lives of participants like Byron but also their campus communities. LGBT student groups can indeed succeed in transforming official nondiscrimination policies; for example, Bridge Builders organized sit-ins, rallies, prayer walks, and other activities to successfully pressure Belmont University to adopt a nondiscrimination policy inclusive of sexual orientation; furthermore, following a similar direct action campaign, students in the Open Letter movement at Goshen College convinced their school to adopt an inclusive nondiscrimination policy. Even when schools initially resist such policies, LGBT groups play a significant role in raising awareness about issues facing LGBT students; for example, participants in CUAllies say that the Catholic University community has moved from relative silence on LGBT issues to wider campus discussion of LGBT issues. In all of these cases, a strategy of embracing conversations about religion and LGBT rights—transforming prevailing understandings of what it means to be a Christian university, a Christian community, and an LGBT Christian—seems to pay dividends. Given current law that allows religious universities to discriminate on the basis of sexual orientation and gender identity, and given many religious denominations' stances against LGBT rights, students in LGBT activist groups at Christian colleges and universities may very well be the central agents of change on one of the new frontiers for the LGBT movement.

Notes

Introduction

1. For more on the importance of socialization, see Bosi (2012); Demerath, Marwell, and Aiken (1971); Isaac, Mutran, and Stryker (1980); Klatch (1999); McAdam (1988); Nepstad (2004a); and Viterna (2006).

2. For more on the importance of prior activism, see Bosi (2012); Corrigall-Brown (2012); Isaac, Coley, Cornfield, and Dickerson (2016); Klatch (1999); McAdam (1988); Viterna (2006); and Wiltfang and McAdam (1991).

3. For more on the role of attitudinal affinity, see Cohn, Barkan, and Whitaker (1993); Corrigall-Brown (2012); Jasper (1997); Jasper and Poulsen (1995); Klandermans and Oegema (1987); Klatch (1999); McAdam (1986); and Schussman and Soule (2005); though also see Blee (2003), Han (2009), and Munson (2008).

4. For more on the link between personal networks and activist group participation, see Beyerlein and Bergstrand (2016); Bosi (2012); Cunningham (2013); Dixon and Roscigno (2003); Jasper and Poulsen (1995); Klandermans and Oegema (1987); Klatch (1999); McAdam (1986); McAdam and Paulsen (1993); Nepstad and Smith (1999); Snow, Zurcher, and Ekland-Olson (1980); and Viterna (2006). For more on the link between organizational networks and activist group participation, see Bosi (2012); Fernandez and McAdam (1988); Klandermans and Oegema (1987); Klatch (1999); McAdam (1986); Schussman and Soule (2005); and Viterna (2006).

5. For more on biographical availability, see Beyerlein and Hipp (2006) and McAdam (1986).

6. For more on the role of attitudinal affinity, microstructural availability, and biographical availability in activist commitment, see Baggetta, Han, and Andrews (2013); Barkan, Cohn, and Whitaker (1993, 1995); and Cohn, Barkan, and Halteman (2003).

7. For more on how meso-level constraints detract from activist group commitment, see Baggetta et al. (2013); Dorius and McCarthy (2011); and Knoke (1981).

8. See studies on the impacts of activist group participation on political behavior and views, such as Demerath et al. (1971); Fendrich (1993); Giguni and Grasso (2016); Isaac et al. (2016); Klatch (1999); McAdam (1988, 1989); Terriquez (2015); and Whalen and Flacks (1989).

9. See studies on the impacts of activist groups on family plans, such as Klatch (1999); McAdam (1989, 1999); Sherkat and Blocker (1997); Van Dyke, McAdam, and Wilhelm (2000); Whalen and Flacks (1989); Whittier (2016); and Wilhelm (1998).

10. For other work on activism within institutions, see, for example, Banaszak (2010); Bell (2014); Davis and Robinson (2012); Kucinskas (2014); McCammon and McGrath (2015); and Santoro and McGuire (1997). For other work on activist

group-induced cultural change, see, for example, Armstrong and Bernstein (2008); Bruce (2016); Earl (2004); and an extended discussion in chapter four.

11. For other work on activist safe spaces and communities, see Fetner, Elafros, Bortolin, and Dreschler (2012); Kelner (2008); Nepstad (2004b); Reger (2012); Rupp and Taylor (1987); Staggenborg (1998); Taylor and Whittier (1992); and Whittier (1995). For other work on intentional activist group-induced personal change, see, for example, Bernstein and De la Cruz (2009); Reger, Myers, and Einwohner (2008); Whittier (2011); Woehrle (2014); and an extended discussion in chapter five.

12. For example, Armstrong (2002), Armstrong and Bernstein (2008), Crossley (2017), Reger (2012), Van Dyke, Soule, and Taylor (2004), and Whittier (1995) all highlight the varieties of goals and tactics that are pursued and deployed by activists.

13. For studies on bullying and harassment toward sexual and gender minorities in schools, see Pascoe (2012); Poteat et al. (2013); and Toomey and Russell (2013, 2016). For a recent study on violence against queer people more generally, see Meyer (2015).

14. For studies on experiences of LGBT students at Christian universities, see Craig, Austin, Rashidi, and Adams (2017) and Wolff, Himes, Soares, and Miller Kwom (2016).

15. For studies on conservative religiosity and homophobia, see Schnabel (2016); Sherkat (2016); Whitley (2009); Wolff, Himes, Miller Kwom, and Bollinger (2012); and Woodford, Levy, and Walls (2013).

16. For studies on the impacts of high school Gay–Straight Alliances, see Currie, Mayberry, and Chenneville (2012); Fetner, Elafros, Bortolin, and Dreschler (2012); Fetner and Elafros (2015); Heck, Flentje, and Cochran (2011); Marx and Kettrey (2016); Mayberry (2006, 2013a, 2013b); Poteat et al. (2013, 2015); Renn (2007); Renn and Bilodeau (2005); Toomey and Russell (2013); and Walls, Kane, and Wisneski (2010).

17. Although both Loyola University Chicago and Catholic University are associated with the Roman Catholic Church—a religious tradition with a body of social justice teachings—I exploited variation within the Catholic Church by selecting one school associated with the social justice-oriented Jesuits (Loyola University Chicago) and another school associated with the more conservative wing of the Roman Catholic Church (Catholic University).

18. I interviewed participants rather than nonparticipants given my goal of understanding variation among participants rather than understanding differences between participants and nonparticipants (an objective that has historically characterized studies of micromobilization but that tends to homogenize participants). This approach is consistent with other recent studies on variation among activists (e.g., Bosi 2012; Isaac et al. 2016).

19. By interviewing Belmont students during two waves, I was able to assess the potential role of changing school policies on students' pathways to activism while holding other contextual variables constant. Furthermore, by interviewing some students during both waves, I was able to verify that recall bias was not an issue—students recalled the details of their initial participation just as well three to four years after they joined as they did in the first few months after they joined.

20. I was not able to identify the earliest participants in the group at Loyola University Chicago given that group's early founding date.

21. Note that I generally avoid referencing respondents' race or gender identity throughout the book; because people of color and trans people were greatly outnumbered within all of these groups, identifying a respondent as a person of color or transgender might compromise their anonymity.

22. Students repeatedly mentioned that Advocate was known for being a male-dominated club.

23. Students similarly mentioned that straight allies dominated the leadership of Advocates.

Chapter 1

1. For research on the same-sex marriage campaigns, see Becker (2014); Bernstein and Taylor (2013); Kimport (2013); and Taylor, Kimport, and Van Dyke (2009).

2. The Mattachine Society was predated by the Society for Human Rights, a homophile-like organization founded in Chicago, Illinois, in 1924. However, the organization lasted for only a few months, because police arrested many of the organization's members (Licata 1981).

3. Beemyn (2003) notes that students at Stanford formulated plans for a gay student organization prior to students at Columbia, but the students never moved past the planning process.

4. For further research on the 1960s civil rights, feminist, and working-class movements, see studies such as Gitlin (1987); Isaac and Christiansen (2002); McAdam (1982); Morris (1986); and Roth (2003).

5. There was an attempt by some activists to revive the contentious tactics that marked the gay liberation and lesbian feminist movements of the late 1960s, as evidenced by the formation of the radical group ACT UP in 1987, which staged high-profile direct actions in such cities as New York City and Los Angeles to fight the AIDS pandemic (Gould 2009; Roth 2017). However, these groups were the exception to the more general trend toward moderation, and most did not last long.

6. An incomplete list of these organization includes A Common Bond (Jehovah's Witnesses); Affirmation (the Mormon Church); Axios (Eastern Orthodox, Byzantine Rite, and Eastern Catholic Christians); Association of Welcoming and Affirming Baptists (American Baptist Churches USA and other mainline Baptist denominations); Brethren Mennonite Council (Church of the Brethren); Changing Attitude (Anglican Church); Courage (Roman Catholic Church); Dignity USA (Roman Catholic Church); Emergence International (Christian Scientists); Friends for Lesbian, Gay, Bisexual, Transgender, and Queer Concerns (Quakers); GLAD Alliance (Disciples of Christ); Integrity USA (Episcopal Church in the United States of America); Lutherans Concerned/North America (Evangelical Lutheran Church in America); Methodists in New Directions (United Methodist Church USA); More Light Presbyterians (Presbyterian Church USA); Nazarene Ally (Church of the Nazarene); New Ways Ministries (Roman Catholic Church); Pink Menno (Mennonite Church USA); Reconciling Ministries Network (United Methodist Church USA); Seventh-Day Adventist Kinship International (Seventh-Day Adventists); and the UCC Open and Affirming Coalition (United Church of Christ). See Fuist, Stoll, and Kniss (2012) for

an analysis of many of these organizations, and see Loseke and Cavendish (2001) and Radojcic (2016) for an analysis of Dignity in particular.

7. For fuller theoretical statements on political opportunity structures, see McAdam (1982, 1997); Meyer (2004); Tarrow (2011); and Tilly (1978).

8. For fuller theoretical statements on resource mobilization theory, see Edwards and Kane (2014) and McCarthy and Zald (1977).

9. I use the terms "individualist" and "communal" rather than related terms such as "libertarian" and "communitarian" because these latter terms generally conflate a focus on individuals versus communities with conservative versus liberal social beliefs (see Davis and Robinson 2012). Specifically, the term "libertarian" often implies that those who are focused on the plights of individuals also hold liberal social beliefs, and the term "communitarian" implies that those who are focused on reforming wider communities also hold conservative social beliefs, whereas I wish to avoid these assumptions.

10. Specifically, scholars have documented strong support for social movements among communal religious traditions (Braunstein, Fuist, and Williams 2017; Shepherd 2009; C. Smith 1996; Wood 2002; Wood and Fulton 2015), including black Protestant churches and colleges (e.g., work on the civil rights movement by Isaac et al. 2012; Morris 1986; R. H. Williams 2002), mainline Protestant denominations (e.g., work on LGBT movements by H. White 2015 and on peace and economic justice movements by Snarr 2011; Wuthnow and Evans 2002; though see mixed findings in Mirola 2015), and the Catholic Church (e.g., other work on peace and economic justice movements by Nepstad 2004a, 2004b, 2008; Palacios 2007; C. Smith 1991). In comparison, mobilization within individualist traditions, such as evangelical Protestant denominations, has mostly been limited to issues of personal piety (e.g., R. H. Williams 2002; R. H. Williams and Blackburn 1996; though see Steensland and Goff 2013). See also Perry's (2017) discussion of how social engagement by conservative evangelicals is self-limiting.

11. For example, Gary T. Marx (1967, 67) shows that African Americans in individualist denominations, which seek to "solace the individual" and "divert concern away from efforts at collective social change," were unlikely to support nonviolent protests in support of civil rights. However, members of denominations that followed a "social gospel" (or communal) tradition often supported civil rights protests. More recently, Barnes (2004) distinguished between individualist functions of religion (such as attendance to "spiritual/religious needs of members") and communal functions of religion (such as the promotion of community empowerment), showing that black churches specializing in communal functions are more involved in providing social services than black churches specializing in individualist functions (also see Reed, Williams, and Ward 2015). Finally, Davidson and Garcia (2014) find that black Protestants are much more likely than evangelical Protestants to support social services for undocumented immigrants given their history of teachings on social justice.

12. There is, of course, an alternative explanation—perhaps a more intuitive one—that would suggest that it is liberal or conservative teachings on the morality of same-sex relationships, rather than these more general theological orientations, that drive Christian colleges and universities to support or oppose LGBT groups (e.g.,

Wuthnow 1988, 1989). However, schools that were associated with religious traditions that view same-sex relationships as "sinful"—including the United Methodist Church and the Roman Catholic Church—comprise the majority of LGBT-inclusive schools in my database, and, in additional multivariate analyses, a variable indicating whether a school was associated with a denomination viewing same-sex relationships as sinful was an insignificant predictor of LGBT group presence and inclusive nondiscrimination policy adoption (see Coley 2017). As I argue, then, it is not teachings on same-sex relationships but rather theological orientations that best explain schools' support for LGBT groups and nondiscrimination statements. This is not to say that conservative or liberal readings of scriptures do not matter. However, it is to argue that religious traditions guided by conservative or liberal teachings on scriptures will not necessarily seek to impose those teachings on their wider communities; those who read scriptures as condemning certain moral practices might still tolerate those practices in their communities in the interest of ensuring universal rights.

Chapter 2

1. Beyond McAdam's (1986, 1988) work, studies ranging from Snow et al.'s (1980) early work on micromobilization into religious movements, Klandermans's (1997) study of social movement participation in an overseas context (the Netherlands), Klatch's (1999) work on participation in both right- and left-wing movements during the 1960s, Schussman and Soule's (2005) analysis of nationally representative U.S. survey data on activist group participation, and Swank and Fahs's (2012) article on college student participation in LGBT activism all support the idea that a prototypical activist exists, although they each make their own unique contributions to the micromobilization literature. Snow et al. (1980) found that religious and student movements were more effective at recruitment when they were rich in personal ties and when they targeted those at a life course stage conducive to movement participation. McAdam (1988) showed that, although factors such as childhood socialization, prior activist group participation, and attitudinal affinity seemed to be "necessary" for participation in Freedom Summer, they were not "sufficient," because such characteristics were also shared by a group of "no-shows" to the Freedom Summer project; instead, microstructural availability in particular seems to distinguish actual participants from no-shows. Klandermans (1997); Klandermans and Oegema (1987) argued that scholars should take seriously the "stages" that would-be participants must progress through en route to activist group participation: specifically, people must first adopt attitudes conducive to movement participation before they are targeted for recruitment by their friends or organizations; they must then decide that the benefits of participation outweigh any costs to participation before they overcome personal constraints on participation. Klatch (1999) showed that socialization, prior movement participation, attitudinal affinity, and microstructural availability matter just as much for right-wing activists as they do for left-wing activists. Schussman and Soule (2005) found that membership in existing organizations can lead to invitations to participate in protests, and prior political and activist engagement and biographical availability explain actual participation in protests. Finally, Swank and

Fahs (2012) found that adopting pro-LGBT attitudes and frames, having personal ties to activists, and maintaining an activist identity are all linked to participation in LGBT rights protest.

2. For examples of studies that highlight the role of socialization, see Bosi (2012); Demerath et al. (1971); Isaac et al. (1980); Klatch (1999); McAdam (1988); Nepstad (2004a); and Viterna (2006).

3. For examples of studies that discuss the role of prior activist group participation, see Bosi (2012); Corrigall-Brown (2012); Isaac et al. (2016); Klatch (1999); McAdam (1988); Viterna (2006); and Wiltfang and McAdam (1991).

4. For examples of studies discussing attitudinal affinity, see Cohn et al. (1993); Corrigall-Brown (2012); Jasper (1997); Jasper and Poulsen (1995); Klandermans and Oegema (1987); Klatch (1999); McAdam (1988); Schussman and Soule (2005); and Swank and Fahs (2012). For a related perspective, see Farrell's (2011) work on moral schemas. But for important exceptions, see Blee (2003), who shows that many women develop intensely racist attitudes only after they begin participating in hate groups; Han (2009), who showed that people's commitment to certain political issues came only after they began participating in a political or civic organization; and Munson (2008), who speaks to many members of pro-life organizations who initially identify as pro-choice or were ambivalent about abortion rights.

5. For examples of studies emphasizing microstructural availability, see Beyerlein and Bergstrand (2016); Bosi (2012); Cunningham (2013); Dixon and Roscigno (2003); Fernandez and McAdam (1988); Jasper and Poulsen (1995); Klandermans and Oegema (1987); Klatch (1999); McAdam (1988); McAdam and Paulsen (1993); Nepstad and Smith (1999); Schussman and Soule (2005); Snow et al. (1980); Suh (2014); Swank and Fahs (2012); and Viterna (2006). But note that studies on participants in animal rights, homeless, and religious movements have shown that the recruitment of strangers who are not otherwise embedded in personal and organizational networks supportive to social movements can be effective (Corrigall-Brown et al. 2009; Jasper 1997; Jasper and Poulsen 1995; Snow et al. 1980, 1986). Even a large-scale study of participation across a variety of activist groups found that a significant minority of people "participate in protest despite never being asked to do so" (Schussman and Soule 2005, 1098).

6. But note that the study that initially offered the idea of biographical availability, McAdam's (1986) study of applicants to the 1964 Freedom Summer voter registration drives in Jim Crow Mississippi, was quite limited in its ability to demonstrate the role of biographical availability—the sample of college-age students was fairly homogenous in terms of life course stage. Also, McAdam's (1986, 85) own analysis of Freedom Summer applicants showed that the "sum of personal constraints" makes "no significant contribution to likelihood of participation" in Freedom Summer when controlling for other variables. Finally, other studies have showed that, in different movements, middle-age people have been more likely to participate in certain activist groups than younger people (Beyerlein and Hipp 2006; Cohn et al. 1993; Nepstad and Smith 1999), people who are fully employed have been more likely to participate in activist groups than underemployed people (Corrigall-Brown 2012; Nepstad and Smith 1999), and parents have been more likely to participate in activ-

ist groups than childless people (Corrigall-Brown 2012; Corrigall-Brown et al. 2009; Wiltfang and McAdam 1991).

7. Although it may seem odd that someone who believes homosexuality is sinful would be involved in LGBT activism, Heather White (2015) discusses how many people of faith were active in the early homophile movement despite similarly believing that same-sex relationships were morally inferior to opposite-sex relationships.

8. For this study, information on organizational ties was not useful for explaining activist group participation, because all potential participants were already embedded in the most important organization relevant to their LGBT group—their school. Furthermore, because so many students joined these groups at the beginning of their first years, they were seldom members of other organizations.

9. Social movement scholars often refer to the concept of *collective identity* when discussing identities relevant to activist group participation. However, as Klatch (1999, 6) notes, this term has been used in highly contradictory ways. Some scholars, including Klatch (1999), consider collective identity to be the identity of an organization; others consider collective identity to be the property of an individual—for example, "an individual's cognitive, moral, and emotional connection with a broader community, category, practice, or institution" (Polletta and Jasper 2001, 285). My use of the term *identity* is most similar to this latter definition, but to avoid some of the confusion surrounding the term *collective identity*, I instead use the term *social identity*, following Klatch's (1999, 6) formulation: "When I speak of *identity* here I am referring to an individual or personal identity that defines a person as a social actor. In answer to the question 'Who am I?' it conveys a sense of 'the real me.' Individual identity is necessarily a social identity. It is the situated self. Individuals gain a sense of identity by locating themselves within a meaningful social world and seeking recognition within this web of social relationships."

10. For examples of studies discussing identity and activist group participation, see Corrigall-Brown (2012); Heaney and Rojas (2015); Klandermans and De Weerd (2000); Klandermans, Sabucedo, Rodriguez, and De Weerd (2002); Klatch (1999); McAdam and Paulsen (1993); and Viterna (2013).

11. Participants with salient religious identities generally held conservative religious views because conservative religious teachings about same-sex relationships are in tension with participation in LGBT activist groups, thus making religion highly salient in these participants' decisions about whether to join LGBT activist groups. Many people in my sample held liberal religious views, but because same-sex relationships are not a big deal in their religion, they did not report those views as being relevant when they decided to join LGBT activist groups; rather, their liberal political views or their own LGBT identities were much larger factors in their participation.

12. This certainly makes them similar to people in other movements who participate primarily because they stand to benefit from the things they achieve (e.g., Fendrich 1993).

13. In separate analyses, I also assessed potential *contextual influences* on participation in these LGBT activist groups—that is, characteristics of a surrounding state or the university itself that might shape students' pathways into LGBT groups. Although such analyses are rare in studies of micromobilization (though see studies by Biggs

2006; Bosi 2012; Cable, Walsh, and Warland 1988; Cunningham 2013; Viterna 2006), it is possible in this study because I rely on multiple sites. However, I found that factors like the "red" (Republican) or "blue" (Democratic) leanings of a state in which a school is located, and the absence or presence of inclusive nondiscrimination policies at a school, did not seem to shape pathways into these LGBT activist groups.

14. For example, a famous study by Snow et al. (1986), drawing partially on data from religious movements, showed that those who recruit others to a movement often have to work to convince recruits that the movement in question has valid goals and values, including through "frame alignment" processes such as "frame amplification" and "frame extension," where recruiters interact with those who are indifferent about the movement, and "frame transformation," where recruiters interact with those who are initially hostile to the movement. More recently, a study by Munson (2008) showed that numerous pro-life activists initially lacked attitudinal affinity (or at least a fully articulated pro-life ideology) when they first joined the movement, although it should be acknowledged that the pro-life movement has been a rare conservative movement in the United States that has indeed often turned to more confrontational (and even violent) tactics.

15. For example, Mayberry's (2006) and Renn's (2007) studies of Gay–Straight Alliances show that these groups draw LGBT students who develop "politicized consciousness" and adopt "activist identities" only after participating in the group (although Fetner et al. [2012] question whether they ever come to see themselves as activists at all).

Chapter 3

1. The question of activist commitment has received little attention from scholars and has been labeled a "black box in the social-movement and voluntary-association literatures" (Cohn, Barkan, and Halteman 2003, 311). Few scholars have studied commitment in part because there is little agreement about what commitment actually entails. Many scholars conflate "commitment" with concepts such as "persistence," or the decision to participate in an activist group over time (see studies on persistence by Bunnage 2014; Corrigall-Brown 2012; Downton and Wehr 1997; Fisher and McInerney 2012; Klatch 1999; McAdam 1988; Nepstad 2004a, 2004b; Passy and Giugni 2000; Rohlinger and Bunnage 2015; Simi, Futrell, and Bubolz 2016; Taylor and Rupp 1987; Van Dyke and Dixon 2013; R. W. White 2010; Whittier 1995). However, other scholars define "commitment" as the level of time, energy, and activity one devotes to or expends on an activist group (e.g., Bagetta et al. 2013; Barkan et al. 1993, 1995; Cohn et al. 2003; Dorius and McCarthy 2011; Isaac et al. 2016; Knoke 1981). Although "commitment" and "persistence" are related—Barkan et al. (1993, 1995) and Cohn et al. (2003) find that "commitment" measured as level of activity in an organization is correlated with "persistence" measured as years of membership in an organization—the two concepts are analytically distinct. I focus here on level of activity in an organization in part because many of my own respondents were in the early stages of their participation in activist groups, meaning data on their persistence are not yet available, and in part because the nature of college-based activism is that participation has a natural end point—graduation.

2. For research linking rational choice calculations and biographical availability to commitment, see Bagetta et al. (2013); Barkan et al. (1993, 1995); Cohn et al. (2003); Dorius and McCarthy (2011); Isaac et al. (2016); and Knoke (1981).

3. The concept of group ethos is distinct from related concepts such as organizational identity, which place emphasis on official titles and mission statements and which may miss nuances in how groups actually operate in practice (see, e.g., Eliasoph and Lichterman's [2003] extended discussion of how peoples can interpret the same "collective representations" in very different ways). Instead, the concept of group ethos has its roots in the scholarship of Weber ([1905] 2002), who argued that the character of certain Protestant groups (as communicated through beliefs and embodied in practices) could be linked to the spread of capitalism. More recently, Xu (2013) argued that the correspondence of certain Chinese student organizations' group ethos (those with an "ethical" ethos, which indicated a collective interest in self-transformation and moral cultivation) with the Bolshevik organizational culture (which similarly emphasized "ascetic self-discipline and subjugation of the self to collective ends"; Xu 2013, 774) led student groups to join the emerging communist movement in China. I draw heavily on Xu's (2013) conceptualization of group ethos (i.e., the character of a group, as communicated through beliefs and embodied in practices) here. However, whereas Xu constructs his argument such that a meso-level variable (group ethos) must correspond with a macro-level variable (the communist movement's organizational culture) to explain a macro-level outcome (movement spillover), I am interested here in how the meso-level variable group ethos corresponds with an individual-level variable (participants' salient identities) to produce an individual-level outcome (participants' commitment to activist groups). Furthermore, I illustrate the applicability of Xu's insights on group ethos to a very different context.

4. For an early theoretical statement on the problem of "identity correspondence," see Snow and McAdam (2000). For other perspectives on the connection between the identities of individuals and groups, see Simi et al. (2016) and Valocchi (2001).

5. Note that being a Christian certainly did not preclude activists from considering more contentious tactics in my sample. Those Christians from denominations with social justice traditions, who were more likely to consider themselves "activists" first (and are thus not classified as having more salient religious identities), certainly employed such tactics. McVeigh and Sikkink (2001, 1425) have shown that churchgoing Protestants can approve contentious tactics when they report the following characteristics: "volunteering for church organizations, a perception that religious values are being threatened, a belief that individuals should not have a right to deviate from Christian moral standards, and a belief that humans are inherently sinful."

6. As noted, a few scholars have argued that an activist considers whether the potential collective benefits that the group might secure—for example, the potential to achieve goals like nondiscrimination ordinances that all people could benefit from (whether they participate in the group or not)—and especially the potential selective incentives one might gain through participation in the group—for example, practical leadership skills one might gain only if one actually participates in the group—merit his or her commitment to the group (Barkan et al. 1993, 1995; Cohn et al. 2003). Yet,

when I asked my respondents what they thought would come about as a result of their participation, I found that different groups I studied tended to value different types of benefits (e.g., direct action group members anticipated changing the policies of their school, educational groups anticipated changing the culture or climate of their schools, and solidarity group members anticipated making new friends). Regardless, there was no one type of organization that produced more committed members than others—the most committed members of each type of organization tended to devote five to six hours per week to their group. Similarly, with regard to biographical availability—another explanation of activist group commitment offered in past studies (Barkan et al. 1993, 1995; Cohn et al. 2003)—I found that my respondents were homogeneous in terms of most traits generally linked to biographical availability: age (they were young), student status (they were all enrolled at their college or university at the time of their participation), marital status (they were mostly single), and parental status (none had children). Thus, biographical availability does not seem to be a helpful explanation for groups where members are at a similar life course stage.

7. For example, Baggetta et al. (2013) show that leaders who spend a smaller proportion of time in meetings devote more time to the organization overall. For the LGBT groups examined here, the attitude toward meetings was generally all or nothing: groups either had no meetings or had weekly meetings. Among those groups that held no meetings, the number of hours students participated each week was above three; among groups that held weekly meetings, the number of hours students participated each week was just above five. If one assumes that students in the meeting groups spent up to two hours each week in meetings (which was usually the case), this means that the overall level of participation in LGBT activism outside of meetings did not significantly vary according to whether groups held meetings. The LGBT groups I studied also varied in terms of bureaucracy and centralization—factors emphasized by Dorius and McCarthy (2011) and Knoke (1981)—but I found no consistent link between organizational structure and commitment. Finally, another relevant study by Isaac et al. (2016) highlights the role of "movement schools" that provide formal training in nonviolent direct action, but I did not uncover much evidence that my respondents attended movement schools.

Chapter 4

1. For other studies on social movements mobilizing within higher education, see Binder and Wood (2013); Cole (2014); Crossley (2017); Dixon, Tope, and Van Dyke (2008); McCammon, McGrath, Dixon, and Robinson (2016); McEntarfer (2011); Munson (2010); Poulson, Ratliff, and Dollieslager (2013); Van Dyke (1998, 2003); and Vespone (2016).

2. For studies on movement-induced artistic products, see Coley (2015); Isaac (2009, 2012); Mai (2016); Morrison and Isaac (2012); Roscigno and Danaher (2001); Rosenthal and Flacks (2012); and S. J. Williams (2016).

3. For studies on movement communities, see Kelner (2008); Nepstad (2004b); Reger (2012); Rupp and Taylor (1987); Staggenborg (1998); Taylor and Whittier (1992); and Whittier (1995).

4. Studies that show that cultural change can accomplish political goals include Armstrong (2002); Armstrong and Bernstein (2008); Bail (2015); Best (2012); Ellingson (2016); Hess (2016); Hess and Coley (2014); Jasper (1997, 2014); Polletta (1997, 2004, 2008); and Taylor, Rupp, and Gamson (2004).

5. Most of the activists involved in the protests believed that enforcing a prohibition on sex outside of marriage was a way of discriminating against lesbian and gay people without actually acknowledging discrimination against lesbian and gay people, because same-sex marriage was not then recognized in Tennessee.

6. Both Belmont and the soccer coach, citing an exit agreement, have refused to comment on the circumstances of her departure—for instance, why she left and whether she was fired, was asked to resign, or resigned voluntarily.

7. One person did bring a sign comparing the Belmont administration to the Nazis, but students quickly asked him to hide the sign and announced rules for future protests banning any language that might be perceived as anti-Belmont.

8. For more on religious and sexual identity conflicts and reconciliation, see Creek (2013); Fuist (2017); Loseke and Cavendish (2001); Moon (2004); Pitt (2010a, 2010b); Rodriguez (2010); Sumerau, Cragun, and Mathers (2016); Wilcox (2003, 2009); Winder (2015); and Wolkomir (2006).

Chapter 5

1. Specifically, works ranging from Demerath et al.'s (1971) study on white civil rights activists who participated in the Southern Christian Leadership Conference's voter registration drives, Fendrich's (1993) analysis of black and white civil rights activists who participated in the 1960s Florida civil rights movement, Giugni and Grasso's (2016) analysis of a representative sample of trajectories of activists in Switzerland, Isaac et al.'s (2016) study of participants in the 1960s Nashville civil rights movement, Klatch's (1999) study of participants in the 1960s Young Americans for Freedom and Students for a Democratic Society organizations, McAdam's (1988, 1989) famous studies on Freedom Summer, McAdam and his team's (McAdam 1999; Van Dyke et al. 2000; Wilhelm 1998) later analyses of a representative sample of 1960s activists, Sherkat and Blocker's (1997) work on high school students who came of age in the 1960s, Terriquez's (2015) study on the political trajectories of nonprofit youth activists, Whalen and Flacks's (1989) study of left-wing bank burners in 1970 Santa Barbara, California, and Whittier's (2016) research on biographical outcomes of lesbian and gay movements have all sought to identify the biographical impacts of activist groups. For an early literature review, see Giugni (2004), and for a recent meta-analysis, see Vestergren, Drury, and Chiriac (2017).

2. For important exceptions to the general rule that scholars analyzing the biographical consequences of activism often downplay differences among activists themselves, see Fendrich (1993); and Van Dyke et al. (2000).

3. For scholarship taking a longer view on the biographical impacts of activist groups, see work on the lives of civil rights activists fifty years following their participation in sit-ins by Isaac et al. (2016); Coley, Cornfield, Isaac, and Dickerson (2017); and Cornfield, Coley, Isaac, and Dickerson (2018).

4. For example, McAdam's (1988) famous study on Freedom Summer showed that participants were much more likely to become active in the student free speech, women's, and antiwar movements of the later 1960s, as well as social justice struggles in the 1970s and 1980s. Other studies (Demerath et al. 1971; Fendrich 1993; Klatch 1999; Sherkat and Blocker 1997; Whalen and Flacks 1989), often relying on smaller, noncomparative samples, largely replicated McAdam's findings.

5. A helpful study of civil rights activists in Florida by Fendrich and Tarleau (1973, 249) constructed a typology of occupations "classified along a continuum, ranging from those chiefly offering rewards of money and status in the private sector of the economy to those that offered the opportunity to express creativity and a chance of humanistic service: (1) proprietors, managers, officials, and salesmen in the private sector of the economy; (2) private practice professionals such as doctors and lawyers; (3) government workers; (4) academic professionals; and (5) those in social service and creative occupations." The study found that former activists almost exclusively pursued jobs in the fourth and fifth categories—collectively known as the "humanistic" professions—while nonactivists pursued jobs in the first three categories. Scholars examining biographical trajectories of other 1960s activists reported similar results (Klatch 1999; McAdam 1988, 1989, 1999; Sherkat and Blocker 1997; Whalen and Flacks 1989).

6. One reason for this is that, as Robbie's story indicates, organizing can be a full-time career.

7. For example, in terms of activists' subsequent family lives, McAdam (1988, 1989) showed that Freedom Summer participants were no less likely to marry compared with no-shows, but they were perhaps more intentional about selecting a partner who agreed with their political and religious views, and they reported more volatile marital trajectories. Other studies largely replicated these findings (Klatch 1999; McAdam 1999; Sherkat and Blocker 1997; Whalen and Flacks 1989), also adding that participants of 1960s movements adopted more egalitarian gender views (Sherkat and Blocker 1997) and that the 1960s generation would facilitate a broader shift in attitudes regarding cohabitation (Wilhelm 1998).

8. Although Renn (2007; Renn and Bilodeau 2005) documents how many sexual minorities involved in a GSA-like group at a Midwestern research university moved from identifying as "student leaders" to identifying as "activists," studies that examine GSA participants' future activist behaviors find mixed evidence that participants engage in behaviors like voting or political campaigns (Mayberry 2013b; Poteat et al. 2015; Russell et al. 2009; Toomey and Russell 2013).

9. This is slightly higher than the 31 percent of students whom I placed in the "politicized participants" category in chapter three, because some students initially identified not only as "activists" but also as persons of faith or LGBT people prior to joining, and for some of these respondents, their faith or sexuality was a greater "pull" for joining the LGBT group.

10. Note that three respondents said they preferred stronger terms—such as "radical" or "rebel"—and I included these people in the "activist" group. However, I exclude people who said they were uncomfortable with the term "activist" (in any sense) and preferred softer terms such as "advocate" or "ally."

References

Adler, Gary. 2012. "An Opening in the Congregational Closet? Boundary-Bridging Culture and Membership Privileges for Gays and Lesbians in Christian Religious Congregations." *Social Problems* 59 (2): 177–206.

Advocate. 2010. "A Letter in Response to the Advocate's Drag Show Being Moved." *Loyola University Chicago.* Retrieved January 6, 2015 (https://orgsync.com/13620/custom_pages/3971).

Anderson, Nick. 2015, December 18. "Religious Colleges Get Exemptions to Anti-Bias Law; Critics Denounce 'Hidden Discrimination' against LGBT Students." *Washington Post.*

Armstrong, Elizabeth A. 2002. *Forging Gay Identities: Organizing Sexuality in San Francisco, 1950–1994.* Chicago: University of Chicago Press.

Armstrong, Elizabeth A., and Mary Bernstein. 2008. "Culture, Power, and Institutions: A Multi-Institutional Approach to Social Movements." *Sociological Theory* 26 (1): 74–99.

Armstrong, Elizabeth A., and Suzanna M. Crage. 2006. "Movements and Memory: The Making of the Stonewall Myth." *American Sociological Review* 71 (5): 724–51.

Association of Statisticians of American Religious Bodies. 2015. "U.S. Congregational Memberships: Reports." Retrieved June 20, 2015 (http://www.thearda.com/rcms2010/).

Baggetta, Matthew, Hahrie Han, and Kenneth T. Andrews. 2013. "Leading Associations: How Individual Characteristics and Team Dynamics Generate Committed Leaders." *American Sociological Review* 78 (4): 544–73.

Bail, Christopher. 2015. *Terrified: How Anti-Muslim Fringe Organizations Became Mainstream.* Princeton, NJ: Princeton University Press.

Banaszak, Lee Ann. 2010. *The Women's Movement Inside and Outside the State.* New York: Cambridge University Press.

Baptist Press. 2006. "Belmont Names 7 Non-Baptists to Join Trustee Board." Retrieved March 8, 2017 (http://www.bpnews.net/24650/belmont-names-7-nonbaptists-to-join-trustee-board).

Barkan, Steven E., Steven F. Cohn, and William H. Whitaker. 1993. "Commitment across the Miles: Ideological and Microstructural Sources of Membership Support in a National Antihunger Organization." *Social Problems* 40 (3): 362–73.

———. 1995. "Beyond Recruitment: Predictors of Differential Participation in a National Antihunger Organization." *Sociological Forum* 10 (1): 113–34.

Barnes, Sandra L. 2004. "Priestly and Prophetic Influences on Black Church Social Services." *Social Problems* 51 (2): 202–21.

Barton, Bernadette C. 2014. *Pray the Gay Away: The Extraordinary Lives of Bible Belt Gays.* New York: New York University Press.

Becker, Jo. 2014. *Forcing the Spring: Inside the Fight for Marriage Equality*. New York: Penguin Press.

Beemyn, Brett. 2003. "The Silence Is Broken: A History of the First Lesbian, Gay, and Bisexual College Student Groups." *Journal of the History of Sexuality* 12 (2): 205–23.

Bell, Joyce M. 2014. *The Black Power Movement and American Social Work*. New York: Columbia University Press.

Belmont University. 2010. "Dr. Fisher's Statement to the Media, Dec. 8, 2010." Retrieved March 8, 2017 (http://www.belmont.edu/oc/presidents-statement /index.html).

———. 2011. "Dr. Fisher's Statement to the Media, Jan. 26, 2011." Retrieved March 8, 2017 (http://www.belmont.edu/oc/presidents-statement/12611.html).

———. 2015. *Belmont University Faculty Handbook*. Retrieved March 8, 2017 (http:/ /www.belmont.edu/hr/pdf/2015-2016%20FACULTY%20HANDBOOK.pdf).

Bernstein, Mary, and Marcie De la Cruz. 2009. "'What Are You?': Explaining Identity as a Goal of the Multiracial Hapa Movement." *Social Problems* 56 (4): 722–45.

Bernstein, Mary, and Nancy A. Naples. 2015. "Altared States: Legal Structuring and Relationship Recognition in the United States, Canada, and Australia." *American Sociological Review* 80 (6): 1226–49.

Bernstein, Mary, and Verta Taylor, eds. 2013. *The Marrying Kind? Debating Same-Sex Marriage within the Lesbian and Gay Movement*. Minneapolis: University of Minnesota Press.

Best, Rachel Kahn. 2012. "Disease Politics and Medical Research Funding: Three Ways Advocacy Shapes Policy." *American Sociological Review* 77 (5): 780–803.

Beyerlein, Kraig, and Kelly Bergstrand. 2016. "It Takes Two: A Dyadic Model of Recruitment to Civic Activity." *Social Science Research* 60 (November): 163–80.

Beyerlein, Kraig, and John Hipp. 2006. "A Two-Stage Model for a Two-Stage Process: How Biographical Availability Matters for Social Movement Mobilization." *Mobilization* 11 (3): 219–40.

Biggs, Michael. 2006. "Who Joined the Sit-Ins and Why: Southern Black Students in the Early 1960s." *Mobilization* 11 (3): 321–36.

Binder, Amy, and Kate Wood. 2013. *Becoming Right: How Campuses Shape Young Conservatives*. Princeton, NJ: Princeton University Press.

Blee, Katlheen. 2003. *Inside Organized Racism: Women in the Hate Movement*. Berkeley: University of California Press.

Bosi, Lorenzo. 2012. "Explaining Pathways to Armed Activism in the Provisional Irish Republican Army, 1969–1972." *Social Science History* 36 (Fall): 347–90.

Bosi, Lorenzo, and Donatella Della Porta. 2012. "Micro-Mobilization into Armed Groups: Ideological, Instrumental, and Solidaristic Paths." *Qualitative Sociology* 35: 361–83.

Braunstein, Ruth, Todd Nicholas Fuist, and Rhys H. Williams. 2017. *Religion and Progressive Activism: New Stories about Faith and Politics*. New York City: New York University Press.

Braunstein, Ruth, Brad R. Fulton, and Richard L. Wood. 2014. "The Role of Bridging Cultural Practices in Racially and Socioeconomically Diverse Civic Organizations." *American Sociological Review* 79: 705–25.

Brenner, Philip S. 2014. "Testing the Veracity of Self-Reported Religious Practice in the Muslim World." *Social Forces* 92 (3): 1009–37.

Brooks, Clem, and Jeff Manza. 1999. *Social Cleavages and Political Change: Voter Alignments and U.S. Party Coalitions.* New York: Oxford University Press.

Brown, Kate Pride. 2016. "The *Prospectus* of Activism: Discerning and Delimiting Imagined Possibility." *Social Movement Studies* 15 (6): 547–60.

Bruce, Katherine McFarland. 2016. *Pride Parades: How a Parade Changed the World.* New York: New York University Press.

Buckley, William F., Jr. 1955. "Our Mission Statement." *National Review.* Retrieved March 8, 2017 (http://www.nationalreview.com/article/223549/our-mission -statement-william-f-buckley-jr).

Bunnage, Leslie A. 2014. "Social Movement Engagement over the Long Haul: Understanding Activist Retention." *Sociology Compass* 8 (4): 433–45.

Cable, Sherry, Edward J. Walsh, and Rex H. Warland. 1988. "Differential Paths to Political Activism: Comparison of Four Mobilization Processes after the Three Mile Island Accident." *Social Forces* 66 (4): 951–69.

Caress, Jordan. 2010, December 9. "After Forcing out Lisa Howe, Can Belmont Be Both a Progressive University and a Fundamentalist Scold?" *Nashville Scene.* Retrieved June 7, 2017 (http://www.nashvillescene.com/news/article/13036573 /after-forcing-out-lisa-howe-can-belmont-be-both-a-progressive-university -and-a-fundamentalist-scold).

Carpenter, Dale. 2012. *Flagrant Conduct: The Story of Lawrence v. Texas.* New York: W. W. Norton.

Catholic University. 2016. "Community Expectations Guide." Retrieved March 8, 2017 (http://deanofstudents.cua.edu/res/docs/Community-Standards-Guide -2016.pdf).

Cohn, Steven F., Steven E. Barkan, and William A. Halteman. 2003. "Dimensions of Participation in a Professional Social-Movement Organization." *Sociological Inquiry* 73 (3): 311–37.

Cohn, Steven F., Steven E. Barkan, and William H. Whitaker. 1993. "Activists against Hunger: Membership Characteristics of a National Social Movement Organization." *Sociological Forum* 8 (1): 113–31.

Cole, Brian E. 2014. "Student Activism within Christian College Cultures: A Symbolic Interactionist Perspective." *Christian Higher Education* 13 (5): 317–39.

Coley, Jonathan S. 2013. "Theorizing Issue Selection in Advocacy Organizations: An Analysis of Human Rights Activism around Darfur and the Congo, 1998– 2010." *Sociological Perspectives* 56 (2): 191–212.

———. 2014. "Social Movements and Bridge Building: Religious and Sexual Identity Conflicts." *Research in Social Movements, Conflicts, and Change* 37: 125–51.

———. 2015. "Narrative and Frame Alignment in Social Movements: Labor Problem Novels and the 1929 Gastonia Strike." *Social Movement Studies* 14 (1): 58–74.

———. 2017. "Reconciling Religion and LGBT Rights: Christian Universities, Theological Orientations, and LGBT Inclusion." *Social Currents* 4 (1): 87–106.

Coley, Jonathan S., Daniel B. Cornfield, Larry W. Isaac, and Dennis C. Dickerson. 2017. "The Career Consequences of the Nashville Civil Rights Movement:

A Qualitative Comparative Analysis." Presented at the Annual Meeting of the American Sociological Association, Montreal, QC.

Comer, Matt. 2007. "A Second Christian College Changes Anti-Gay Policy, after Visit from Equality Ride." *Interstate: Q.* Retrieved December 10, 2014 (http://interstateq.com/archives/2309/).

Cornfield, Daniel B. 2015. *Beyond the Beat: Musicians Building Community in Nashville.* Princeton, NJ: Princeton University Press.

Cornfield, Daniel B., Jonathan S. Coley, Larry W. Isaac, and Dennis C. Dickerson. 2018. "Occupational Activism and Race Desegregation at Work: Activist Careers after the Nonviolent Nashville Civil Rights Movement." *Research in the Sociology of Work* 32.

Corrigall-Brown, Catherine. 2012. *Patterns of Protest: Trajectories of Participation in Social Movements.* Stanford, CA: Stanford University Press.

Corrigall-Brown, Catherine, David A. Snow, Kelly Smith, and Theron Quist. 2009. "Explaining the Puzzle of Homeless Mobilization: An Examination of Differential Participation." *Sociological Perspectives* 52 (3): 309–35.

Craig, Shelley L., Ashley Austin, Mariam Rashidi, and Marc Adams. 2017. "Fighting for Survival: The Experiences of Lesbian, Gay, Bisexual, Transgender, and Questioning Students in Religious Colleges and Universities." *Journal of Gay & Lesbian Social Services* 29 (1): 1–24.

Creek, S. J. 2013. " 'Not Getting Any Because of Jesus': The Centrality of Desire Management to the Identity Work of Gay, Celibate Christians." *Symbolic Interaction* 36 (2): 119–36.

Crockett, Jason Lee, and Melinda D. Kane. 2012. "Mobilizing in Response to Threat: The Case of the Ex-Gay Movement." *Research in Social Movements, Conflicts, and Change* 33: 227–56.

Crossley, Alison Dahl. 2017. *Finding Feminism: Millennial Activists and the Unfinished Gender Revolution.* New York: New York University Press.

Cunningham, David. 2013. *Klansville, U.S.A.: The Rise and Fall of the Civil Rights-Era Ku Klux Klan.* New York: Oxford University Press.

Curran, Charles E. 2006. *Loyal Dissent: Memoir of a Catholic Theologian.* Washington, DC: Georgetown University Press.

Currie, Sean, Maralee Mayberry, and Tiffany Chenneville. 2012. "Destabilizing Anti-Gay Environments through Gay–Straight Alliances: Possibilities and Limitations through Shifting Discourses." *The Clearing House: A Journal of Educational Strategies, Issues, and Ideas* 85 (2): 56–60.

Davidson, Theresa C., and Carlos Garcia. 2014. "Welcoming the Stranger: Religion and Attitudes toward Social Justice for Immigrants in the U.S." *Journal of Religion & Society* 16 (1): 1–21.

Davis, Nancy J., and Robert V. Robinson. 2012. *Claiming Society for God: Religious Movements and Social Welfare.* Bloomington: Indiana University Press.

DeBernardo, Francis. 2012. "Was Cardinal George's Apology Enough? Catholic Students Don't Think So." *New Ways Ministries, Bonding 2.0.* Retrieved January 9, 2015 (https://newwaysministryblog.wordpress.com/2012/01/18/was-cardinal-georges-apology-enough-catholic-students-dont-think-so/).

Demerath, N. Jay, Gerald Marwell, and Michael T. Aiken. 1971. *Dynamics of Idealism: White Activists in a Black Movement*. San Francisco: Jossey-Bass.

D'Emilio, John. 1983. *Sexual Politics, Sexual Communities: The Making of a Homosexual Minority in the United States, 1940–1970*. Chicago: University of Chicago Press.

Dixon, Marc, and Vincent J. Roscigno. 2003. "Status, Networks, and Social Movement Participation: The Case of Striking Workers." *American Journal of Sociology* 108 (6): 1292–1327.

Dixon, Marc, Daniel Tope, and Nella Van Dyke. 2008. "'The University Works Because We Do': On the Determinants of Campus Labor Organizing in the 1990s." *Sociological Perspectives* 51 (2): 375–96.

Doan, Long, Annalise Loehr, and Lisa R. Miller. 2014. "Formal Rights and Informal Privileges for Same-Sex Couples: Evidence from a National Survey Experiment." *American Sociological Review* 79 (6): 1172–95.

Donadio, Rachel. 2013, July 29. "On Gay Priests, Pope Francis Asks, 'Who Am I to Judge?'" *New York Times*.

Dorius, Cassandra, and John D. McCarthy. 2011. "Understanding Activist Leadership Effort in the Movement Opposing Drinking and Driving." *Social Forces* 90 (2): 453–73.

Downton, James, and Paul Wehr. 1997. *The Persistent Activist: How Peace Commitment Develops and Survives*. Boulder, CO: Westview Press.

Earl, Jennifer. 2004. "The Cultural Consequences of Social Movements." In *The Blackwell Companion to Social Movements*, edited by David A. Snow, Sarah A. Soule, and Hanspeter Kriesi, 508–30. Malden, MA: Blackwell.

Edwards, Bob, and Melinda Kane. 2014. "Resource Mobilization and Social and Political Movements." In *Handbook of Political Citizenship and Social Movements*, edited by Hein-Anton van der Heijden, 205–32. Cheltenham, UK: Edward Elgar.

Eliasoph, Nina, and Paul Lichterman. 2003. "Culture in Interaction." *American Journal of Sociology* 108 (4): 735–94.

Ellingson, Stephen. 2016. *To Care for Creation: The Emergence of the Religious Environmental Movement*. Chicago: University of Chicago Press.

Erzen, Tanya. 2006. *Straight to Jesus: Sexual and Christian Conversions in the Ex-Gay Movement*. Berkeley: University of California Press.

Fain, Paul. 2017. "Title IX Enforcement and LGBT Students." *Inside Higher Ed*. Retrieved March 3, 2017 (https://www.insidehighered.com/news/2017/02/27/liberty-and-bob-jones-universities-may-run-afoul-obama-title-ix-protections-lgbt).

Faith in America. 2014. "Our Mission." Retrieved December 8, 2014 (http://www.faithinamerica.org/about-fia/our-mission/).

Farrell, Justin. 2011. "Environmental Activism and Moral Schemas: Cultural Components of Differential Participation." *Environment and Behavior* 45 (3): 399–423.

Fendrich, James M. 1993. *Ideal Citizens: The Legacy of the Civil Rights Movement*. Albany: State University of New York Press.

Fendrich, James M., and Alison T. Tarleau. 1973. "Marching to a Different Drummer: Occupational and Political Correlates of Former Student Activists." *Social Forces* 52 (2): 245–53.

Fernandez, Roberto M., and Doug McAdam. 1988. "Social Networks and Social Movements: Multiorganizational Fields and Recruitment to Mississippi Freedom Summer." *Sociological Forum* 3 (3): 357–82.

Fetner, Tina. 2008. *How the Religious Right Shaped Lesbian and Gay Activism.* Minneapolis: University of Minnesota Press.

Fetner, Tina, and Athena Elafros. 2015. "The GSA Difference: LGBTQ and Ally Experiences in High Schools with and without Gay–Straight Alliances." *Social Sciences* 4 (3): 563–81.

Fetner, Tina, Athena Elafros, Sandra Bortolin, and Coralee Dreschler. 2012. "Safe Spaces: Gay–Straight Alliances in High Schools." *Canadian Review of Sociology* 49 (2): 188–207.

Fetner, Tina, and Kristin Kush. 2008. "Gay–Straight Alliances in High Schools: Social Predictors of Early Adoption." *Youth & Society* 40 (1): 114–30.

Fine, Leigh E. 2012. "The Context of Creating Space: Assessing the Likelihood of College LGBT Center Presence." *Journal of College Student Development* 53 (2): 285–99.

Fisher, Dana R., and Paul-Brian McInerney. 2012. "The Limits of Networks in Social Movement Retention: On Canvassers and Their Careers." *Mobilization* 17 (2): 109–28.

Fuist, Todd Nicholas. 2017. "'It Just Always Seemed Like It Wasn't a Big Deal, yet I Know for Some People They Really Struggle with It': LGBT Religious Identities in Context." *Journal for the Scientific Study of Religion* 55 (4): 770–86. doi:10.1111/jssr.12291.

Fuist, Todd Nicholas, Laurie Cooper Stoll, and Fred Kniss. 2012. "Beyond the Liberal–Conservative Divide: Assessing the Relationship between Religious Denominations and Their Associated LGBT Organizations." *Qualitative Sociology* 35 (1): 65–87.

Gamson, William A. 1991. "Commitment and Agency in Social Movements." *Sociological Forum* 6 (1): 27–50.

Gecas, Viktor. 2000. "Value Identities, Self Motives, and Social Movements." In *Self, Identity, and Social Movements*, edited by Sheldon Stryker, Timothy J. Owens, and Robert W. White, 93–109. Minneapolis: University of Minnesota Press.

Ghaziani, Amin. 2014. *There Goes the Gayborhood?* Princeton, NJ: Princeton University Press.

Gitlin, Todd. 1987. *The Sixties: Years of Hope, Days of Rage.* New York: Bantam Books.

Giugni, Marco G. 2004. "Personal and Biographical Consequences." In *The Blackwell Companion to Social Movements*, edited by David A. Snow, Sarah A. Soule, and Hanspeter Kriesi, 489–507. Malden, MA: Blackwell.

Giugni, Marco, and Maria T. Grasso. 2016. "The Biographical Impact of Participation in Social Movement Activities: Beyond Highly Committed New Left Activism." In *The Consequences of Social Movements*, edited by Lorenzo Bosi, Marco Giugni, and Katrin Uba, 85–105. Cambridge: Cambridge University Press.

Goshen College. 2015. "Goshen College Board of Directors Updates Non-Discrimination Policy." Retrieved March 7, 2017 (https://www.goshen.edu/about/leadership/president/non-discrimination-policy-decision/).

Gould, Deborah B. 2009. *Moving Politics: Emotion and ACT UP's Fight Against AIDS.* Berkeley: University of California Press.

Gramsci, Antonio. 1971. *Selections from the Prison Notebooks.* Edited by Q. Hoare and G. N. Smith. New York: International Publishers.

Guhin, Jeffrey. 2014. "Religion as Site Rather than Religion as Category: On the Sociology of Religion's Export Problem." *Sociology of Religion* 75 (4): 579–593.

Hadaway, C. Kirk, Penny Long Marler, and Mark Chaves. 1993. "What the Polls Don't Show: A Closer Look at U.S. Church Attendance." *American Sociological Review* 58 (6): 741–52.

Han, Hahrie. 2009. *Moved to Action: Motivation, Participation, and Inequality in American Politics.* Stanford, CA: Stanford University Press.

Heaney, Michael T., and Fabio Rojas. 2015. *Party in the Street: The Antiwar Movement and the Democratic Party after 9/11.* New York: Cambridge University Press.

Heck, Nicholas C., A. Flentje, and Bryan N. Cochran. 2011. "Offsetting Risks: High School Gay-Straight Alliances and Lesbian, Gay, Bisexual, and Transgender (LGBT) Youth." *Social Psychology Quarterly* 26 (2): 161–74.

Heim, Kevin. 2010, December 6. "Sit-In Second of Planned Student Protests." *Belmont Vision.*

Hess, David J. 2016. *Undone Science: Social Movements, Mobilized Politics, and Industrial Transitions.* Cambridge, MA: MIT Press.

Hess, David J., and Jonathan S. Coley. 2014. "Wireless Smart Meters and Public Acceptance: The Environment, Limited Choices, and Precautionary Politics." *Public Understanding of Science* 23 (6): 688–702.

Hotchkiss, Sam. 2013. "Disputes between Christian Schools and LGBT Students: Should the Law Get Involved?" *UMKC Law Review* 81 (3): 701–24.

Human Rights Campaign. 2015. "Faith Positions." Retrieved December 9, 2014 (http://www.hrc.org/resources/entry/faith-positions).

Hunter, James Davison. 1992. *Culture Wars: The Struggle to Define America.* New York: Basic Books.

Integrity USA. 2011. "Frequently Asked Questions." Retrieved December 8, 2014 (http://www.integrityusa.org/archive/FAQs/index.htm).

Isaac, Larry. 2009. "Movements, Aesthetics, and Markets in Literary Change: Making the American Labor Problem Novel." *American Sociological Review* 74 (6): 938–65.

———. 2012. "Literary Activists and Battling Books: The Labor Problem Novel as Contentious Movement Medium." *Research in Social Movements, Conflicts, and Change* 33 (1): 17–49.

Isaac, Larry, and Lars Christiansen. 2002. "How the Civil Rights Movement Revitalized Labor Militancy." *American Sociological Review* 67 (5): 722–46.

Isaac, Larry W., Jonathan S. Coley, Daniel B. Cornfield, and Dennis C. Dickerson. 2016. "Preparation Pathways and Movement Participation: Insurgent Schooling and Nonviolent Direct Action in the Early Nashville Civil Rights Movement." *Mobilization* 21 (2): 155–76.

Isaac, Larry W., Daniel B. Cornfield, Dennis C. Dickerson, James M. Lawson, Jr., and Jonathan S. Coley. 2012. "Movement Schools and Dialogical Diffusion of

Nonviolent Praxis: Nashville Workshops in the Southern Civil Rights Movement." *Research in Social Movements, Conflicts, and Change* 34: 155–84.

Isaac, Larry, Elizabeth Mutran, and Sheldon Stryker. 1980. "Political Protest Orientations among Black and White Adults." *American Sociological Review* 45 (2): 191–213.

Jasper, James M. 1997. *The Art of Moral Protest: Culture, Biography, and Creativity in Social Movements.* Chicago: University of Chicago Press.

———. 2014. *Protest: A Cultural Introduction to Social Movements.* Malden, MA: Polity Press.

Jasper, James M., and Dorothy Nelkin. 1991. *The Animal Rights Crusade: The Growth of a Moral Protest.* New York: The Free Press.

Jasper, James M., and Jane D. Poulsen. 1995. "Recruiting Strangers and Friends: Moral Shocks and Social Networks in Animal Rights and Anti-Nuclear Protests." *Social Problems* 42 (4): 493–512.

Kane, Melinda D. 2013a. "Finding 'Safe' Campuses: Predicting the Presence of LGBT Student Groups at North Carolina Colleges and Universities." *Journal of Homosexuality* 60 (6): 828–52.

———. 2013b. "LGBT Religious Activism: Predicting State Variations in the Number of Metropolitan Community Churches, 1974–2000." *Sociological Forum* 28 (1): 135–58.

Kaplan, Judy, and Linn Shapiro. 1998. *Red Diapers: Growing up in the Communist Left.* Urbana Champaign: University of Illinois Press.

Kelner, Shaul. 2008. "Ritualized Protest and Redemptive Politics: Cultural Consequences of the American Mobilization to Free Soviet Jewry." *Jewish Social Studies* 14 (3): 1–37.

Kimport, Katrina. 2013. *Queering Marriage: Challenging Family Formation in the United States.* New Brunswick, NJ: Rutgers University Press.

Klandermans, Bert. 1997. *The Social Psychology of Protest.* Cambridge, MA: Wiley-Blackwell.

Klandermans, Bert, and Marga De Weerd. 2000. "Group Identification and Political Protest." 2000. In *Self, Identity, and Social Movements,* edited by Sheldon Stryker, Timothy Joseph Owens, and Robert W. White, 68–90. Minneapolis: University of Minnesota Press.

Klandermans, Bert, and Dirk Oegema. 1987. "Potentials, Networks, Motivations, and Barriers: Steps towards Participation in Social Movements." *American Sociological Review* 52 (4): 519–31.

Klandermans, Bert, Jose Manuel Sabucedo, Mauro Rodriguez, and Marga De Weerd. 2002. "Identity Processes in Collective Action Participation: Farmers' Identity and Farmers' Protest in the Netherlands and Spain." *Political Psychology* 23 (2): 235–51.

Klatch, Rebecca. 1999. *A Generation Divided: The New Left, the New Right, and the 1960s.* Berkeley: University of California Press.

Kniss, Fred. 2003. "Mapping the Moral Order: Depicting the Terrain of Religious Conflict and Change." In *Handbook of the Sociology of Religion,* edited by Michele Dillon, 331–47. New York: Cambridge University Press.

Knoke, David. 1981. "Commitment and Detachment in Voluntary Associations." *American Sociological Review* 46 (2): 141–58.

Kubicki, Paul. 2014, February 25. "Loyola Marriage Policy Is Unjust." *Loyola Phoenix*. Retrieved January 9, 2015 (www.loyolaphoenix.com/loyola-marriage -policy-unjust).

Kucinskas, Jaime. 2014. "The Unobtrusive Tactics of Religious Movements." *Sociology of Religion* 75 (4): 537–50.

Kwon, Lillian. 2009. "ELCA Opens Ordination to Noncelibate Homosexuals." *Christian Post*. Retrieved December 10, 2014 (http://www.christianpost.com /news/elca-opens-ordination-to-noncelibate-homosexuals-40439/).

———. 2010. "PCUSA Assembly OKs Lifting Gay Ordination Ban." *Christian Post*. Retrieved December 10, 2014 (http://www.christianpost.com/news/pcusa -assembly-oks-removing-gay-ordination-ban-45837/).

———. 2014. "PCUSA Votes to Allow Clergy to Marry Same-Sex Couples." *Christian Post*. Retrieved December 10, 2014 (http://www.christianpost.com /news/pcusa-votes-to-allow-clergy-to-marry-same-sex-couples-approves -redefining-marriage-121874/).

Licata, Salvatore J. 1981. "The Homosexual Rights Movement in the United States: A Traditionally Overlooked Area of American History." *Journal of Homosexuality* 6 (1): 161–89.

Linden, Annette, and Bert Klandermans. 2007. "Revolutionaries, Wanderers, Converts, and Compliants: Life Histories of Extreme Right Activists." *Journal of Contemporary Ethnography* 36 (2): 184–201.

Lofland, John. 1985. *Protest: Studies of Collective Behavior and Social Movements*. New York: Routledge.

Loseke, Donileen R., and James C. Cavendish. 2001. "Producing Institutional Selves: Rhetorically Constructing the Dignity of Sexually Marginalized Catholics." *Social Psychology Quarterly* 64 (4): 347–62.

Mai, Quan D. 2016. "All the Labor Problems Fit to Print: The *New York Times* and the Cultural Production of the U.S. 'Labor Problem,' 1870–1932." *Labor History* 57 (2): 141–69.

Mannheim, Karl. (1928) 1952. "The Problem of Generations." In *Essays on the Sociology of Knowledge*, edited by Paul Kecskemeti, 276–322. New York: Routledge.

Mansbridge, Jane. 2013. "Everyday Activism." In *The Wiley-Blackwell Encyclopedia of Social and Political Movements*, edited by David Snow, Donatella Della Porta, Bert Klandermans, and Doug McAdam, 437–39. London: Wiley-Blackwell.

Martinez, Jessica. 2013. "Disciples of Christ Church Votes to Affirm Homo-sexuality, Transgenderism; Allows Openly Gay Leaders." *Christian Post*. Retrieved December 10, 2014 (http://www.christianpost.com/news/disciples-of-christ -church-votes-to-affirm-homosexuality-transgenderism-allows-openly-gay -leaders-100495/).

Marx, Gary T. 1967. "Religion: Opiate or Inspiration of Civil Rights Militancy among Negroes?" *American Sociological Review* 32 (1): 64–72.

Marx, Robert A., and Heather Hensman Kettrey. 2016. "Gay–Straight Alliances Are Associated with Lower Levels of School-Based Victimization of LGBTQ+ Youth:

A Systematic Review and Meta-Analysis." *Journal of Youth and Adolescence* 45 (7): 1269–82.

Masci, David. 2008. "An Overview of the Same-Sex Marriage Debate." *Pew Research Center*. Retrieved November 13, 2014 (http://www.pewresearch.org/2008/04/01/an-overview-of-the-samesex-marriage-debate/).

Mayberry, Maralee. 2006. "Identity Work and LGBT Youth: The Story of a Salt Lake City Gay–Straight Alliance." *Journal of Gay and Lesbian Issues in Education* 4 (1): 13–32.

———. 2013a. "Challenging the Sounds of Silence: A Qualitative Study of Gay–Straight Alliances and School Reform Efforts." *Education and Urban Society* 45 (4): 307–39.

———. 2013b. "Gay–Straight Alliances: Youth Empowerment and Working toward Reducing Stigma of LGBT Youth." *Humanity & Society* 37 (1): 35–54.

McAdam, Doug. 1982. *Political Process and the Development of Black Insurgency, 1930–1970*. Chicago: University of Chicago Press.

———. 1986. "Recruitment to High-Risk Activism: The Case of Freedom Summer." *American Journal of Sociology* 92 (1): 64–90.

———. 1988. *Freedom Summer*. Oxford: Oxford University Press.

———. 1989. "The Biographical Consequences of Activism." *American Sociological Review* 54 (5): 744–60.

———. 1997. "Conceptual Origins, Current Problems, Future Directions." In *Comparative Perspectives on Social Movements: Political Opportunities, Mobilizing Structures, and Cultural Framings*, edited by Doug McAdam, John D. McCarthy, and Mayer N. Zald, 23–40. Cambridge: Cambridge University Press.

———. 1999. "The Biographical Impact of Activism." In *How Movements Matter*, edited by Marcio Giugni, Doug McAdam, and Charles Tilly, 119–46. Minneapolis: University of Minnesota Press.

McAdam, Doug, and Hilary Boudet. 2012. *Putting Social Movements in Their Place: Explaining Opposition to Energy Projects in the United States, 2000–2005*. New York: Cambridge University Press.

McAdam, Doug, and Ronnelle Paulsen. 1993. "Specifying the Relationship between Social Ties and Activism." *American Journal of Sociology* 99 (3): 640–67.

McAdam, Doug, Robert J. Sampson, Simon Weffer, and Heather MacIndoe. 2005. " 'There Will Be Fighting in the Streets': The Distorting Lens of Social Movement Theory." *Mobilization: An International Journal* 10 (1): 1–18.

McCammon, Holly J., and Allison R. McGrath. 2015. "Litigating Change? Social Movements and the Court System." *Sociology Compass* 9 (2): 128–39.

McCammon, Holly J., Allison R. McGrath, Ashley Dixon, and Megan Robinson. 2016. "Targeting Culture: Feminist Legal Activists and Critical Community Tactics." *Research in Social Movements, Conflicts, and Change* 41: 243–78.

McCarthy, John D., and Mayer N. Zald. 1977. "Resource Mobilization and Social Movements: A Partial Theory." *American Journal of Sociology* 82 (6): 1212–41.

McEntarfer, Heather Killelea. 2011. " 'Not Going Away': Approaches Used by Students, Faculty, and Staff Members to Create Gay–Straight Alliances at Three Religiously Affiliated Universities." *Journal of LGBT Youth* 8 (4): 309–31.

McPherson, Miller, Lynn Smith-Lovin, and James M. Cook. 2001. "Birds of a Feather: Homophily in Social Networks." *Annual Review of Sociology* 27: 415–44.

McVeigh, Rory, and David Sikkink. 2001. "God, Politics, and Protest: Religious Beliefs and the Legitimation of Contentious Tactics." *Social Forces* 79 (4): 1425–58.

Meyer, David S. 2004. "Protest and Political Opportunities." *Annual Review of Sociology* 30: 125–45.

Meyer, Doug. 2015. *Violence against Queer People: Race, Class, Gender, and the Persistence of Anti-LGBT Discrimination.* New Brunswick, NJ: Rutgers University Press.

Miceli, Melinda. 2005. *Standing out, Standing Together: The Social and Political Impact of Gay–Straight Alliances.* New York: Routledge.

Mills, C. Wright. (1959) 2000. *The Sociological Imagination.* Reprint, New York: Oxford University Press.

Mirola, William A. 2015. *Redeeming Time: Protestantism and Chicago's Eight-Hour Movement, 1866–1912.* Urbana: University of Illinois Press.

Mitchell, Peter. 2015. *The Coup at Catholic University: The 1968 Revolution in American Catholic Education.* San Francisco: Ignatius Press.

Moon, Dawne. 2004. *God, Sex, and Politics: Homosexuality and Everyday Theologies.* Chicago: University of Chicago Press.

Morris, Aldon. 1986. *The Origins of the Civil Rights Movement: Black Communities Organizing for Change.* New York: The Free Press.

Morrison, Daniel R., and Larry W. Isaac. 2012. "Insurgent Images: Genre Selection and Visual Amplification in IWW Cartoon Art." *Social Movement Studies* 11 (1): 61–78.

Munson, Ziad W. 2008. *The Making of Pro-Life Activists: How Social Movement Mobilization Works.* Chicago: University of Chicago Press.

———. 2010. "Mobilizing on Campus: Conservative Movements and Today's College Students." *Sociological Forum* 25 (4): 769–86.

Nashville Scene Staff. 2011, October 6. "Best of Nashville 2011: Media & Politics Writers' Choice." *Nashville Scene.*

National Public Radio. 2015. "GOP Pushes First Amendment Defense Act after Same-Sex Marriage Ruling." Retrieved March 3, 2017 (http://www.npr.org/2015/07/09/421528477/gop-pushes-first-amendment-defense-act-after-same-sex-marriage-ruling).

Nepstad, Sharon Erickson. 2004a. *Convictions of the Soul: Religion, Culture, and Agency in the Central America Solidarity Movement.* New York: Oxford University Press.

———. 2004b. "Persistent Resistance: Commitment and Continuity in the Plowshares Movement." *Social Problems* 51 (1): 43–60.

———. 2008. *Religion and War Resistance in the Plowshares Movement.* New York: Cambridge University Press.

Nepstad, Sharon Erickson, and Christian Smith. 1999. "Rethinking Recruitment to High-Risk/Cost Activism: The Case of Nicaragua Exchange." *Mobilization* 4 (1): 25–40.

Office of Civil Rights. 2016. "Religious Exemptions List." *U.S. Department of Education.* Retrieved June 7, 2016 (http://www2.ed.gov/about/offices/list/ocr/docs/t9-rel-exempt/z-index-links-list-2009-2016.html).

Open and Affirming Coalition. 2014. "History." Retrieved December 9, 2014 (http://openandaffirming.org/about/history/).

Palacios, Joseph M. 2007. *The Catholic Social Imagination: Activism and the Just Society in Mexico and the United States.* Chicago: University of Chicago Press.

Pascoe, C. J. 2012. *Dude, You're a Fag: Masculinity and Sexuality in High School.* 2nd ed. Berkeley: University of California Press.

Passy, Florence, and Marco Giugni. 2000. "Life-Spheres, Networks, and Sustained Participation in Social Movements: A Phenomenological Approach to Political Commitment." *Sociological Forum* 15 (1): 117–44.

Payne, Ed. 2013. "Group Apologizes to Gay Community, Shuts down 'Cure' Ministry." *CNN.* Retrieved December 10, 2014 (http://www.cnn.com/2013/06/20/us/exodus-international-shutdown/).

Perry, Samuel L. 2017. *Growing God's Family: The Global Orphan Care Movement and the Limits of Evangelical Activism.* New York: New York University Press.

Pew Research Center. 2015. "Same-Sex Marriage, State by State." Retrieved August 2, 2016 (http://www.pewforum.org/2015/06/26/same-sex-marriage-state-by-state/).

Pfund, Emily. 2014, May 19. "Goshen College Staff Member Comes out as Lesbian, Resigns Library Job." *Elkhart Truth.*

Pitt, Richard N. 2010a. "'Killing the Messenger': Religious Black Gay Men's Neutralization of Anti-Gay Religious Messages." *Journal for the Scientific Study of Religion* 49 (1): 56–72.

———. 2010b. "'Still Looking for My Jonathan': Gay Black Men's Management of Religious and Sexual Identity Conflicts." *Journal of Homosexuality* 57 (1): 39–53.

Piven, Frances Fox, and Richard A. Cloward. 1977. *Poor People's Movements: Why They Succeed, How They Fail.* New York: Vintage Books.

Polletta, Francesca. 1997. "Culture and Its Discontents: Recent Theorizing on Culture and Protest." *Sociological Inquiry* 67 (4): 431–50.

———. 2004. "Culture in and outside Institutions." *Research in Social Movements, Conflicts, and Change* 25 (1): 161–83.

———. 2008. "Culture and Movements." *Annals of the American Academy of Political and Social Science* 619 (1): 78–96.

Polletta, Francesca, and James M. Jasper. 2001. "Collective Identity and Social Movements." *Annual Review of Sociology* 27: 283–305.

Poteat, V. Paul, Jillian R. Scheer, Robert A. Marx, Jerel P. Calzo, and Hirokazu Yoshikawa. 2015. "Gay–Straight Alliances Vary on Dimensions of Youth Socializing and Advocacy: Factors Accounting for Individual and Setting-Level Differences." *American Journal of Community Psychology* 55 (3–4): 422–32.

Poteat, V. Paul, Katerina O. Sinclair, Craig D. DiGiovanni, Brian W. Koenig, and Stephen T. Russell. 2013. "Gay–Straight Alliances Are Associated with Student Health: A Multischool Comparison of LGBTQ and Heterosexual Youth." *Journal of Research on Adolescence* 23 (2): 319–30.

Poulson, Stephen C., Thomas N. Ratliff, and Emily Dollieslager. 2013. "You Have to Fight! For Your Right! To Party! Structure, Culture, and Mobilization in a University Party Riot." *Research in Social Movements, Conflicts, and Change* 36: 269–305.

Powell, Rachel. 2011. "Frames and Narratives as Tools for Recruiting and Sustaining Group Members: The Soulforce Equality Ride as a Social Movement Organization." *Sociological Inquiry* 81 (4): 454–76.

Public Religion Research Institute. 2014. "A Shifting Landscape: A Decade of Change in American Attitudes about Same-Sex Marriage and LGBT issues." Retrieved November 16, 2014 (http://publicreligion.org/research/2014/02/2014 -lgbt-survey/).

Pullella, Philip. 2016, June 27. "Pope Says Church Should Ask Forgiveness from Gays for Past Treatment." *Reuters*. Retrieved July 8, 2016 (http://in.reuters.com /article/pope-church-idINKCN0ZD07O).

Radojcic, Natasha. 2016. "Building a Dignified Identity: An Ethnographic Case Study of LGBT Catholics." *Journal of Homosexuality* 63 (10): 1297–1313.

Rankin, Susan R. 2003. *Campus Climate for Gay, Lesbian, and Transgender People: A National Perspective.* New York: National Gay and Lesbian Task Force Policy Institute.

Reed, Jean-Pierre, Rhys H. Williams, and Kathryn B. Ward. 2015. "Civil Religious Contention in Cairo, Illinois: Priestly and Prophetic Ideologies in a 'Northern' Civil Rights Struggle." *Theory and Society* 45 (1): 25–55.

Reger, Jo. 2012. *Everywhere and Nowhere: Contemporary Feminism in the United States.* New York: Oxford University Press.

Reger, Jo, Daniel J. Myers, and Rachel L. Einwohner, eds. 2008. *Identity Work in Social Movements.* Minneapolis: University of Minnesota Press.

Reichard, David A. 2010. "'We Can't Hide and They Are Wrong': The Society for Homosexual Freedom and the Struggle for Recognition at Sacramento State College, 1969–1971." *Law and History Review* 28 (3): 629–74.

Renn, Kristen A. 2007. "LGBT Student Leaders and Queer Activists: Identities of Lesbian, Gay, Bisexual, Transgender, and Queer Identified College Student Leaders and Activists." *Journal of College Student Development* 48 (3): 311–30.

Renn, Kristen A., and Brent Bilodeau. 2005. "Queer Student Leaders: An Exploratory Case Study of Identity Development and LGBT Student Involvement at a Midwestern Research University." *Journal of Gay & Lesbian Issues in Education* 2 (4): 49–71.

Ringenberg, William C. 2006. *The Christian College: A History of Protestant Higher Education in America.* Grand Rapids, MI: Baker Academic.

Robertson, Campbell. 2010, December 17. "Lesbian Coach's Exit from Belmont U. Has Nashville Talking." *New York Times.*

Rodriguez, Eric M. 2010. "At the Intersection of Church and Gay: A Review of the Psychological Research on Gay and Lesbian Christians." *Journal of Homosexuality* 57 (1): 5–38.

Rohlinger, Deana A. 2015. *Abortion Politics, Mass Media, and Social Movements in America.* New York: Cambridge University Press.

Rohlinger, Deana A., and Leslie A. Bunnage. 2015. "Connecting People to Politics over Time? Internet Communication Technology and Retention in MoveOn.org and the Florida Tea Party Movement." *Information, Communication, & Society* 18 (5): 539–52.

Roscigno, Vincent J., and William Danaher. 2001. "Media and Mobilization: The Case of Radio and Southern Textile Worker Insurgency, 1929 to 1934." *American Sociological Review* 66 (1): 21–48.

Rosenthal, Rob, and Richard Flacks. 2012. *Playing for Change: Music and Musicians in the Service of Social Movements*. New York: Paradigm Publishers.

Roth, Benita. 2003. *Separate Roads to Feminism: Black, Chicana, and White Feminist Movements in America's Second Wave*. New York: Cambridge University Press.

———. 2017. *The Life and Death of ACT UP/LA: Anti-AIDS Activism in Los Angeles from the 1980s to the 2000s*. New York: Cambridge University Press.

Rupp, Leila J., and Verta Taylor. 1987. *Survival in the Doldrums: The American Women's Rights Movement, 1945 to 1960s*. New York: Oxford University Press.

Santoro, Wayne A., and Gail M. McGuire. 1997. "Social Movement Insiders: The Impact of Institutional Activists on Affirmative Action and Comparable Worth Policies." *Social Problems* 44 (4): 503–19.

Schnabel, Landon. 2016. "Gender and Homosexuality Attitudes across Religious Groups from the 1970s to 2014: Similarity, Distinction, and Adaptation." *Social Science Research* 55 (1): 31–47.

Schussman, Alan, and Sarah Soule. 2005. "Process and Protest: Accounting for Individual Protest Participation." *Social Forces* 84 (2): 1083–1108.

Selden, Abby. 2009, October 28. "Bruin Guide No Longer Specifically Addresses 'Homosexual Behavior.'" *Belmont Vision*. Retrieved April 25, 2016 (http://belmontvision.com/2009/10/bruin-guide-no-longer-specifically-addresses-homosexual-behavior/).

Shepherd, Frederick M., ed. 2009. *Christianity and Human Rights: Christians and the Struggle for Global Justice*. Lanham, MD: Lexington Books.

Sherkat, Darren E. 2016, August 11. "Intersecting Identities and Support for Same-Sex Marriage in the United States." *Social Currents*. doi:10.1177/2329496516663221.

Sherkat, Darren E., and T. Jean Blocker. 1997. "Explaining the Political and Personal Consequences of Protest." *Social Forces* 75 (3): 1049–70.

Simi, Pete, Robert Futrell, and Bryan F. Bubolz. 2016. "Parenting as Activism: Identity Alignment and Activist Persistence in the White Power Movement." *Sociological Quarterly* 57 (3): 491–519.

Simon, Bernd, and Bert Klandermans. 2001. "Politicized Collective Identity: A Social Psychological Analysis." *American Psychologist* 56 (4): 319–31.

Smietana, Bob. 2010, December 5. "Belmont's Morality Policy Not Unique." *Tennessean*.

Smith, Christian. 1991. *The Emergence of Liberation Theology: Radical Religion and Social Movement Theory*. Chicago: University of Chicago Press.

———. 1996. *Disruptive Religion: The Force of Faith in Social Movement Activism*. New York: Routledge.

Snarr, C. Melissa. 2011. *All You That Labor: Religion and Ethics in the Living Wage Movement*. New York: New York University Press.

Snow, David A., and Doug McAdam. 2000. "Identity Work Processes in the Context of Social Movements: Clarifying the Identity/Movement Nexus." In *Self, Identity, and Social Movements*, edited by Sheldon Stryker, Timothy Joseph Owens, and Robert W. White, 41–67. Minneapolis: University of Minnesota Press.

Snow, David A., and Dana M. Moss. 2014. "Protest on the Fly: Toward a Theory of Spontaneity in the Dynamics of Protest and Social Movements." *American Sociological Review* 79 (6): 1122–43.

Snow, David A., E. Burke Rochford Jr., Steven K. Worden, and Robert D. Benford. 1986. "Frame Alignment Processes, Micromobilization, and Movement Participation." *American Sociological Review* 51 (4): 464–81.

Snow, David A., Sarah A. Soule, and Hanspeter Kriesi. 2004. "Mapping the Terrain." In *The Blackwell Companion to Social Movements*, edited by David A. Snow, Sarah A. Soule, and Hanspeter Kriesi, 3–16. Malden, MA: Wiley-Blackwell.

Snow, David A., Louis A. Zurcher, Jr., and Sheldon Ekland-Olson. 1980. "Social Networks and Social Movements: A Microstructural Approach to Differential Recruitment." *American Sociological Review* 45 (5): 787–801.

Spencer, Leland G., and Joshua Trey Barnett. 2013. "Touring Homophobia: Understanding the Soulforce Equality Ride as a Toxic Tour." *Southern Communication Journal* 78 (1): 25–41.

Staggenborg, Suzanne. 1998. "Social Movement Communities and Cycles of Protest: The Emergence and Maintenance of a Local Women's Movement." *Social Problems* 45 (2): 180–204.

Steensland, Brian, and Philip Goff, eds. 2013. *The New Evangelical Social Engagement*. New York: Oxford University Press.

Stone, Amy L. 2016. "The Impact of Anti-Gay Politics on the LGBTQ Movement." *Sociology Compass* 10 (6): 459–467.

Stryker, Sheldon. 2000. "Identity Competition: Key to Differential Social Movement Participation?" In *Self, Identity, and Social Movements*, edited by Sheldon Stryker, Timothy J. Owens, and Robert W. White, 21–40. Minneapolis: University of Minnesota Press.

Sue, Derald Wing. 2010. *Microaggressions in Everyday Life: Race, Gender, and Sexual Orientation*. New York: John Wiley & Sons.

Suh, Chan. 2014. "Differential Participation in Professional Activism: The Case of the Guantanamo Habeas Lawyers." *Mobilization* 19 (3): 287–307.

Sumerau, J. E., Ryan T. Cragun, and Lain A. B. Mathers. 2016. "'I Found God in the Glory Hole': The Moral Career of a Gay Christian." *Sociological Inquiry* 86 (4): 618–40. doi:10.1111/soin.12134.

Swank, Eric, and Breanne Fahs. 2012. "Resources, Social Networks, and Collective Action Frames of College Students Who Join the Gay and Lesbian Rights Movement." *Journal of Homosexuality* 59 (1): 67–89.

Tarrow, Sidney G. 2011. *Power in Movement: Social Movements and Contentious Politics*. 3rd ed. New York: Cambridge University Press.

Taylor, Verta, Katrina Kimport, and Nella Van Dyke. 2009. "Culture and Mobilization: Tactical Repertoires, Same-Sex Weddings, and the Impact on Gay Activism." *American Sociological Review* 74 (6): 865–90.

Taylor, Verta, and N. C. Raeburn. 1995. "Identity Politics as High-Risk Activism: Career Consequences for Lesbian, Gay, and Bisexual Sociologists." *Social Problems* 42 (2): 252–73.

Taylor, Verta, Leila J. Rupp, and Joshua Gamson. 2004. "Performing Protest: Drag Shows as Tactical Repertoire of the Gay and Lesbian Movement." *Research in Social Movements, Conflicts, and Change* 25: 105–38.

Taylor, Verta, and Nancy E. Whittier. 1992. "Collective Identity in Social Movement Communities: Lesbian Feminist Mobilization." In *Frontiers in Social Movement Theory*, edited by Aldon D. Morris and C. M. Mueller, 104–29. New Haven, CT: Yale University Press.

Terriquez, Veronica. 2015. "Training Young Activists: Grassroots Organizing and Youths' Civic and Political Trajectories." *Sociological Perspectives* 58 (2): 223–42.

Tilly, Charles. 1978. *From Mobilization to Revolution*. New York: Random House.

Toomey, Russell B, and Stephen T. Russell. 2013. "Gay–Straight Alliances, Social Justice Involvement, and School Victimization of Lesbian, Gay, Bisexual, and Queer Youth: Implications for School Well-Being and Plans to Vote." *Youth & Society* 45 (4): 500–522.

———. 2016. "The Role of Sexual Orientation in School-Based Victimization: A Meta-Analysis." *Youth & Society* 48 (2): 176–201.

Valocchi, Stephen. 2001. "Individual Identities, Collective Identities, and Organizational Structure: The Relationship of the Political Left and Gay Liberation in the United States." *Sociological Perspectives* 44 (4): 445–467.

———. 2013. "Activism as a Career, Calling, and Way of Life." *Journal of Contemporary Ethnography* 42 (2): 169–200.

Van Dyke, Nella. 1998. "Hotbeds of Activism: Locations of Student Protest." *Social Problems* 45 (2): 205–20.

———. 2003. "Crossing Movement Boundaries: Factors that Facilitate Coalition Protest by American College Students, 1930–1990." *Social Problems* 50 (2): 226–50.

Van Dyke, Nella, and Marc Dixon. 2013. "Activist Human Capital: Skills Acquisition and the Development of Commitment to Social Movement Activism." *Mobilization* 18 (2): 197–214.

Van Dyke, Nella, Doug McAdam, and Brenda Wilhelm. 2000. "Gender Outcomes: Gender Differences in the Biographical Consequences of Activism." *Mobilization* 5 (2): 161–77.

Van Dyke, Nella, Sarah A. Soule, and Verta A. Taylor. 2004. "The Targets of Social Movements: Beyond a Focus on the State." *Research in Social Movements, Conflicts, and Change* 25: 27–51.

Vespone, Brianna M. 2016. "Integrating Identities: Facilitating a Support Group for LGBTQ Students on a Christian Campus." *Christian Higher Education* 15 (4): 215–229.

Vestergren, Sara, John Drury, and Eva Hammar Chiriac. 2017. "The Biographical Consequences of Protest and Activism: A Systematic Review and a New Typology." *Social Movement Studies* 16 (2): 203–21.

Vines, Matthew. 2013. "The Reformation Project: Training Christians to Eradicate Homophobia from the Church." *Huffington Post*. Retrieved December 11, 2014 (http://www.huffingtonpost.com/matthew-vines/the-reformation-project-christians-homophobia_b_2790039.html).

Viterna, Jocelyn. 2006. "Pulled, Pushed, and Persuaded: Explaining Women's Mobilization into the Salvadoran Guerilla Army." *American Journal of Sociology* 112 (1): 1–45.

———. 2013. *Women in War: The Micro-Processes of Mobilization in El Salvador*. New York: Oxford University Press.

Waidzunas, Tom. 2015. *The Straight Line: How the Fringe Science of Ex-Gay Therapy Reoriented Sexuality*. Minneapolis: University of Minnesota Press.

Walls, N. Eugene, Sarah B. Kane, and Hope Wisneski. 2010. "Gay–Straight Alliances and School Experiences of Sexual Minority Youth." *Youth & Society* 41 (3): 307–32.

Weber, Max. (1905) 2002. *The Protestant Ethic and the Spirit of Capitalism*. Reprint, New York: Penguin Books.

Westhues, Kenneth. 1976. "The Church in Opposition." *Sociological Analysis* 37 (4): 299–314.

Whalen, Jack, and Richard Flacks. 1989. *Beyond the Barricades: The Sixties Generation Grows Up*. Philadelphia: Temple University Press.

White, Heather. 2015. *Reforming Sodom: Protestants and the Rise of Gay Rights*. Chapel Hill: University of North Carolina Press.

White, Robert W. 2010. "Structural Identity Theory and the Post-Recruitment Activism of Irish Republicans: Persistence, Disengagement, Splits, and Dissidents in Social Movement Organizations." *Social Problems* 57 (3): 341–70.

Whitehead, Andrew L. 2013. "Religious Organizations and Homosexuality: The Acceptance of Gays and Lesbians in American Congregations." *Review of Religious Research* 55 (2): 297–317.

Whitley, Bernard E., Jr. 2009. "Religiosity and Attitudes toward Lesbians and Gay Men: A Meta-Analysis." *International Journal for the Psychology of Religion* 19 (1): 21–38.

Whittier, Nancy. 1995. *Feminist Generations: The Persistence of the Radical Women's Movement*. Philadelphia: Temple University Press.

———. 1997. "Political Generations, Micro-Cohorts, and the Transformation of Social Movements." *American Sociological Review* 62 (5): 760–78.

———. 2011. *The Politics of Child Sex Abuse: Emotion, Social Movements, and the State*. New York: Oxford University Press.

———. 2016. "Aggregate-Level Biographical Outcomes for Gay and Lesbian Movements." In *The Consequences of Social Movements*, edited by Lorenzo Bosi, Marco Giugni, and Katrin Uba, 130–56. Cambridge: University of Cambridge Press.

Wilcox, Clyde. 1991. *God's Warriors: The Christian Right in Twentieth-Century America*. Baltimore, MD: Johns Hopkins University Press.

Wilcox, Melissa M. 2001. "Of Markets and Missions: The Early History of the Universal Fellowship of Metropolitan Community Churches." *Religion and American Culture* 11 (1): 83–108.

———. 2003. *Coming Out in Christianity: Religion, Identity, and Community.* Bloomington: Indiana University Press.

———. 2009. *Queer Women and Religious Individualism.* Bloomington: Indiana University Press.

Wilhelm, Brenda. 1998. "Changes in Cohabitation across Cohorts: The Influence of Political Activism." *Social Forces* 77 (1): 289–310.

Williams, Daniel K. 2010. *God's Own Party: The Making of the Christian Right.* New York: Oxford University Press.

Williams, Rhys H. 2002. "From the 'Beloved Community' to 'Family Values': Religious Language, Symbolic Repertoires, and Democratic Cultures." In *Social Movements: Identity, Culture, and the State*, edited by David Meyer, Nancy Whittier, and Belinda Robnett, 247–65. New York: Oxford University Press.

Williams, Rhys H., and Jeffrey Blackburn. 1996. "Many Are Called but Few Obey: Ideological Commitment and Activism in Operation Rescue." In *Disruptive Religion: The Force of Faith in Social Movement Activism*, edited by Christian Smith, 167–88. New York: Routledge.

Williams, Stacy J. 2016. "Hiding Spinach in the Brownies: Frame Alignment in Suffrage Community Cookbooks, 1886–1916." *Social Movement Studies* 15 (2): 146–63.

Wiltfang, Gregory L., and Doug McAdam. 1991. "The Costs and Risks of Social Activism: A Study of Sanctuary Movement Activism." *Social Forces* 69 (4): 987–1010.

Winder, Terrell J. A. 2015. "'Shouting It Out': Religion and the Development of Black Gay Identities." *Qualitative Sociology* 38 (4): 375–94.

Woehrle, Lynne M, ed. 2014. *Intersectionality and Social Change.* Bingley, UK: Emerald Group Publishing.

Wolff, Joshua R., and Heather L. Himes. 2010. "Purposeful Exclusion of Sexual Minority Youth in Christian Higher Education: The Implications of Discrimination." *Christian Higher Education* 9 (5): 439–60.

Wolff, Joshua R., Heather L. Himes, Ellen Miller Kwon, and Richard A. Bollinger. 2012. "Evangelical Christian College Students and Attitudes toward Gay Rights: A California University Sample." *Journal of LGBT Youth* 9 (3): 200–224.

Wolff, Joshua R., Heather L. Himes, Sabrina D. Soares, and Ellen Miller Kwom. 2016. "Sexual Minority Students in Non-Affirming Religious Higher Education: Mental Health, Outness, and Identity." *Psychology of Sexual Orientation and Gender Diversity* 3 (2): 201–12.

Wolkomir, Michelle. 2006. *Be Not Deceived: The Sacred and Sexual Struggles of Gay and Ex-Gay Christian Men.* New Brunswick, NJ: Rutgers University Press.

Wood, Richard L. 2002. *Faith in Action: Religion, Race, and Democratic Organizing in America.* Chicago: University of Chicago Press.

Wood, Richard L., and Brad R. Fulton. 2015. *A Shared Future: Faith-Based Organizing for Racial Equity and Ethical Democracy.* Chicago: University of Chicago Press.

Woodford, Michael R., Denise Levy, and N. Eugene Walls. 2013. "Sexual Prejudice among Christian College Students, Denominational Teachings, and Personal Religious Beliefs." *Review of Religious Research* 55 (1): 105–30.

Wuthnow, Robert. 1988. *The Restructuring of American Religion: Society and Faith since World War II.* Princeton, NJ: Princeton University Press.

——. 1989. *The Struggle for America's Soul: Evangelicals, Liberals, and Secularism.* Grand Rapids, MI: Eerdmans.

Wuthnow, Robert, and John H. Evans. 2002. *The Quiet Hand of God: Faith-Based Activism and the Public Role of Mainline Protestantism.* Berkeley: University of California Press.

Xu, Xiaohong. 2013. "Belonging before Believing: Group Ethos and Bloc Recruitment in the Making of Chinese Communism." *American Sociological Review* 78 (5): 773–96.

Yip, Andrew K. T. 1997. "Dare to Differ: Gay and Lesbian Catholics' Assessment of Official Catholic Positions on Sexuality." *Sociology of Religion* 58 (2): 165–180.

Yukich, Grace. 2013. *One Family under God: Immigration Politics and Progressive Religion in America.* New York: Oxford University Press.

Zoll, Rachel. 2014. "Evangelical College Gay Rights Stand Causes Uproar." *ABC News.* Retrieved November 11, 2014 (http://abcnews.go.com/Health/wireStory /evangelical-college-gay-rights-stand-uproar-26637940).

Zylan, Yvonne. 2011. *States of Passion: Law, Identity, and Social Construction of Desire.* New York: Oxford University Press.

Zylstra, Sarah Eekhoff, Morgan Lee, and Bob Smietana. 2015, July 8. "Hope College and Belmont University to Offer Benefits to Same-Sex Spouses." *Christianity Today.* Retrieved April 25, 2016 (http://www.christianitytoday.com /ct/2015/july-web-only/hope-college-and-belmont-to-offer-benefits-to-same -sex-spou.html).

Index

Campus climate; Campus Ministries; CUAllies; Nondiscrimination statements; Organization for Gay and Lesbian Rights; Protest

Changing Attitude, 155n6

Chicago, Illinois, 14, 17–18, 71, 84, 155n2

Chicago Metropolitan Sports Association, 84

Christian Century, 27

Christian Church. *See* Disciples of Christ

Christian colleges and universities: historical opportunities for LGBT activism at, 23–35; LGBT issues at, 11–17; nondiscrimination policies at, 35–41, 156n12; presence of LGBT groups at, 35–41, 156n12; understandings of what it means to be, 92–111, 116–18. *See also* Belmont University; Bible colleges; Bob Jones University; Catholic University of America; Eastern Mennonite University; Georgetown University; Goshen College; Loyola University Chicago

Christianity: apathy toward, 83; changing understandings of, 92–118; communalist and individualist divisions within, 38–41, 156nn9–12; conversion to, 81–83, 112–14; historical responses to LGBT activism, 24–35; moderating effect on biographical impacts of LGBT activism, 111–16; rejection of, 62, 109–11; role in opposition to same-sex marriage, 14, 16, 33–34, 44, 95–96, 102–3; role in shaping campus climates, 102–11; role in shaping campus policies, 94–102; role in shaping identities relevant to commitment, 4–8, 71, 76–83, 87–89, 145–46; role in shaping identities relevant to micromobilization, 4–7, 52, 58, 65, 145; role in support for same-sex marriage, 34, 47, 130. *See also* Catholic Church; Protestants

Christianity Today, 27

Christian Life Communities (organizations at Loyola University Chicago), 111, 118

Christian Scientists, 155n6

Church of God in Christ, 34

Church of Jesus Christ of Latter-day Saints. *See* Mormon Church

Church of the Brethren, 155n6

Church of the Nazarene, 34, 155n6

Cisgender. *See* Gender identity

Civil rights movement, 26, 32, 147–48, 155n4, 156nn10–11, 163n1, 163n3, 164n5

Clinton, Bill, 29–30

CNN, 98

Cohort replacement, 83, 90, 148

Collective action, 3, 7, 9, 71, 123. *See also* Letter-writing campaign; Marches; Prayer vigil; Prayer walk; Protest; Rally; Sit-in

Collective benefits, 68, 74, 89–90, 161n6

Collective identity, 159n9. *See also* Identity

College Democrats, 16

Columbia University, 24–25, 155n3

Coming out, 57, 63, 67, 82, 108, 115, 118–19, 135

Commitment: definition of, 5, 67, 160n1; role of attitudinal affinity in, 5–7, 153n6; role of biographical availability in, 5–7, 68, 73, 76, 83, 89–90, 153n6, 161n2, 161n6; role of group ethos in, 4–8, 11, 68–91, 145–48, 151, 161n3; role of identity in, 4–8, 11, 67–69, 71–91, 145–48, 151, 161n3; role of meso-level constraints, 5–7, 68, 89–90, 161n7; role of microstructural availability in, 5–7, 153n6; role of rational choice calculations in, 68, 73–74, 89–90, 161n2, 161n6; to Advocate, 69–74, 83–87; to Advocates, 67–68; to Bridge Builders, 80–83; to CUAllies, 5–7, 77–80; to direct action groups, 7, 69–76, 87–89, 145; to educational

Institutional tactics. *See* Tactics: institutional

Integrity USA, 155n6

Intentional relationships, 4, 135–40, 148

Iowa, 31

Iraq War, 67, 75

Jehovah's Witnesses, 155n6

Jesuits, 14, 18, 136, 154n17

Jesus, 97–99, 109, 118

Ku Klux Klan, 16

Labor movement, 26, 155n4

Lesbian. *See* Sexual orientation

Lesbian, Bisexual, and Gay Alliance (LGBT organization at Goshen College), 30

Lesbian feminist movement, 26, 155n5

Letter-writing campaign, 15, 47, 74–75, 127, 133. *See also* Open Letter movement

LGBT movement: attitudinal affinity with, 5, 49, 61, 64–65; history of, 24–35; post-graduation participation in, 125–26, 128–29. *See also* Gay liberation movement; Homophile movement; Lesbian feminist movement

LGBT participants: commitment to solidarity groups, 8, 71, 83–89, 146; involvement in Advocate, 59, 61–62, 72–73, 83–87, 135–38, 140, 143–46; involvement in Bridge Builders, 59–60, 63; involvement in CUAllies, 2–3, 6–7; involvement in Open Letter movement, 127–29; pathways to activism, 1–7, 58–65, 145

LGBT rights. *See* Nondiscrimination statements; Same-sex marriage

Los Angeles, California, 24, 26, 28, 155n5

Los Angeles Times, 98

Love in Action, 28

Loyola University Chicago: characteristics of respondents at, 18–19, 154n20; history of LGBT activism at, 13–14, 30, 33, 70; religious identity of, 18, 143, 154n17. *See also* Advocate; Campus climate; Campus Ministries; Christian Life Communities; Gay, Lesbian, and Bisexual Association; Nondiscrimination statements; Protest; Rainbow Connection; Spectrum

Lutherans Concerned, 155n6

Maine, 31

Mannheim, Karl, 119, 121

Marches, 9, 27, 71, 85

Marriage equality. *See* Same-sex marriage

Massachusetts, 29, 31

Mattachine Society, 24, 155n2

McAdam, Doug, 10, 44, 157n1, 158n6, 164n4, 164n7

McCain, John, 96

Medium, 137

Mennonite Church USA, 12–13, 46–48, 75, 100–101, 128, 155n6

Methodists in New Directions, 155n6

Metropolitan Community Church, 26–27

Microaggressions, 2, 8, 148

Micromobilization: definition of, 5, 44; findings for Advocate, 61–62; findings for Bridge Builders, 43–44, 55–56, 63; findings for CUAllies, 1–7, 51–58; findings for Open Letter movement, 46–49; patterns for LGBT participants, 4–7, 58–65, 145; patterns for politicized participants, 4–7, 45–52, 65, 145; patterns for religious participants, 4–7, 52–58, 65, 145; role of attitudinal affinity in, 5–7, 44–50, 52, 54–55, 58, 61, 64–66, 153n3, 157n1, 158n4, 160n14; role of biographical availability in, 5–7, 44–46, 50, 55, 63–65, 153n5, 157n1,

Pope, 30, 34, 109
Prayer vigil, 76–78, 109
Prayer walk, 82, 98, 152
Presbyterian Church in America, 34
Presbyterian Church USA, 32, 155n6
Presidential elections: of 1968, 28; of
1976, 28; of 1988, 28; of 1992, 29–30;
of 2000, 31; of 2004, 31; of 2008, 31–32;
of 2012, 31–32
PRISM (LGBT organization at Goshen
College), 13, 31, 67–68, 74, 127
Protest: at Belmont University, 15, 17,
43, 92, 95, 97–100, 104, 106–7, 112, 117,
163n5, 163n7; at Catholic University
of America, 27, 78–79, 101, 130; at
Goshen College, 46, 74, 100, 127; at
Loyola University Chicago, 71; at
religious conventions, 32, 75;
post-graduation participation in, 122;
tactic of direct action groups, 64,
78–79, 145, 149
Protestants, 13, 29, 33—35, 156nn10–11,
161n3, 161n5. *See also* African
Methodist Episcopal Church;
American Baptist Churches USA;
Anglican Church; Assemblies of
God; Christian Scientists; Church of
God in Christ; Church of the
Brethren; Church of the Nazarene;
Disciples of Christ; Episcopal
Church USA; Mennonite Church
USA; Metropolitan Community
Church; Presbyterian Church in
America; Presbyterian Church USA;
Quakers; Southern Baptist Conven-
tion; Tennessee Baptist Convention;
United Church of Christ; United
Methodist Church

Quakers, 52, 155n6
Queer. *See* Gender identity; Sexual
orientation
Queer Straight Student Organization
(LGBT organization at Belmont
University), 150

Rainbow Connection (LGBT organization at Loyola University
Chicago), 70
Rally, 9, 15, 67, 71, 80, 97–99, 152
Rational choice theory, 7, 68, 73, 90,
147, 161n2
Ratzinger, Josef, 30
Reagan, Ronald, 28
Reconciling Ministries Network, 155n6
Red-diaper babies, 8, 53
Reformation Project, 32
Religion: apathy toward, 83; as an
academic discipline, 1, 39–41, 51;
communalist and individualist
divisions within, 38–41, 156nn9–12;
conflict with LGBT identities,
55, 62, 105, 111–16, 132, 145, 152;
conversion to, 81–83, 112–14;
rejection of, 62, 109–11; role in
opposition to same-sex marriage,
14, 16, 33–34, 44, 95–96, 102–3; role
in shaping campus climates, 102–11;
role in shaping campus policies,
94–102; role in shaping identities
relevant to commitment, 4–8, 71,
76–83, 87–89, 145–46; role in
shaping identities relevant to micromobilization, 4–7, 52–58, 65, 145;
role in shaping opportunities for
LGBT activism, 23–35; role in
support for same-sex marriage, 34,
47, 130. *See also* Christianity
Religious participants: commitment to
educational groups, 7–8, 71, 76–83,
87–89, 145–46; involvement in
Advocate, 72–73, 139–40; involvement
in Advocates, 109; involvement in
Bridge Builders, 43–44, 55–56, 80–83,
113–16; involvement in CUAllies, 1–2,
6, 53–58, 77–80, 109, 125–26, 130–33;
pathways to activism, 1–7, 52–58, 65,
145
Reparative therapy, 2, 28, 54, 61
Republican Party, 17, 26, 28–29, 31,
159n13

Tactics (cont.)
26, 46, 61, 66, 68, 76–78, 123, 130, 149, 155n5, 160n14, 161n5; extra-institutional, 7, 9–11, 71, 121, 123, 145, 149; institutional, 9–10, 30–31, 71, 123. *See also* Collective action; Letter-writing campaign; Marches; Prayer vigil; Prayer walk; Protest; Rally; Sit-in

Takeover, 77, 83, 90, 148

Tennessean, 96–97

Tennessee, 15, 17–18, 95, 163n5

Tennessee Baptist Convention, 15, 95, 100

Theological orientations, 17–18, 38–42, 100, 156nn9–12

Title IX, 12, 34

Transgender. *See* Gender identity

Transgender rights, 12, 33–34

Transphobia, 16, 105

Trump, Donald, 12, 34

Twelfth Night, 144

UCC Open and Affirming Coalition, 155n6

United Church of Christ, 29, 32, 155n6

United Federation of Metropolitan Community Churches. *See* Metropolitan Community Church

United Methodist Church, 33, 155n6

University Ministries (organization at Belmont University), 56, 80–82, 103–6, 108, 117–18, 150

U.S. Department of Education, 34

U.S. Supreme Court, 29, 31–32

Value identity, 4, 7, 50, 65, 71–72, 145–47

Vermont, 31

Washington, 31

Washington, D.C., 1, 5, 14, 16–18, 27

White, Mel, 32

Women's movements, 10, 26, 155n4, 164n4

World War II, 24

CPSIA information can be obtained
at www.ICGtesting.com
Printed in the USA
LVHW01s0745011018
591856LV00002B/3/P